D0443363

Beyond Addiction

HOW SCIENCE AND KINDNESS HELP PEOPLE CHANGE

A Guide for Families

JEFFREY FOOTE, PHD, CARRIE WILKENS, PHD,
AND NICOLE KOSANKE, PHD
WITH STEPHANIE HIGGS

SCRIBNER

New York   London   Toronto   Sydney   New Delhi

SCRIBNER
A Division of Simon & Schuster, Inc.
1230 Avenue of the Americas
New York, NY 10020

Copyright © 2014 by Psychological Motivation and Change Group, PLLC.

All rights reserved, including the right to reproduce this book or portions thereof
in any form whatsoever. For information, address Scribner Subsidiary Rights Department,
1230 Avenue of the Americas, New York, NY 10020.

First Scribner hardcover edition February 2014

SCRIBNER and design are registered trademarks of The Gale Group, Inc.,
used under license by Simon & Schuster, Inc., the publisher of this work.

For information about special discounts for bulk purchases,
please contact Simon & Schuster Special Sales at 1-866-506-1949
or business@simonandschuster.com.

The Simon & Schuster Speakers Bureau can bring authors to your live event.
For more information or to book an event, contact the Simon & Schuster Speakers Bureau
at 1-866-248-3049 or visit our website at www.simonspeakers.com.

Manufactured in the United States of America

3   5   7   9   10   8   6   4

Library of Congress Control Number: 2013032603

ISBN 978-1-4767-0947-5
ISBN 978-1-4767-0949-9 (ebook)

Clients and cases discussed are based on composites.

For everyone who is hoping and working for change.

In a gentle way, you can shake the world.
—MAHATMA GANDHI

Contents

PART THREE

How to Help

PART FOUR

Live Your Life

Beyond
Addiction

Foreword

It is with the greatest pleasure that we write this preface. Jane and I have known and worked for more than a decade with the directors and staff of the Center for Motivation and Change (CMC), and we have conducted workshops and staff trainings in CRAFT (Community Reinforcement and Family Training) at CMC with Jeff Foote. The first workshop drew an international audience from three continents. CMC's absolute commitment to change the way family treatment is done, and their determination to do whatever it takes, are unsurpassed, and it is also significant that CMC had been using and promoting evidenced-based treatments long before they became popular.

CMC has embraced the task of working with families—not just the individual with the substance use problem but the whole family. Many treatment centers in the United States still use old-school treatments that have not been tested by rigorous randomized clinical trials, whereas CMC has developed several programs for substance-abusing individuals and their families based on solid evidence-based treatments. Without question, CMC has been innovative and progressive in their evaluation and treatment of people suffering either directly or indirectly (i.e., family members) from substance use.

I can personally attest to the pain caused by having a family member who abuses alcohol or drugs. I came from one of those families and I understand the anguish firsthand. As my father's out-of-control drinking continued, I also witnessed my mother suffering incredible pain. As a result of her frustrations, my brother and I also suffered. My mother passed away at the young age of forty-five. It is because of this troubled history that I carved out my path of investigating humane and positive ways to help substance users and family members. My early years in the field brought me to the stark reality that there was no reliable or reasonable treatment for family members at the time. "Family Days" at treatment centers typically centered around viewing a film on the effects of alcohol.

The addiction field as a whole has struggled to find effective ways to help distraught family members. During my long tenure in the substance abuse field, I developed a program called Community Reinforcement and Family Training. CRAFT is designed specifically to empower family members. It teaches them how to take control of their lives, and as part of this process to change their interactions with the substance user in ways that promote positive behavioral change. Clinical trials on CRAFT have shown that when family members use these positive, supportive, nonconfrontational techniques, not only do they find ways to get their loved one into treatment, but the family members themselves feel better—specifically showing decreases in depression, anger, anxiety, and medical problems—when they participate in CRAFT. Clinical trials also have shown that the family members benefit emotionally even if their loved one does not enter treatment.

The Center for Motivation and Change has taken CRAFT, motivational interviewing, and cognitive behavioral therapy and woven them into a powerful treatment system under the expert guidance of its directors, Drs. Jeff Foote and Carrie Wilkens. Jane and I became fans of CMC years ago, due to their kindred spirit and their commitment to doing the right thing. It is a true honor to know and work with such dedicated people.

We believe this book will have a huge positive impact on the addiction community, beginning with therapists and researchers. But we also hope it opens the eyes of directors, legislators, and families to a novel way of thinking about how to approach and address the family's substance use problem.

—Robert J. Meyers, PhD, Emeritus Associate
 Research Professor of Psychology, University
 of New Mexico, and Director of Robert J.
 Meyers, PhD & Associates

—Jane Ellen Smith, PhD, Professor and Chair,
 Department of Psychology, University of New
 Mexico, Albuquerque, NM

Where to Start

who struggles with drinking, drugs, eating, or other compulsive behaviors. Often, it is the critical difference.

We also know that people get better, and there are many reasons to be hopeful. However, you're probably more familiar with the popular notions of intractable character defects and progressive, chronic disease. There's widespread pessimism about the possibility of real change. Addiction can be terrible—at times life-threatening. But change is possible, and there are clear paths leading to it.

This is why, ten years ago, we created a new treatment program, the Center for Motivation and Change (CMC), in New York City, where we are part of a revolution in addiction treatment based on evidence and on a new model for change.

We built our practice on optimism, not because it made us feel good, though it does, but because it works. We base our optimism, our clinical practice, and now this book on forty years of well-documented research on how substances and other compulsive behaviors affect people, why people use them, and how and why people stop self-destructive behavior and start on paths toward health and happiness. In turn, our experiences with thousands of clients bear out the research findings.

There is in fact a *science of change*.

Every day at CMC we see clients put it into practice, using the knowledge, attitudes, and skills you'll find in this book. It takes time, and it is not usually a straight or smooth path. But it is a better way. Things can and do change. The process already started when you picked up this book.

The Science of Change

It's been five hundred years since the scientific revolution, and we've had modern medicine for at least a century. Yet shockingly, the understanding and treatment of substance use in the United States has been exempt from scientific standards and separate from mainstream healthcare until quite recently.

Researchers in America only began to collect evidence in earnest in the 1970s. The National Institute on Alcohol Abuse and Alcoholism (NIAAA) was established in 1970, followed by the National Institute on Drug Abuse (NIDA) in 1974. Finally, after years of folk wisdom running the gamut from truly helpful to ineffective to harmful, federal money flowed toward scientific studies of what works, including what family and friends like you can do to help. The increasing number of controlled studies, including our own, over these forty-odd years, has created a mountain of evidence—scientists have separated the wheat from the chaff, revealing that certain approaches and treatment strategies are more successful than others. That's good news, and we hope that it will help you find your own optimism.

Most people equate treatment with intensive, residential "rehab" and believe rehab is the starting point of all change. In fact, there are *many* treatment options and substantial evidence that outpatient treatment is at least as effective in most cases and often a better place to start. Since 1996, the American Society of Addiction Medicine recommends starting with the *least* intensive treatment that is safe. Dr. Mark Willenbring, former director of the Treatment and Recovery Research Division of NIAAA, describes how the vast majority of people who could benefit from help don't get it, in part because the system is designed to treat the most severe problems, while the culture dictates waiting until someone "hits bottom"—in other words, waiting until problems become severe. Family members and friends are left with few options other than to stand by and watch things get worse, then get their loved one into rehab if they can. This despite strong evidence that reaching people early, when their problems are less severe and more treatable, leads to better outcomes. Thankfully, the treatment system is starting to change.

The evidence supports many ways to address substance use disorders, as many ways as there are reasons people have them. Treatment is not always necessary; it turns out that many people get better without ever seeking professional help. There is also clear evidence that certain treatment approaches consistently outperform others. Cognitive-behavioral and motivational approaches, for example, which treat substance abuse like any other human behavior, are significantly more effective than confrontational approaches aimed to challenge a person's "denial" about his "disease."

Research has demonstrated that the popular belief that if someone "just stops" using a substance, then the rest of his problems will take care of themselves is simplistic and untrue. Substance problems are complex and multidetermined, often driven by underlying psychiatric disorders such as depression, anxiety, bipolar disorder, or attention deficit disorders that require specialized attention over and beyond just treating the substance problem. In other words, good treatment often includes psychiatric care, which has historically been overlooked or even discouraged in some drug and alcohol treatment settings.

Science has also given us a better understanding of the brain's role in substance use and compulsive behaviors. With that science, there are new medications that reduce cravings and compulsivity, block drug effects, ease withdrawal, and treat underlying issues. Neuroimaging research provides new insights into the effects of substances on the brain; and recent discoveries in neuroscience have shown the power of neuroplasticity in the brain's healing itself.

And science has revealed that teenagers are not simply grown-ups who text a lot; they are neurologically, psychologically, socially, and legally different from adults, and they have different treatment needs. Until about fifteen years ago, most of the services available for adolescents were barely modified adult treatments. Clinical trials have shown us that teenagers respond well to appropriate treatment and just as with adults, some treatments are considerably more effective than others. You might be surprised to learn that they all involve parents as active treatment participants (and often siblings, peers, and school systems).*

Finally, research has shown how you can play a role in change. Our work with families and friends of people with substance problems is informed by CRAFT—Community Reinforcement and Family Training—a scientifically supported, evidence-based, clinically proven approach to helping families of substance abusers. CRAFT grew out of treatment innovations that began in the 1970s. A group of researchers in Illinois, led by behavioral psychologist Nathan Azrin, developed what is still the most effective behavioral treatment for substance users, and called it the Community Reinforcement Approach, or CRA. In the process, they discovered that family involvement was a crucial factor in successful change. Robert J. Meyers, PhD (one of the original Illinois group), expanded the CRA approach to work with families when their loved one *refused* help, and called it CRAFT. After moving to the Center on Alcoholism, Substance Abuse and Addictions (CASAA) at the University of New Mexico, Dr. Meyers conducted further research and clinical trials (teaming with Jane Ellen Smith, PhD), and they and others investigating CRAFT have given us robust evidence that given the right tools, families can effect change.

CRAFT has three goals: 1.) to teach you skills to take care of yourself; 2.) to teach you skills you can use to help your loved one change;

---

*The parent-child relationship is different from other relationships, too, even when the "child" is an adult. This book is for everyone, parents included. However, we recognize that parenting comes with unique challenges, responsibilities, and feelings, and so we partnered with the Partnership at Drugfree.org to offer a supplementary guide for parents. You can download it from our website at http://www.the20minute guide.com.

and 3.) to reduce substance use, period, whether your loved one gets formal treatment or not. CRAFT is behavioral in that it employs strategies for real-world, observable change. CRAFT is also motivational, drawing its strength from collaboration and kindness rather than confrontation and conflict. This motivational and behavioral approach is the core of our work with families, the substance of the helping strategies in this book, and an opportunity for profound change.

Drs. Meyers and Smith and other research groups have studied CRAFT with family members from a variety of socioeconomic, ethnic, and age groups struggling with a range of different substances, with the following results:

- Two-thirds of people using substances who had been initially resistant to treatment agreed to go to treatment (typically after family members had around five sessions of CRAFT).
- The majority of participating spouses and parents reported being happier, less depressed, less angry, and having more family cohesion and less family conflict than prior to their CRAFT sessions, *whether or not their loved one engaged in treatment.*
- CRAFT's effectiveness in engaging substance users and improving family functioning is found across substance types, relationship types, and ethnicities.

Good News: Things get better with CRAFT. Families feel better, substance use often decreases, and people with substance problems usually enter treatment when a family member uses CRAFT.

CRAFT works, first, because it understands substance problems holistically, in the context of family, community, and work. People do not use substances in a vacuum. Their relationships impact their substance use just as their substance use impacts their relationships. CRAFT recognizes that most family members and friends, for their part, have good intentions, good instincts, and a healthy desire to help. CRAFT treats the problems families face as a deficit of skills rather than as a disease of codependence. These skills can be learned.

Second, CRAFT recognizes that "just stopping" is not a sustainable long-term solution. While change depends at first on stopping (or reducing), the $64,000 question is what promotes *staying stopped*. CRAFT asks you to see what makes substance use rewarding to your loved one, so that you can introduce the "competition"—more constructive activities that serve the same needs—into her world. To this end, CRAFT will feel strange at first. If you have been viewing her substance problem as the cause of all other problems for some time, you may wonder what taking her bike in for a tune-up could have to do with anything. Plenty, as we'll see.

What We Offer

First, we offer a new perspective on *why* your loved one does what he does. "Why" is a key to change. Second, we will teach you skills: positive communication, reinforcement strategies, and problem-solving skills to transform your relationship with your loved one and your life. Third, we will help you navigate what is often a one-toned, ideologically tinged treatment system, because there are treatment approaches and settings, medications, and knowledge available that you run a high risk of never encountering through traditional channels. Fourth, we will show you how to take better care of *yourself* so you'll have the energy to keep going, keep changing, keep helping. Finally, we will teach you skills to make peace with the things you cannot change.

Questions You Might Have

Here are the primary questions from families who come to us. While there is no quick fix, we do have some answers.

Can I really help him if he doesn't want to change?
Yes! This is perhaps the best question you could ask, and really the heart of the matter. With a motivational approach, part of helping people change is helping them *want* to change. You, the one at his side, worried, distraught, and horrified, don't have to stand by in detachment or go ballistic as your only alternatives (though you might do these things sometimes anyway). If you give people the right encouragement, stay connected to them, provide good options (not ultimatums), respect their right to be part of the solution, and keep your balance by taking care of yourself and setting healthy limits, things get better. Change doesn't always happen as quickly as we want and it can be messy, but it happens.

Even when people say repeatedly that they don't want to or simply can't change, they do so all the time—even in the face of long odds. Why? Because change becomes worth it to them. The balance shifts enough for them to say, "Enough! Let me try another way." The pain of continuing what they are doing and the benefits of changing begin to seem *to them* to outweigh the benefits of continuing to use and the pain of changing. The little-known but well-documented secret of our field is that many people change on their own, including recovering from terrible substance problems, because change becomes worth it.

The reality is that people by nature have a self-righting mechanism—but you don't need to wait passively for this righting mechanism to kick in. Your involvement can help bring about an internal shift in your loved one toward positive change. Most people do not need to "hit rock bottom" and "admit they are addicts" for real change to occur. Though some people change this way, it's not the only way. In fact, when people use these phrases to describe how they changed, they are expressing their versions of exactly what we mean—something shifted to make it worth it to them. What you will learn here is how to help your loved one make this shift, without stepping away from him, and sooner rather than later. This book will help you trust *and* influence the process of change.

What if I feel as though I've already tried everything?

Depending on what has transpired by the time you picked up this book, some skepticism at the idea of doing more is understandable. It's also natural for you to despair sometimes, but this doesn't mean your situation is actually hopeless. At some level you know this: you're reading this book because even if you feel as though you've tried everything, you're still trying! It can be hard to feel hopeful when change doesn't seem to be happening, despite best intentions and major investments of time, money, and emotions. However, we know that you haven't tried everything, though you may feel like you have. How do we know? Because at this point only a few treatment providers in North America share our approach for working with families and friends. The system is starting to change, but for now we can be pretty sure you'll find something new here.

You'll discover, for instance, that how you communicate has a major impact on your loved one's attitude toward change, her willingness to take more responsibility for herself, the atmosphere in your home, and how you feel when your head meets your pillow at night. While many of us feel like we can communicate well enough, when it comes to stressed interactions with our loved one, communication typically breaks down. Stepping away from the fight and using new communication skills will make a difference.

You'll see that lapses and relapses—commonly seen as crises—are a natural part of getting better for most people. They are not failures to change but opportunities to learn. Most people go through many stages of change—resistance, willingness, learning and progress, frustrations and setbacks, more resistance, more willingness, more learning and progress. Understandably, your loved one's setbacks may try your patience and equanimity. With new understanding, resilience, and skills to tolerate the downs with the ups, you won't have to feel as though your life is on hold (or coming apart) until she gets it perfectly.

You'll learn that you can help by seeing your loved one's point of view; by knowing your full range of options; by understanding how change works. You can help by treating her with kindness and respect; by learning how to problem-solve; by learning how to have patience. You can help her navigate the treatment system and you can support her aftercare plan. You can let her understand that while you may be upset sometimes, you're on her side. You can help by getting out of the way to let her realize the consequences of her behavior. You can help by taking care of yourself. There are many ways you can help your loved one change. We will show you how.

And, what about me? How can I begin to feel better?

In other words, how can you help yourself? You may feel exhausted from helping so much and you may doubt whether you can help any more. At the same time, you may believe that putting your needs last is the hallmark of a good helper. But the captain doesn't help by going down with the ship (however heroic it seems); taking care of yourself is a skill you can't afford to ignore.

If you're like most people, you've probably been living for some time— for many people it's been years—with a toxic combination of fear, anger, and wishing that there weren't really a problem or that the problem would just go away. Chronic worrying affects your physical and mental health. It can disrupt your sleep, interfere with your concentration, and play havoc with your moods. It wears on your heart, figuratively and physiologically. You may have gotten to the point where the only way you show love toward this person is by worrying. You may not have noticed the effect worry is having on you because you've been so busy worrying about someone else. This book will help *you* change too.

And, finally: What can I DO right now?

First, change the way you *think* about substance use, compulsive behavior, and change. This is important: thinking *is* doing. How you think about a problem is the first step to a solution and the first thing you can change. To help you do this, we've distilled the ten most revolutionary discoveries by scientists and clinicians in our field over the past forty years—ten evidence-based reasons to have hope.

1. You can help.

We can't emphasize enough that *you can help*.

The research evidence is clear: involving family and friends in helping a loved one struggling with substances significantly increases the odds of improvement and helps maintain positive changes. Family influence is a commonly cited reason for seeking treatment for substance use problems. In other words, you have an impact and you have leverage.

The opposite has been said too often, that the best way to help is not to help. You have probably run into terms like "tough love," "enabling," "codependency," and "detach with love." They're everywhere, so it's no wonder so many people are confused—maybe even feeling guilty and blamed.

Our clients who have read books on codependency worry about doing *anything* nice for their loved ones for fear that it might be "enabling" their destructive behavior. One client asked if it was okay to make waffles for his daughter on Sunday morning. He knew she still smoked pot sometimes, and he was scared of inadvertently encouraging the behavior by being nice. Of course it's okay to make your loved one breakfast. We will teach you how to take care of your loved one without condoning or supporting the behavior you don't want.

Conversely, when frustrations and disappointments mount, you may, understandably, want to get "tough"—yell or turn your back. But when you yell at your loved one to stop drinking, are you straightening her out, or giving her more reason to drink? When you don't yell at your loved one to stop drinking, are you sending the message that it's not important to you?

These are all good questions. Our answers may surprise you. We'll show you how to extricate yourself from negative patterns, not by "detaching" but by encouraging positive, nonusing behaviors instead.

2. Helping yourself helps.

It's not either/or. You don't have to choose between your self-preservation and his. The evidence is clear about this too. You might feel distant; you might feel like you hardly know him anymore, but you and your loved one are on parallel paths. When you help yourself, you help your loved one.

Your emotional resilience, physical health, social supports, and perspective on change can contribute to his. First, you will be setting an example. Second, you need internal resources to do what is most helpful for your loved one.

As you read this book you'll notice that what we will ask of you will be similar to what you will ask of your loved one. We want you to feel better about *you* and learn how to take care of *you*. We want you to feel hopeful about your life and remember how to have fun. We want you to notice what's not working for you, try something different, and practice, practice, practice.

To paraphrase the classic airplane safety announcement: you both need oxygen; we want you to put on your oxygen mask first.

3. *Your loved one isn't crazy.*

Nor is your loved one a bad person. From your perspective, her behavior may seem to lie somewhere on a spectrum between ill-advised and demonic. From her perspective, it makes a certain kind of sense—and *her perspective matters.* People don't use substances because they're crazy. People don't use substances because they're bad people. People use substances because they get something they like out of it.

Maybe it makes socializing easier, or makes business doable, or makes sex possible, or makes depression go away. Maybe it's fun (one of the hardest reasons to accept when the downsides are so apparent to you). The reasons are different for different people. You wouldn't be reading this if there weren't a serious downside to the way your loved one uses substances, and the suggestion that you try to understand her point of view may seem galling to you. But understanding—not condoning—why people do what they do gives us a much better chance of helping.

It may seem like a leap, but most people, including people with substance problems, are capable of making rational decisions. Studies have found repeatedly that most people stop abusing substances on their own, without formal treatment or intervention. If you believe, however, that a person is incapable of honesty, reasoning, and constructive collaboration with you, there will be no chance of engaging on these terms. And probably she will live *down* to your expectations. Research has shown that the more you criticize someone, presumably (and understandably) in the hopes of "getting through" to her, the more defensive she'll become—which is often taken for "denial." This book offers strategies based on respect and optimism that are proven to lower defenses and get you on the same side, working together against the problem.

You may feel you have lost touch completely with your loved one's good qualities. That's a sad place to be, but understandable. One of our hopes in writing this book is to help you find the good again.

4. The world isn't black-and-white.

Traditional notions of addiction give you two, and only two, options. People are said to be addicts or not. Addicts are said to be ready to change or not. They're either recovering or they're in denial, "with the program" or not. (In the black-and-white view, there's only one program.) Treatment is rehab or nothing. Success or failure. Healthy or sick. "Clean" or dirty. Abstinent or relapsing. And for friends and family: "intervening" or "enabling." The good news? It's not true!

The truth is, problems with substances vary; and individual differences matter. The current scientific evidence supports an explanatory model involving psychological, biological, and social factors. And, while you might fantasize about a lever you can pull that will send your loved one straight to rehab and he will come back cured, that's black-and-white thinking, too. The truth is that people are more likely to make big changes and continue with those changes if they are given time and help to choose among reasonable alternatives.

Black-and-white thinking is not just a philosophical problem; it's a barrier to change.

5. Labels do more harm than good.

Studies have shown repeatedly that one of the major impediments to seeking help for substance problems is stigma. Many people don't seek help because they expect to be offered only one way to get it—accepting a label of alcoholic or addict.

Black-and-white thinking naturally leads to labeling, which involves an us-and-them mentality that divides people into "addicts" and "the rest of us." In fact, by branding more than 20 million Americans with a single label and treating them according to that label, the media and parts of the treatment community have given people the wrong idea, that everyone struggling with these problems is basically the same.

You may not be sure whether your loved one is an addict. Or you may be sure, and you're wasting a lot of energy trying to argue her into agreeing with you. We recommend you to put aside the question of whether someone is an "addict" or "alcoholic."

The label simply doesn't matter.

What matters is what matters to you and to her: What effect is the substance use having in her life and in yours? What will motivate your loved one to change? The answers will be based on how well you know your loved one as an individual and the particular ways you matter to each other.

Rather than reach for a label, save your energy for the more constructive work of problem solving.

6. Different people need different options.

Inpatient, outpatient. Group therapy, individual therapy. Outpatient once a week, twice a week, every day. Anticraving medications, medications for symptoms of withdrawal. Treatment for co-occurring disorders like depression or attention deficit. Extended care facilities. Sober companions. Self-help support groups. Cognitive-behavioral therapy. "90 in 90." Talking with a rabbi or priest. Starting to exercise. There are many therapeutic options—some not as widely available as others; some approaches better supported by evidence than others. The most important things to bear in mind are 1.) no single size fits all, and 2.) having a choice among treatment plans and plans for change in general predicts positive outcomes. *On these points the evidence is crystal clear.* Giving people options helps them get invested in the resulting plan.

Backing people into a corner and telling them what they should do—the "rehab or else" approach—might get them into rehab. But rehab might not be the best option for them, and coercion may kill their motivation to even participate while in treatment, and may also undermine their motivation to continue making changes afterward. (If there is a moment of truth in rehab, it's not when people enter, it's when they leave.) Then again, an ultimatum might not get them into rehab at all and only succeed in increasing their defensiveness.

For more than half a century, high-confrontation addiction treatment in this country has aimed at "breaking through" an addict's supposed "denial" or resistance to treatment. Some of us in the field now have recognized—and studies have proven—that this kind of confrontation *increases* resistance. The evidence-based treatments we describe give you the option—many options, in fact—to opt out of the awful, self-fulfilling prophecy of confrontation and resistance. The point is not to force your loved one into just any treatment. It's more helpful to find the best kinds of treatment for her particular problems, and engage her motivation to be part of the plan.

We will lay out the considerations that go into good treatment planning and describe the major evidence-based treatment approaches. We will help you ask questions that help you assess the nature and quality of prospective treatment providers, including how (or if) they would individualize a plan for your loved one.

7. Treatment isn't the be-all and end-all.

You can make significant changes in your life, including your relationship, whether or not your loved one enters treatment. You might have been relieved to learn there's a good chance that he may even get better without treatment. One national survey found that 24 percent of people diagnosed with alcohol dependence (the most severe category of alcohol problem) recovered *on their own within a year.*

Remember, CRAFT results in better communication and relationship satisfaction, increased happiness on the part of the family member or friend, and reduced substance use *even when the loved one doesn't enter treatment.* In other words, you can be a positive influence and your loved one can get better, all without ever crossing the threshold of a treatment center or self-help group.

We recommend that you think less about getting your loved one to admit to an addiction and more about what it takes to build a better life. For you, that might entail reaching out to friends, treatment for depression, more exercise, kinder self-talk, starting a morning meditation routine, revisiting an old hobby. For your loved one, it might mean talking to her pastor, talking to her mom, revisiting an old hobby, being more honest. People get better in a variety of ways—so many ways that we don't know them all. Our clients surprise us and your loved one may surprise you. And if your loved one does enter treatment, or is already in treatment, we will help you support that process, during and after.

We're not saying this will be easy or that there is one sure thing that will make all the difference. We're saying that the way people sustain ongoing, long-term change is through building a better life in ways that matter to them as individuals.

8. Ambivalence is normal.

When a person is motivated in two opposing directions at the same time, that's ambivalence. Ambivalence is a defining feature not just of struggles with substance use, but of change in general. How can people define a goal for change when they're pulled in two directions? That pull is a big part of relapsing to old behaviors ("I don't want to, but I also do").

Psychological theories of motivation explain how working with ambivalence is critical to helping someone change. Unfortunately, traditional treatment has not handled ambivalence particularly well, shutting out people who can't commit unequivocally to abstinence up front, and kicking out the very people who need treatment most when they lapse. The assumption has been that people can't be helped until they are willing to never use again. That assumption is wrong.

Empirical evidence indicates that people can be helped long before they're that certain, if they ever are. The data about how people really behave and change contradicts the view that a commitment to absolute, lifelong abstinence is the only legitimate option. One major clinical study found that believing lifelong abstinence to be a requirement of change predicted higher rates of relapse. For most people, use falls somewhere along a continuum of unproblematic, problematic in varying ways and degrees, and destructive. For many people, change is gradual, a process of weighing costs and benefits and experimenting to find out what works. Change often happens incrementally, rarely in a straight line, and continues until the problem has improved to the satisfaction of the one making changes.

At the time they enter treatment, many people need to abstain from using a substance to eliminate its negative effects and establish a steady path. As providers, we support their efforts and teach them the skills to be successful. The evidence suggests, however, that for others, moderation is a reasonable and viable goal. Moderation can be a terrifying concept for families and friends when they've witnessed someone repeatedly lose control; but it has been demonstrated in research and in everyday life to work for some people.

Perhaps more important is the revelation that more people may find their way to abstinence when given a choice. Some of our outpatient clients start with moderation as their goal and wind up with abstinence based on their own experience. Even in inpatient settings, where abstinence is the goal, it's not uncommon for people to express concerns about staying sober forever. Working *with* ambivalence, we help people realize what it is they want to do and how to do it, and weigh benefits and costs and make positive choices that make sense to them. Over time, our clients discover for themselves what works, knowing that the advice they are getting from us is geared toward helping them, not forcing or condemning them. They feel respected and in turn gain self-respect. "I never thought I would want to stop drinking altogether," they say. If we had told them in the beginning, "You must stop drinking," they would never have gotten there. By understanding their ambivalence, people can better internalize their own profound and lasting reasons to change.

9. People can be helped at any time.

Motivation for change can occur whenever the costs of a behavior perceptibly outweigh the benefits. Sometimes external factors influence motivation. For example, as public awareness of the health costs of smoking cigarettes increased, many people quit. Internal factors can also move a person to change. If a person who used to drag herself into a job she hated gets a new job that she likes very much, she may start to consider whether the mild hangover she has every morning from drinking three glasses of wine at night interferes with her work. Instead of rolling her hangovers into her overall resentment of her job, she may start to feel that they are getting in the way of her enjoyment.

We can't stress this enough: what looks like unwillingness to change is often a defensive reaction. People with substance problems respond with significantly less resistance to kindness and respectful treatment (as do the rest of us). So don't wait for your loved one to "hit bottom"—it can be dangerous, and problems are more treatable the sooner they are caught. And don't lose hope in the face of resistance from your loved one. Resistance is subject to change.

The positive communication skills you'll learn will help lower defenses. You'll also find strategies for increasing the costs and decreasing the benefits of your loved one's substance use. You'll learn how to recognize, reward, invite, and support turns for the better. You will begin to allow the natural, negative consequences of your loved one's use to weigh in (on him, not you!). The questions we recommend you ask of prospective treatment providers are designed to help you home in on those who will meet your situation respectfully and tailor treatment to particular needs, hopes, and goals.

10. Life is a series of experiments.

Try thinking like a scientist. This doesn't mean having all the answers or being overly analytical; it means adopting an open-ended questioning, experimental approach to life. Observe, try, notice what works and what doesn't, and adjust your strategies accordingly. Be proactive instead of reactive. As difficult as it is when your buttons have been pushed and you're impatient for change, try to stay calm. Think of Copernicus, who was open-minded enough to recognize something as counterintuitive as the Earth revolving around the sun. Think of Gandhi, observing people to understand them, acting according to his reason as well as his heart. Be yourself, but be as willing to change as you want your loved one to be. And try not to take things personally; behavior is the issue here, not character. Behavior can change. Try to temper your emotions enough to observe how things are going and how you affect them—not because your feelings aren't valid, but because a calm, clear-eyed approach gets better results. Easier said than done, yes, but the tools are available to help you do it.

In short, you can hope for change, and you can do something about it. Not all at once, because change takes time, and effort, and practice. It is more a process than an end result. This is actually good news, because it means change starts here and now; it is not something that happens later. Reading this book is an opportunity to think about changes you would like to make, on your own and with your loved one. Throughout this book you'll find examples to spark your imagination, and skills and strategies to help you implement change. (All the clinical examples in this book are based on composites.)

Some Things Our Clients Have Changed

A nineteen-year-old college student started taking OxyContin, an opioid painkiller, for headaches and found that some of her friends used it at parties. Over time, she ended up taking it daily for pain and a little extra for fun on the weekends. At home she tried not to use the drug but then she'd feel sweaty and sick. Ashamed and confused about what was happening to her, she tried to hide it from her parents when she returned home for the summer. She struggled with this for a while until she couldn't stand it and asked her parents for help.

Her mother, Alice, dedicated herself to helping her daughter. She attended an Al-Anon support group and returned to therapy, stayed in touch with her daughter's doctors, read books about addiction, and worried. From many of these sources she gathered that there wasn't much she could do to help. But "detaching" went against her instincts and sense of responsibility as a mother. It made her furious, actually. She fought with her husband because he didn't seem to worry enough. She took her anger out on her daughter as well. In turn, her daughter almost stopped talking to her altogether, which seemed to confirm that there was nothing she could do.

Alice did not tell anyone what was going on in her family. She had a close network of girlfriends and two sisters, but she didn't want to burden them, knowing it was a difficult time for the family for other reasons. She also wanted to protect her daughter's reputation. Finally, Alice felt deeply ashamed and blamed herself for her daughter's problems, which seemed much more frightening than her friends' children's problems.

Alice came to CMC initially to find out how to support her daughter's treatment. Her CMC therapist quickly recognized the bind Alice was in: she desperately wanted to help her daughter but feared anything she did would only "enable" drug use, as people had warned her. Her support group had told her to "get honest" with her sisters and everyone else,

but she felt she had good reasons to keep things to herself. The therapist assured Alice she could help her daughter, by starting to feel better
and less angry herself. They talked about how important it was to have
the support of people who cared about her, but that she didn't need to
go around telling everyone everything. They brainstormed together and
Alice decided whom she felt safe confiding in and how much. Still it was
hard. She had been covering up so much that she now felt ashamed of this
too. With her therapist, they role-played how to tell her sisters over and
over until she was ready to do it.

When she did talk to her sisters, it was a profound relief. They had been
worried about her anyway; now they could help. One sister took on a bigger role of caring for their mother; the other reached out to her niece
about her own struggle with drugs in college. As Alice's mood improved,
she found it easier to talk to her daughter without yelling. At the suggestion of her CMC therapist, she began going on weekly dates with her husband and remembered what it was like to not be angry with him all the
time. These changes emboldened her to open up more, which led to more
support, help, and communication with her daughter and to constructive
involvement with her treatment. She also learned to trust herself to figure out when to make sacrifices and when to set limits, as well as which
parts of her daughter's struggle were hers to help with and which were her
daughter's to solve for herself. Perhaps most rewarding of all, she regained
her confidence as a mother.

Kim was a woman in her early thirties who came to us for help after dis-
covering that her husband had been hiding his heavy drinking for years.
With two children under the age of three, her own full-time job, her husband finishing his doctorate, and now his drinking problem revealed, the
stresses on their marriage had skyrocketed. Her husband seemed to have
changed from a thoughtful, fun, smart partner to a distracted, brooding
guy who didn't care about her anymore and, even worse, had apparently
lost interest in their children.

Working with her CMC therapist, Kim began to understand that many
of her husband's distressing habits—terrible snoring and disrupted sleep,
chronic lateness, not remembering discussions they'd had at night, indif-
ference to the babies, and their worsening sex life—were alcohol-related
behaviors. This helped her to understand what was happening and to take
it less personally, which made it easier for her to practice yelling at him
less and taking care of herself more.

After Kim had been coming to CMC for a few months, her husband began his own treatment with an addiction psychiatrist to help him drink less. Eventually he succeeded in stopping drinking for months at a time. Kim's next challenge was to understand that though her husband's not drinking was a relief, abstinence would come, at first, with his own distressing behaviors. During periods of abstinence, he became irritable, short-tempered, and even more disengaged than when he drank. Appreciating that he was sober was not her first thought when he'd just snapped at her over dinner. It took effort on her part and support from her friends, family, and therapist to put aside her reactions to his sober moodiness, go ahead with her strategies to encourage abstinence anyway.

Toward the end of her husband's treatment, Kim began to recogn person she remembered, who was sober and sweet at the same time although he struggled with relapses several times over the next yea became increasingly more communicative and engaged with the far Kim regained her trust that his good mood didn't mean he was drinki Their relationship improved so much that he felt he could tell her direc when he lapsed and ask for her help to get back on track. Together the knew that the worst was behind them, as the process of change becam increasingly rewarding for both of them.

Because people change for different reasons and in different ways, there can be no perfect example, but we will share many more stories throughout this book to show you how things actually work, and to inspire you. Hopefully you will recognize something in each example, and feel less alone.

How to Use This Book

Whether or not you realize it, things started to change when you picked up this book, and they will continue to change as you read and think about your situation in light of what we're saying. In research we call this "measurement reactivity," meaning the therapeutic effect of simply answering questions. It's measurable.

As you have seen, the changes we address involve more than your loved one's behavior. This is your change process too, and it has already begun.

In the four sections of this book you'll find four profound possibilities: understanding, coping, helping, and thriving. Each chapter will help you develop the attitudes and learn the facts, skills, and strategies that make understanding, coping, helping, and thriving possible.

Throughout the book we will prompt you to skip around, depending on what feels most helpful to you. The chapter order follows a certain logic, but we made sure each chapter and even parts of chapters work on their own. If you left your bookmark in the chapter on treatment options but you've had three big fights in the last week, maybe it's a good time to go back to the positive communication chapter. If you get there and realize you're too emotional to do what it's asking, return to the self-care section. If you're worried it might be an emergency, see "When Is It an Emergency?" Making these choices will help develop your awareness, and awareness will empower you to customize your own path through the book.

We do recommend that you often take the "You Are Here" self-awareness questionnaire at the end of chapter 4. And you can do them in any order you want, but do the exercises. Practice the skills. Change has already started, and it will only continue with practice.

Words of Encouragement

Our hope—and challenge is to encourage you to take off your black-and-white glasses and try to see the many shades of your situation. We encourage you to step back and think through what might be effective (a kind word), not just what would feel justified (a loud shout). We encourage you to care for yourself as much as you care for your loved one. We encourage you to listen: to your loved one, because what he or she thinks, feels, and wants matters and needs to be understood; and to yourself, because the same holds true for you.

We know these encouragements are hard to take in at times, and that the simpler world of labels and ultimatums beckons. It takes courage to be encouraged. We encourage you to copy a pocket-size version of the ten reasons to have hope, listed below, and carry it around, stick it to your bathroom mirror, and generally let these concepts lead you toward a more loving, trusting, and satisfying relationship with the person you're worried about.

You *can* help.
Helping yourself helps.
Your loved one isn't crazy.
The world isn't black-and-white.
Labels do more harm than good.
Different people need different options.
Treatment isn't the be-all and end-all.
Ambivalence is normal.
People can be helped at any time.
Life is a series of experiments.

Now we come full circle: we're optimistic because the evidence supports many ways to help, and we're optimistic because there's plenty of evidence that *optimism helps*. People don't try what they don't think they can do. This book is about what you can do.

Things You Can Change

How comfortable you are right now
How optimistic you are in general
What behaviors you encourage
How much you argue
How often you smile
How much you sleep
How strong you feel
Your habitual reactions
Your tone of voice
What you pay attention to
Your point of view
The atmosphere in your home
How isolated you feel
How you deal with stress
How much you worry
Your heart rate
How you spend your money
How you express concern
What substances you use
How you help
How you get help
What kind of help you get
The first thing you do when you wake up in the morning
Whether anything good happens today
How much you enjoy life

If You're the "Loved One" We're Talking About . . .

If you found this book lying around and suspect you're the "reason" some-one is reading it . . . *Shhhh!* . . . And welcome to this book. What your friend/spouse/mom/dad/son/daughter/sister/brother/grandma/grandpa/grandson/granddaughter might not know how to tell you is that they are worried (and sometimes scared, angry, sad, frustrated, or hopeless, some-times all at the same time) about what they perceive as your not-so-great relationship to some sort of substance or behavior. They're reading this book because they are trying to figure out how to help—help you and help themselves.

What we're telling them in these pages is that people change in different ways and use substances for different reasons, many of which are reason-able, though they might be causing considerable harm. We're telling them you're not crazy. We're telling them they're not crazy either, for being upset and caring, and not always handling things perfectly. We're teaching them how to care without yelling. We're suggesting that talking and actually lis-tening to your perspective (and you to theirs) helps. We're encouraging them to take care of themselves as well as help you sort things out. There, the cat's out of the bag. Please read on, if you choose.

PART ONE

What to Know

Hey, there's one simple way of never being in that position. Don't take [the drug]. But there's probably a million different reasons you do.

—KEITH RICHARDS, *LIFE*

CHAPTER 1.

What Is Addiction?

This is the first of a trio of chapters that will help you understand your loved one's behavior, your own behavior, and how they can change. Changing the way you understand a problem changes lots of things: the way you feel about it, the way you react to it, the way you go about solving it, and your expectations and sense of hopefulness for the outcome. With better understanding of addiction and how people change, you won't be stuck standing there helplessly staring at your problems; you'll see how to pick up the tools in the chapters that follow and put them to good use.

People usually arrive in the "Addiction and Recovery" section of the bookstore with assumptions, some of them helpful, some of them not. This chapter lets you reconsider your assumptions in the light of new information and evidence—and the good news about addiction—gathered by scientists, researchers, and clinicians.

What Is Addiction?

The Webster's definition of addiction is a "compulsive need for and use of a habit-forming substance characterized by tolerance and by well-defined physiological symptoms upon withdrawal." Does that capture the problems you see in your loved one? What if there are no substances involved; your husband is betting on football games in a way that makes you worried about your ability to retire? What if your sister could care less about a cocktail for months at a time, only to disappear for a weekend of drinking and using cocaine, and then seems to bounce back as if nothing happened? The dictionary doesn't begin to describe the range of substance use problems and compulsive behaviors.

The term *addiction* in popular culture is even less helpful. It has come to mean one of two things: for some it represents a package of undesirable, socially reprehensible lifestyle choices presumed to stem from laziness, weak will, or a broken moral compass. For others, addiction is a "disease" for which there is only one treatment: complete abstinence. Likewise, for many in our culture, the label *addict* defines a *type* of person. Yet it doesn't help us see, let alone understand, an individual's particular behaviors.

Assuming that one description fits all makes the problem of addiction seem more manageable, the outcome more predictable. One problem, one solution, sounds more approachable than multiple problems with multiple possible solutions and the often tangled mess of cause and effect that substance problems really are. If there's one thing that's generally true about addiction, however, it's that one description *does not* fit all.

Research has found no evidence to support the idea that there is a type of person who becomes an "addict" or a set of "addictive personality" traits (commonly believed to be dishonesty, self-centeredness, et cetera). Yet we live in a culture that has come to lump its assumptions about addiction together, despite the evidence that people come to their substance problems from all directions, for all sorts of reasons, and get through these problems in different ways. This is why, with our clients and throughout the rest of this book, we never refer to a person as an "addict."

We're not mincing words here: labeling has a demonstrated negative impact. It blinds us to the specifics of an individual's situation, specifics we need to understand to help that particular person. A label like *addict*, loaded as it is with negative associations, affects how we feel about people and how we treat them, and how people feel about themselves and their ability to change. In one study, primary care providers had more negative views of patients who had been described as "substance abusers" as compared to the same group of patients when they were described as having a "substance use disorder." Even in settings designed to treat substance problems, a survey of counselors found that they identified the term *addict* with lying, irresponsibility, and denial. Some people with substance problems find it helpful to identify as "addicts." But "addict" is not a psychiatric diagnosis and "because they're addicts" does not explain any behavior pattern; it's just circular logic.

Another downside to explaining everything through "addiction" is that all other problems tend to get explained through this single prism. If he is flunking classes, withdrawn from the world, emotionally volatile, chronically late, not living up to his potential, unemployed, sexually promiscuous, awake at odd hours of the night, and/or [fill in the blank], the traditional logic dictates that treating the addiction would solve these problems. A host of other psychiatric and social issues too often are attributed to substance abuse, and important information gets lost. Mood disorders, career problems, relationship issues, insomnia, and so on, whether they are the chicken or the egg or both, do not magically resolve when people stop using substances. Left untreated, these factors make it much more likely that the person will resort to using substances again.

The newest edition of the *Diagnostic and Statistical Manual of Mental Disorders,* known as *DSM-5,* classifies "substance use disorder" and describes it on a continuum that has eleven potential criteria ranging from mild to severe. We diagnose substance use disorders according to DSM criteria when they apply, but in day-to-day life we talk about "having problems with substances" (or other behaviors). Because that's what matters: Is the person having a problem or not? What are the specific variables involved with her struggle? We need to understand her *specific* route in and out of the problem, her underlying coping difficulties, her emotional vulnerabilities, and even more importantly her strengths, interests, and supports in her life (including you) that can help her with her problems.

Anyone can have a substance problem, and it's different for different people:

- The fifty-six-year-old construction worker with chronic arthritis in his hands, who started taking prescribed Vicodin and for the past nine months has taken more than prescribed
- The forty-five-year-old mother raising three kids after her husband left her for another woman, who drinks a bottle of wine every night after the children are in bed, to soften her anxiety and fall asleep
- The thirty-seven-year-old who has been drinking heavily since college and needs to entertain clients at work; his wife has threatened to leave him because of his use of cocaine and prostitutes
- The twenty-eight-year-old who uses methamphetamine four times a year, after which he can't function for two days; drug use is part of his art gallery scene, where he is well respected and successful
- The seventeen-year-old who smokes pot every day in her senior year of high school, is clearly not doing much work, and just got into her top three choices for college

Doesn't Science Have a Simple Answer?

The simple answer is no. Science offers no simpler explanation. The compound words commonly used in models of addiction—*bio-psycho-social, neuropsychiatric,* and *neurobehavioral*—reflect our understanding of addiction as a complex interaction of multiple factors, including genetic and psychological makeup and experience, developmental and social history, and the impact of the culture(s) in which a person lives. Problems with substances come about in many ways and are affected by many variables—and not the same variables in each person.

Scientists have not found an addiction gene. They have found evidence of different genetic vulnerabilities, but the relationship between genes and behavior, between what we inherit and what we do, is complicated, even (or especially) for geneticists. For instance, people metabolize substances differently—faster, slower, or not well at all—and the pleasurable effects of substances vary among individuals. One person might feel woozy from two light beers while another person drinks a six-pack to begin to feel a buzz. There are even differences in the taste receptors on our tongues, affecting how good alcohol tastes to each of us. To some extent, our genetic inheritance (which is still not well understood) drives differences in how each of us reacts to a substance, and thus in how rewarding we experience it to be. We also know that people have different propensities to feel pleasure in ordinary life. One person might enjoy sharing a good laugh with friends while another has to drive his car at top speed around hairpin curves to feel pleasure. Differences in baseline levels of emotion—how we usually feel about life—as well as in novelty seeking, risk taking, and impulsivity can all contribute to an increased risk of substance problems.

Heritability refers to how much genetic factors account for a person's propensity to use substances, relative to another person's propensity. Scientists can measure genetically driven differences in risk for all sorts of illnesses and disorders, including cancer, diabetes, and depression. By our best estimates, the heritability of addictions (when measured as a problem that is diagnosable) ranges from 40 to 70 percent, with variation depending on the substance. These rates are in line with those of mood and anxiety disorders and others that are considered moderately genetically driven.

Environmental and social factors such as childhood neglect or abuse, trauma, loss of a parent as a child, and poor parent-child relationship have also been found to predict substance problems somewhat, as has starting use early in life. Availability of substances and peer use are factors too. But again, there is no clear cause and effect; these are "associated variables." In a case of four adult siblings who grew up in the same physically abusive household, one might be depressed, one might have a cocaine problem, one might have a cocaine and anger problem, and one might be happily married and have no mood or behavioral symptoms at all.

Culture has an impact on an individual's vulnerability to substance problems as well, in such forms as acceptability of intoxication within a given culture, gender differences in behavioral norms, and the price of a given substance within a society. (For example, higher taxes have reduced cigarette and alcohol consumption in certain states.) Local cultural factors like store hours, the size of drink containers, and legal consequences also affect use.

There is no clean separation between these influences; genes and biology interact reciprocally with environmental factors. Luckily, this complex mix includes a host of protective factors too, one of the strongest being positive family involvement, which can reduce the risk as well as influence the trajectory of substance problems. In fact, most individuals at risk for substance problems because of their genetics never start to use drugs, much less develop significant problems. Genetic inheritance and past experience do not seal a person's fate.

The Flexible Brain

You don't need diagrams of amygdalae or PET scans showing brain activity lit up in color to see that substances affect the brain. But we would like to share some of what we now know about the brain and its role in substance problems, as well as how it can contribute to change. Some understanding of neurotransmitters and brain functioning can help you respond constructively to your loved one's moods, cravings, and behaviors. It may also help you take her behavior less personally: Is she acting irresponsibly, or is the substance affecting her cerebral cortex in a particular way? Is it hedonism or is it dopamine running amok?

Remember the ad campaign with the motto "This is your brain on drugs"? The image of the fried egg was designed to increase awareness of the effect of substance use on the brain, but, while it got our attention, the fried egg in the poster didn't tell a crucial aspect of the story: the brain changes to *heal* from substance abuse, too. Since it is impossible to unfry an egg, that metaphor isn't so apt; the current evidence suggests that you needn't be as pessimistic as that fried egg led us to believe.

The notion of "permanent brain damage" is less applicable than scientists used to think; we now know that our brains are constantly evolving, even as adults. According to the old model of brain function, there were our formative years in early childhood and adolescence, after which, sometime in our twenties, we coasted and declined. Now we know that our brains continue to hone old pathways of activity and forge new ones long into adulthood. This is good news for everybody—old dogs not only *can* learn new tricks, they *should*, if they want to optimize their brain functioning—and it is especially good news for people affected by substance problems.

Our colleague John Mariani, MD, an addiction psychiatrist, teacher, clinician, and researcher at Columbia University, suggests we think of a broken leg instead of a fried egg. A bone breaks, and with help—a cast and crutches to prevent reinjury while the person returns to a normal routine, physical therapy to regain strength and flexibility, and family and friends to help and to keep up morale—the bone heals and the person can work, play, run, and jump again. The leg may be more vulnerable to breaking after all that, and the person will need to take care to protect it, but the person can adapt and, for the most part, the body heals. The brain is no exception. Given help and time, therapy and sometimes medication, concerted effort, and measures to safeguard against returning to substance use, brains do heal from the effects of drugs—perhaps not without a trace, but with enough resilience to justify optimism.

Good News: The brain can heal from substance abuse and scientists are finding out more about how.

What's the Big Deal About Dopamine?

From another corner of neuroscience, we're learning about a neurotransmitter called dopamine. Though there are more than fifty neurotransmitters (that we know of), scientists studying substance problems have given dopamine much of their attention. The brain's reward system and pleasure centers—the areas most impacted by substance use and compulsive behaviors—have a high concentration of dopamine. Some brains have more of it than others, and some people have a capacity to enjoy a range of experiences more than others, owing to a combination of genetics and environment. The thing about dopamine is that it makes us feel really good. We tend to want more of it. It is naturally generated through ordinary, pleasurable activities like eating and sex, and it is the brain's way of rewarding us—or nature's way of rewarding the brain—for activities necessary to our survival, individually or as a species. It is the "mechanism by which 'instinct' is manifest." Our brains arrange for dopamine levels to rise in anticipation and spike during a pleasurable activity to make sure we do it again. It helps focus our attention on all the cues that contributed to our exposure to whatever felt good (these eventually become triggers to use, as we explain later).

Drugs and alcohol (and certain behaviors) turn on a gushing fire hose of dopamine in the brain, and we feel good, even euphoric. Dopamine produced by these artificial means, however, throws our pleasure and reward systems out of whack immediately. Flooding the brain repeatedly with dopamine has long-term effects and creates what's known as tolerance—when we lose our ability to produce or absorb our own dopamine and need more and more of it artificially just to feel okay. Specifically, the brain compensates for the flood of dopamine by decreasing its own production of it or by desensitizing itself to the neurotransmitter by reducing the number of dopamine receptors, or both. The brain is just trying to keep a balance.

The problem with the brain's reduction in natural dopamine production is that when you take the substance or behavior out of the picture, there's not enough dopamine in the brain to make you feel good. Without enough dopamine, there is no interest or pleasure. Then not only does the brain lose the pleasure associated with using, it might not be able to enjoy a sunset or a back rub, either.

A lowered level of dopamine, combined with people's longing for the rush of dopamine they got from using substances, contributes to "craving" states. Cravings are a physiological process associated with the brain's struggle to regain its normal dopamine balance, and they can influence a decision to keep using a substance even when a person is experiencing negative consequences that matter to him and a strong desire to change. Depending on the length of time and quantities a person has been using, these craving states can be quite uncomfortable and compelling.

The dopamine system can and does recover, starting as soon as we stop flooding it. But it takes time, and in the time between shutting off the artificial supply of dopamine and the brain's rebuilding its natural resources, people tend to feel worse (before they feel better). On a deep, instinctual level, their brains are telling them that by *stopping* using, something is missing; something is wrong. This is a huge factor in relapse, despite good intentions and effort to change. Knowing this can help you and your loved one make it across this gap in brain reward systems. Medication and behavioral strategies can also help, as we will see in the coming chapters.

Dopamine balance in the brain is not the only thing that gets disrupted by repeated use of a substance. It also affects key structures in the brain, such as the prefrontal cortex and limbic system. The prefrontal cortex is where we assess risks, weigh consequences, and make plans—in other words, make considered decisions. It manages input from the other parts of the brain like the limbic system and bodily regions, and has been dubbed the braking system of the brain because it makes possible the judgments and decisions that go along with saying no to an impulse. When flooded with a substance, this part of the brain basically shuts down. (Teenagers have a distinct disadvantage here, as their young cerebral cortexes aren't even fully developed.)

The limbic system, in contrast, is where our sense of drive and urgency comes from, generated through emotion, motivation, and in some ways the formation of memories. In the context of substance use or compulsive behaviors, this part of the brain gets excited into overdrive. So a brain that finds its limbic system acutely activated and anticipating the reward of using, and its judgment and decision-making prefrontal cortex more or less disabled, is a brain that's likely to go forward with the impulse and desire to use—no stop and all go. A brain in this state will register the smell of marijuana being smoked, the desire to smoke it, and anticipate the feeling that comes along with smoking, while the reasons not to smoke disappear. (When, at some point with repeated use, tolerance develops, the desire to use is not so much focused on feeling good, but on just not feeling bad.)

Like cravings from low dopamine, the runaway limbic system is also an automatic, physiological process that is outside conscious control. It just happens.

We hope that understanding this much about the brain's role in substance use and compulsive behaviors will inform your compassion for what your loved one is going through, give you optimism for his brain's capacity to change, and maybe make it all a bit more tolerable for you. When he tries to stop using and seems agitated and cranky, you can understand it as *his brain* struggling to accept the new state of affairs. When you see him returning to old behavior even though he promised he would stop, perhaps you will consider that it happened as a result of craving states generated in his brain rather than assuming he lied to you and doesn't care about your feelings. It's not easy, but with awareness, new coping skills, sometimes medications, practice, and time, brains can heal and learn new behavior patterns that take precedence over old habits. Triggers lose their power to trigger and the brain regains its power to pause, reflect, and choose a different response. Research has proven that learning new hab-

Different for Different People

ve was born into a family with a long history of alcohol problems, and
genetic chances of alcohol dependence were higher than for someone
hout that history. Because of his genes, the effect he got from alcohol
s stimulating but weak. He drank more to get the same effect, and he
nk often because he liked the effect. His brother had been trying for
rs to get him to go to AA meetings with him, but every time the subject
ne up they argued. The brother smoked a pack and a half of cigarettes
ay, but hadn't had a drink in seventeen years.

eventy-eight-year-old Margaret was used to having three drinks a
: a glass of wine with lunch, a bourbon before dinner, and a glass of
e with dinner. When her husband was alive, they had their pre-dinner
rbon together nearly every night for forty-six years of marriage. They
d to tease each other when they forgot things, and say, "The bourbon
t be helping." After her husband died, Margaret lived alone and usually
nk her three drinks alone. Her daughter, who lived two thousand miles
y and called often, tried to convince her to drink less. Her daughter's
eaties annoyed her, but Margaret didn't say so, nor did she mention
own concerns about her memory.

idan had been drinking at parties since he was fourteen but about
t months ago his friend gave him Vicodin, an opioid painkiller, and
ad been using more and more ever since. His friend had taken it
his father's medicine chest and gotten so hooked he started buying
a dealer. Whereas Aidan liked drinking when partying with a big
p, the Vicodin was something he did only with his friend. His par-
knew about the drinking and never made an issue of it. They didn't
about the Vicodin and he didn't want to tell them, even though he
een worried about it since he and his friend tried stopping and felt
ful that they went back to it two days later. Aidan and his dad had a
common and sometimes they had good talks, but he was afraid of
d's temper.

e, a professional woman in her fifties, smoked more than a pack of
ttes a day and felt that, for a long list of reasons she could recite to
lf (and often did), she was a horrible person. Even though she was
ssful in her work, she felt worthless and afraid, and when she smoked
rgot those feelings temporarily. And though she was worried about
alth, she looked forward to stepping out for a cigarette. She also had
tic predisposition to depression, and the cigarettes seemed to help,
always felt better for the moment.

its to replace old habits changes the brain. It then makes
of the most effective treatment techniques for substance
behavior problems do just that: they retrain a brain.

Good News: Scientists in the exciting field of interpersonal
showing us that the nature-nurture divide turns out not to
an ongoing interaction of biology and environment. Our envir
other people, who affect us all the way down to a molecular
are changed by our relationships and our brains impact o
Remember this if you doubt whether you can compete with
effects of a drug on your loved one. You—your love, empathy
and limits—have physiological effects too.

What Is Addiction? Part 2:
What Does It Mean in My House?

Besides the causal theories and diagnostic criteria,
meaning of substance problems for you and your fai
below will help you understand addiction in the conte

1. Is your loved one's substance use causing problems
that you find unacceptable?
The definition of a problem is different for each pe
occur with any amount of substance use, and it's im
urge to compare your situation to others' as you con:
stances in your relationship. For example, a couple
wine with dinner may not pose a problem for either
when one person drinks two big glasses of wine a
doesn't drink anything, the fact that the first perso
a buzz going in the evening might be a problem for
drink. Or it might not: the teetotaler may not min
habit one bit. The problem lies in the negative co
either of you experiences them. All or none of the
ples below may meet the DSM criteria for a Substan
matters is what matters to the individuals themsel
behavior affects their lives and their loved ones.

All of these people are using different substances, for different reasons, with different negative effects. And they are all likely to change their substance use over time in different ways. Ignoring these differences would be like consulting the manual for your hair dryer when you are working on your car. Both have motors, but the wrong manual won't help you understand or tell you how to help.

2. How much of a problem does your loved one think her use is?

Here we don't mean what *you* think, or what *others* think, and not what she would say when backed into a corner. Whatever the negative consequences of substance use may appear to be, how much do they actually bother your loved one? Ultimately, this internal valuation of the costs and benefits is what we call *motivation*. The greater your loved one's sense of the costs of a behavior relative to the benefits, the more motivated she will be to change. Understanding how motivation works is so important, we give it its own chapter.

In Margaret's case, she was aware of memory problems but it wasn't until she underwent—at the suggestion of a longtime friend of her late husband's—a battery of neurological tests to rule out Alzheimer's that she started taking her memory lapses and their connection to her drinking habits seriously. It was at this point that she came to us. Her daughter's nagging hadn't helped. What had helped was her daughter realizing that by pressing her mother on the drinking, she was only irritating her and pushing her away. It had been Margaret's daughter's idea to ask the family friend to call, and they had agreed he would not ask about the drinking; he would just ask how Margaret was doing. Given that room, and the comfort of the connection she felt to her husband through his old friend, she was able to take her own account of the costs of drinking.

Note that Margaret's daughter did not stop calling her mother; they just talked about other things. Recognizing that a benefit of drinking bourbon for Margaret was the sense of connection to her late husband, Margaret and her daughter made a point of talking about him. Margaret also stayed in touch with her husband's old friend. The bourbon itself became less appealing to her as she learned that she didn't need it to remember her husband. At the same time she felt less harassed and defensive and more willing to talk to her daughter about her health issues. Eventually, Margaret replaced her before-dinner drink with a before-dinner call from her daughter.

3. Is he physically or psychologically dependent, or, how dangerous would it be to stop?

People often think of addiction as defined by whether a person can stop without the shakes, nausea, vomiting, aches, and pain. In fact, many substances have no physical withdrawal symptoms associated with stopping. A person can qualify as having a substance abuse disorder, according to the *DSM-5*, without being physically dependent on the substance. A person with a pattern of sporadic bingeing may never have any signs of physical withdrawal, yet be in real danger during each binge.

When a person has been using a substance(s) regularly, the brain notices when it is removed. The removal causes a withdrawal phenomenon that can manifest symptoms ranging from mild (low mood, restlessness, irritability) to severe and potentially life-threatening (insomnia, depression, paranoia, seizure, delirium tremens). Symptoms can be short-lived or last for months.

In some cases, as with alcohol or benzodiazepines, "just stopping" can be outright dangerous, even life-threatening. When Steve told us he drank to "feel it" every night, it was a red flag. We needed to know how much and for how long he'd been doing this before we knew whether it was safe for him to stop cold turkey. A thorough evaluation also revealed that Steve had a history of heart problems and occasionally threw up in the morning but had not seen his doctor in a long time. These are important considerations. If your loved one is in trouble with these substances, he may need to be physically detoxified under medical supervision, preferably with the aid of medications.

With other substances, such as OxyContin, Vicodin, heroin, or other opiates, physical dependence can make stopping intensely painful and distressing, though not in itself life-threatening. Aidan and his friend experienced withdrawal when they tried to quit using painkillers. They were uncomfortable enough to start using again, but it wasn't dangerous for them to stop. In these cases, certain medications can ease the brain's transition from using to not using, and help people manage the craving states that often result in a return to use in spite of their desire to stop.

Some substances produce a fairly intense *psychological* withdrawal upon stopping, especially after a period of heavy or prolonged use. Using cocaine or amphetamines, for instance, can result in a window of depression or emotional flatness in which the person experiences no pleasure. Ending a long period of marijuana use can result in a pronounced spike in anxiety. Either state can be difficult for the abstainer to tolerate, and most people are at high risk of relapse in these early days. It is helpful to educate your-self about the type and quantity of substance(s) that are in your loved one's system and the associated withdrawal symptoms if he were to stop using.

We do not suggest that you take on the responsibility of diagnosing your loved one. We recommend instead that you talk to your doctor or an addiction psychiatrist to find out if medically supervised detoxification is necessary or advisable. Meanwhile, the greater your awareness about your loved one's experience, the more helpful you can be.

4. What are the dangers if he doesn't stop?

Substance abuse can be dangerous—we see lives destroyed and terri-ble things happen. Sometimes people die. AND . . . it's equally true that change doesn't happen in an instant, and often can't be forced. Friends and family understandably worry all through the ebb and flow of their loved one's use and its consequences. This can go on for years, with worry cross-ing over to panic when calm and patience would serve everyone better. Staying calm is easy to say and much harder to do, but it is doable.

Every substance has its own risk profile. Cocaine use can result in strokes and heart attacks; alcohol use can result in liver disease, a variety of can-cers, alcohol poisoning, blackouts, and disinhibited actions such as driv-ing drunk; heroin use can result in overdosing (respiratory depression), or being poisoned from a "bad batch"; methamphetamine use can result in crushing depression, personality transformation, and suicidal ideas; cig-arette use has well-documented and severe, long-term, broad-spectrum physical consequences. Unfortunately, there is a Russian roulette quality to substance use: any of it can happen anytime (but usually doesn't).

The "When Is It an Emergency?" exercise at the end of the book (page 287) is intended to help you sort through what can be a confusing, scary mess of symptoms, urges, feelings, and problems. It can help you learn to distinguish feelings of doom or panic that may have been building for years, from truly unsafe situations for your loved one and/or others involved. Talk to a qualified professional about the particulars of your sit-uation. The information you gather in the exercise will be helpful in that conversation.

Emergency or not, it is always better to have the facts and stay calm.

5. How hard would it be for her to stop and stay stopped?

Or to continue moderating, if that's the goal? The moment of stopping tends to receive more attention than it deserves. For most people, main-taining change over the long run is the real challenge.

Embedded in this question is another one: How much treatment support would your loved one need to make a change? The answer could be anywhere from none to not much to inpatient treatment, and the best answer, according to the American Society of Addiction Medicine's (ASAM) standards for assessment, is always the *least* intrusive level of care that is safe and sufficient to keep the person motivated and involved.

Could she stop on her own, without formal treatment? Remember, most people with substance problems do just that. You can't know the whole answer to this one up front, but you may have an idea. (Plus, keeping this question in mind over time will help you and your loved one assess her evolving needs.) Margaret didn't want inpatient treatment, nor did she need it. With the support of her daughter and her husband's old friend, it was enough to see her CMC therapist once a week for a few months as well as her new medical doctor.

The new paradigm for substance problems recognizes a range of severity and degrees of entrenchment, and calls for *proportional* therapeutic intervention.

6. What strategies would help him stop?

Keep reading! But for now, just bear in mind that a) it's different for different people; b) it matters what he thinks would help; and c) it matters what research has shown to help. Many people have strong opinions about what helps, but unfortunately, people who have the strongest opinions are not always the most informed.

When Steve, the man with the genetic vulnerability for alcohol problems, came across an article suggesting that Alcoholics Anonymous wasn't the only option, he explored others. He also shared the article with his brother, who continued to attend AA himself but backed off from insisting on it for Steve. Among Steve's strategies to stop drinking was spending time outdoors with his brother, which had been a great source of joy for both of them growing up, and was again now that they had (mostly) stopped arguing as adults. Incidentally, Steve's brother found that the less he smoked, the more he enjoyed hiking. He cut back significantly, especially before and during trips, and for the first time in his life started to think seriously about quitting.

Just as different people have different reasons to use substances and different reasons to change, there are many legitimate paths to change. In fact, having a choice among options for change makes it that much more likely to happen, as we will see in the next chapter.

7. What strategies has she tried already and did they work for a time?

A key piece of problem solving is learning from what has or hasn't worked, and making adjustments. Often, people have made attempts at change previously and had some success; it is valuable to acknowledge this and examine it in order to see what might be helpful moving forward (or what might get in the way).

Aidan, the high school student using Vicodin, had tried stopping on his own. From this he learned that he would need help. When his parents found out about it, they suggested he talk to us. We referred the family to an addiction psychiatrist who prescribed buprenorphine, an opiate replacement medication. This bought us time to work with Aidan on making changes in his life that would support his not using Vicodin. Among other things, he joined the cross-country running team and told the friend he'd been using with that he couldn't hang out with him unless he also got help. Later—more than a year later—when Aidan gradually tapered off of the buprenorphine, he was able not only to tolerate life without Vicodin but to enjoy it. Unlike his first attempt, this time he had given himself more reasons not to use, like new hobbies that gave him pleasure, a support system that included psychotherapy (where he learned new ways to cope with social anxiety), and his parents, who he learned were pretty cool and actually kind of fun.

Many of our clients have tried to quit before, often multiple times. By looking closely at these earlier attempts, we can learn what didn't work—for example, what was going on leading up to a relapse after three months of abstinence? Additionally, however (and this is the part that is too often ignored), we acknowledge that three months of abstinence is an achievement in itself. We want to know what *did* work for those three months. Were there attitudes, behaviors, people, medications, and so on that helped then and could again? In changing substance use, as in the rest of life, rarely if ever do we find that *everything* or, conversely, *nothing* is working. Usually it's a mix of both. A black-and-white, success/failure view obscures enormous amounts of information about the learning process that can be crucial to keeping change going.

8. Does he need to stop entirely?

"Sobriety sampling" is the approach our colleague Robert Meyers suggests in dealing with this question. Unlike the traditional model that assumes that total and permanent abstinence is the one-and-only solution for everyone with substance problems, sobriety sampling offers a palatable starting place for many who can't yet imagine never using a substance again. We discuss how it works in more detail in the "Treatment Options" chapter, but in a nutshell, a person agrees to stop using for a week or two weeks or a month or whatever length of time seems doable (with help and encouragement) to that individual at the outset. This sets him up for success, to experience abstinence as tolerable, possible, and confidence building, rather than a prison. The client gathers data in the spirit of an experiment to see what works, what doesn't, and what to do next. In this way, abstinence becomes a personal process, less monolithic and daunting than the traditional, generic imperative of abstinence for life. People are more likely to move forward in a positive direction when they frame their goals this way, as opposed to being dragged along reluctantly with dread and pessimism about a sober future.

For Steve, sobriety sampling was the difference between refusing help of any kind and trying out some changes that made sense to him.

And so, finally, what is addiction? Understanding your particular situation, with all its complexities, will help you more than any diagnostic categorizing. Throughout this book, we hope to show you how understanding—including your perspective and that of your loved one—can guide your actions to foster positive change.

Exercise: What Really Matters

We can tell you why these questions are important, but we can't answer them for you—precisely because your situation is unique. Start to think about the answers to these questions for you and your loved one. Down the road, you may want to refer to your answers if you think you've lost sight of what matters. You may want to revisit the questions, too, since the answers, like everything, will likely change over time.

1. Is your loved one's substance use causing problems that you find unacceptable?
2. What's important to your loved one about his substance use? What does he get out of it? (The Behavior Analysis exercise in the next chapter will help you explore this in detail.)
3. How much of a problem does *your loved one* think her use is?
4. (This one is for a qualified professional.) Is your loved one physically or psychologically dependent?
5. (A professional should help you answer this one too.) What are the dangers if she doesn't stop?
6. Do you have a sense of how hard it would be for him to stop and stay stopped?
7. What strategies would help her stop?
8. What strategies has he tried already, and did they work for a time?
9. Do you think she needs to stop entirely?

CHAPTER 2.

Motivation:
Why Do People Change?

Do you think of your loved one as *unmotivated*? Does his decision to continue using substances seem inexplicable, stubborn, and even crazy to you? You may have given up trying to understand why he does what he does—and why he doesn't do what you wish he would do. You may be so frustrated and angry that you don't care anymore why he does it; you just want it to stop. By the time families come to us for help, they often feel as though they're living in a different universe from their loved one, or at the very least speaking a different language. But substance use and other compulsive behaviors are not as mysterious as they may seem, and your loved one is not as unreachable as you might think.

In fact, your loved one is motivated in at least one direction—to use substances. We're not being flippant. This chapter will help you see the immense value in understanding your loved one's perspective. For the most part, people decide to take an action, for example, to use a substance, because they get something out of it. They are, in other words, "motivated" by the outcome of the action. In the case of substance use, the objective could be to feel happy and excited, to feel less depressed and anxious, or to fit in with peers. As we saw in chapter 1, people use substances for different reasons—usually, for each person, a combination of reasons.

The first, critical step in helping people change is to understand the motivation for their behavior in the first place—not the deep-rooted, historic motivations (though sometimes these too), but what, in the here and now, makes sense about their behavior *to them*. Using substances or engaging in other compulsive behaviors is goal-oriented behavior, not crazy or stupid or immoral. There's nothing crazy about the statement "I like to drink because it makes me feel better." It might even seem disappointingly obvious once we put it that way. Understanding the reason behind a person's behavior, however, contains the seeds of a solution to the problem. It

44

could be that when the person finds another way to feel better and a better way to cope with not feeling better, she won't choose to drink. Of course she probably drinks for other reasons too, and she might drink for different reasons at different times. Regardless of the pattern, understanding what it is doing for her lets you start moving in another direction.

You may feel like you're already doing all the work, and are put off that now we're asking you to be understanding too. You may also be anxious to skip over the understanding part and just get on with the changing part. But understanding motivation is crucial to building an environment where real change, and real collaboration, can begin. In recent decades, researchers and clinicians have made remarkable progress in the science of motivation and change. We want you to have this information, not as the theory behind our practical advice, but as a necessary step to change. Hopefully, too, you will be relieved to know that your loved one is more than "just not motivated" and, in fact, always has the potential to change.

Until recently, traditional methods of treatment for substance problems conceived of motivation as a fixed trait: you have it or you don't. People who supposedly didn't have the motivation to change were told to come back when they were "ready." Family members were coached to disengage, as there was nothing they could do until their loved one was "ready." Unfortunately (and sometimes tragically), this view left clinicians and family members on one of two sides, neither of which was helpful: they could passively wait for motivation to happen, or they could aggressively demand change.

Thanks to good research, we now know that treatment providers, family members, and others important to your loved one can all have a positive impact on his motivation. Conversely, we know that certain ways of interacting cause people to push back, hold on tighter to the status quo, and, what's worse, pretend to comply without a genuine investment in change. Human interaction affects motivation. In this chapter, we share all that we know about how motivation works so you can make it work for your loved one and you.

Janie, a woman in her early thirties, came to us because she was worried about (and fed up with) her husband, Oscar, who often stayed out after work and didn't come home until late. He was not very communicative about his nighttime activities, would often stop answering his phone at a certain point in the evening, compounding Janie's worries about his safety and the state of their marriage. She knew Oscar was drinking a lot because he smelled like alcohol when he came home and in the morning. He also had taken to passing out on their front porch swing and acknowledged having used cocaine several times (as he asked her for cash in the morning). She knew he usually went out with his two best friends, who were also coworkers. She also knew, because she was there, that he drank a lot at family events. Recently, Janie's mother had asked if he had a problem.

Janie for the most part thought her husband was acting like he was still in college—indeed, she had met him in college and they used to go out drinking together—and she couldn't understand why he wouldn't settle down. She wanted to start having kids, something they'd talked about early on in their marriage but not so much lately without the discussion breaking down into yelling and tears. Now their weekends together began with his hangover and her anger. By Sunday night they would have started to repair the damage and reconnect, just in time to start the cycle all over again. Over the past nine months, Janie had tried a number of times to talk to Oscar about his behavior. Her frustration usually showed, and these "talks" usually ended with Oscar storming out of the room.

Was Oscar unmotivated? Was he in denial? Was there nothing Janie could do until he decided he was ready to change? Did she need to just sit tight and let things get worse? Should she have hired an interventionist and tried to push her husband into rehab? Traditionally, the assumptions would be yes on all counts. What we now know from clinical experience as well as research on motivation, however, tells a different story.

What Is Motivation?

Like addiction, motivation can also be understood to be "in the brain." Many neurological systems are involved in goal-directed behavior; the outward signs of motivation—for example, taking action—are a result of complex internal neurological processes. In essence, motivation is the link between emotion ("ahh . . . this feels good" or "wow, I could use some relief") and action (having another drink), involving the parts of the brain that manage attention, pleasure seeking, inhibition, and memory. In the end, motivation gives us the energy to make a decision and take action and is intimately involved in how we recognize a problem and attempt to solve it.

Remember the discussion of dopamine from chapter 1? Since it is instrumental in the human experience of what is enjoyable and worthwhile, it also plays a significant role in motivational states. For example, do you like camping? Do you hate it? Don't have strong feelings about it, or much interest? Whatever your feelings, you'd agree that one has to be pretty motivated to take all the steps of planning and organizing to get on the road for a camping trip.

In neurobiological (and simplified) terms, we are motivated to do things that have been associated with dopamine in our experience. So we are motivated to go camping if dopamine flowed the last time we went or, if you have never been, perhaps when you looked at pictures of a beautiful camping spot. As we look forward to the trip, we summon the drive it takes to pack up backpacks, organize maps, plan meals, and forgo our comfy bed for a week. When we're there, we take in the sounds, smells, and adventure of the experience and dopamine flows and we feel good. In the end, the decision to do all the work associated with a camping trip is motivated by the anticipation and actual reward of smelling pine needles, hearing babbling brooks, and eating s'mores.

Motivation works in the same way with the decision to use a substance. Substance use increases dopamine in the brain (or the substance itself acts like dopamine). If someone who is struggling with depression uses cocaine and feels more alert, engaged, and less tired, they may be motivated to use cocaine to "feel better" again, even though going on a camping trip would also make the person feel better. Camping is a lot more work. According to what we'll call the zero-to-sixty rule, the quicker a substance (or experience) affects the brain, the more powerfully the brain is motivated to use it. And it's relative: if the brain's reward system has learned to release dopamine in response to a drug, it might not get excited by nature, the smell of a campfire, s'mores, and so on. In other words, the benefits of camping will pale in comparison to those of using the drug. For someone using substances, cocaine is rocket fuel, while camping is a can of Sterno.

Thankfully, as we discussed in chapter 1, some of the most exciting and hopeful research in neurobiology is revealing how psychological and social factors like medications, therapy, and family involvement can, in turn, change our brains and motivational states. The brain and the world in which it operates are inextricably intertwined; we literally take in substances, people, and other stimuli, and they affect the very structure and functioning of our brains. Our brains in turn affect our behavior toward substances, people, and other stimuli in the world. Understanding the interactive nature of motivation, you can see the value in staying engaged. Your loved one is affecting his brain chemistry with substances; you can affect his brain chemistry with the way you interact.

In other words, don't leave your loved one's brain alone! You can affect those covert systems with strategically planned overt actions; you can influence your loved one's choices by helping him associate positive experiences with positive actions ("I feel better when my wife . . . " instead of "I feel better when I use . . . "). The "How to Help" section (Part 3) will show you how to do this.

Neuroscience is not the only science supporting the idea that we influence others' motivation. One of the most robust, evidence-supported theories describing human motivation is Self-Determination Theory (SDT), developed by Edward Deci and Richard Ryan, psychologists at the University of Rochester. In explaining the impact of the interpersonal, social environment on human motivation and behavior, SDT identifies two types of motivations behind people's choices: *internal*, or autonomous, and *external*, or controlled motivation.

When we are internally motivated to do something, we have reasons for making a choice or taking action that make sense to us, to our values, desires, and thinking. External motivation comes from reasons outside of us, as in the law, company policy, school rules, parental rules, or anyone else's reasons for why we should do something. While their influence and power tend to fade over time, external forces are often the reasons we do things in the first place ("I don't want to get arrested," "I want to get an A," "I want my coach to be proud of me"). But imagine if the only reason you had to show up for work every day until you retire was "because I'll get fired if I don't." Hopefully you have a number of more positive, internal motivations for doing your work.

Self-determination applies to the whole range of human behaviors and relationships, from children at play to athletes' performance, from parent-child to boss-employee to doctor-patient relations. Within these relationships, the way one person interacts has proved to affect the type of motivation the other person experiences. In other words, your behavior toward your loved one can help to foster her internal motivation.

Some clients who over time made great changes working with us at CMC wouldn't have come through the door in the first place if they hadn't been compelled by external motivators. They were told—sometimes with kindness and a rationale appealing to their point of view; sometimes without—that they needed to choose between their marriage and cocaine, between graduating and getting stoned, between their job and drinking every night. The external motivation added a sudden weight to the costs of continuing the behavior, moving the person to seek help in the moment. However, *maintaining* changes in behavior beyond that first decision usually requires a shift, at least in part, from external motivators to internal ones. Research has shown time and again that it is essential that people develop their own reasons or "buy in" to change.

We need to find our own reasons for doing things. We need internal motivation to change our behavior if we're going to continue caring enough to stick with it. The traditional treatment mandate to "come back when you're ready" partly got it right: maintaining change usually requires that people develop their own reasons for wanting that change. What this mandate did not get, however, is that a person's internal motivation is directly influenced by external factors, including treatment providers. Our mandate has become *How do we help you shift your motivation?*

A husband could strategize to make dinner for his wife and be affectionate toward her when she comes home sober. When she comes home intoxicated, he can tell her he is going to the den to read and let her make dinner for herself. At first, her husband's withdrawal and having to cook dinner for herself would be an external motivator for the wife not to drink. But after they've had some nice dinners together (when she has come home sober) and she's enjoying his company and feeling good about her marriage, the reasons to skip the drinks after work start to become important to her, and she internalizes the motivation. Now she values this time with her husband and knows that if she drinks it won't happen, and she will miss it; this becomes *her* reason to not drink, and as such it will more likely hold over the long haul. In terms of self-determination theory, the husband's behavior contributed to an environment where his wife felt motivated to change.

As we've stressed before, everyone is different, but for most people a combination of external and internal factors has the strongest effect on their motivation and actions. A classic example is the case of physicians, who have one of the highest recovery rates among categories of people struggling with substance abuse. They have tremendous external pressures and structure: urine testing, close monitoring, appearances before the state board, and their careers to lose if they fail. But they also like their lives as doctors—that's why they went to medical school in the first place. They understand their substance use to be incompatible with the life they want. When the external controls are removed, they have enough internal reasons to maintain the changes.

What We Know about Motivation

Motivation is a state, specific to a given behavior,
not a general trait inherent in a person.

Everyone is motivated, just not always in the ways other people would like us to be. Teenagers may be highly motivated to hang out with their friends,

ficial, and not clearly thought through. As a result, they don't hold after those reasons change or those emotions subside. For example, Oscar in the earlier example could decide to stop drinking because Janie threatened to leave him. When Janie was more relaxed, he might decide she wouldn't really mind if he went out. The short-term, reactive motivation doesn't ultimately sustain change—and causes pessimism and discouragement in family and friends.

*Motivation to change can occur whenever the costs
of a behavior outweigh the benefits.*

People who have decided to change their use of substances without ever consulting a professional (which, you'll recall, is *most* people) most frequently cite as their reason for changing some version of "the costs outweighed the benefits." This realization can strike like an epiphany or it can develop over time, but it does happen, often. In fact, in the context of motivational therapies, this cost-benefit analysis (or "decisional balance" in therapy-speak) is one of the most powerful techniques in the therapist's motivational arsenal.

Of course, people's perceptions of costs and benefits can change over time for the same behavior, and it can be maddening when your loved one does not see the equation in the same light you do. You may not want to acknowledge the benefits your loved one perceives in his behavior. And it may be painful and scary to be aware of how much he relies on a substance to get things done, unwind or relax, or just feel okay in his own skin.

If, however, you can understand how your loved one has constructed his ledger—the cost-benefit balance inherent in his behavior—it can help you understand your potential to influence his costs, benefits, and perceptions, which in turn will affect his motivation for change. Specifically, you can change your behavior in a way that shifts the costs of your loved one's behavior back to him so you aren't carrying them on your shoulders. Instead of getting him up in the morning and enduring the fight you usually have, you can let him sleep in and miss his meeting and feel his boss's frustration. You can help your loved one define the costs of his behavior more sharply for himself, and with less conflict between you.

One of our clients made dinner for his wife every night. Often she would come home drunk, they'd fight, and she'd take her plate into the TV room. This made him furious. He would either lash out at her or give her the silent treatment. But he kept making dinner for her, out of habit and because in spite of his anger he wanted to take care of her somehow. His CMC therapist suggested he consider his wife's motivations. He saw that not having dinner made for her could be a cost for her of drinking and, conversely, having dinner made for her could be a benefit of not drinking. He strategized to wait to make dinner until his wife was home and he knew she wasn't intoxicated. They both experienced the difference. As he described it, "Now when she comes home sober she watches TV while I make dinner, and then we eat together, which is really nice for both of us. If she is drinking, I let her make her own food while I read a book by myself." One change like this may not tip the scales, but a number of them will add up; positive change often starts to happen well before the biggest issues are resolved. However long his wife took to weigh the costs and benefits, their fighting and his resentment had already decreased dramatically. Meanwhile, as their relationship improved, his wife felt closer to and more considerate of him, which was intrinsically motivating to both of them.

When people see their behavior as inconsistent with their self-image or goals, their motivation to change can increase.

We can find potential energy for change in any gap between how we see ourselves now and who we want to be. We may look at our current state of affairs and think, *This is not who I am!* and the balance can shift toward making a change. Sometimes this happens organically, as when someone becomes a parent and decides something they used to do or not do is no longer compatible with what it means to them to be a parent. For instance, a couple may have stopped attending synagogue for years, then realize, as they plan for the birth of their first child, that they want their new family to be part of that community and spiritual life. So they start going to synagogue again. Other times the assessment requires soul-searching, trial, and error as we clarify our values and goals and figure out the steps we need to take to realign our lives.

It takes courage for any of us to examine ourselves, to step back and ask, *Is this who I want to be?* It turns out that the right kind of encouragement from others can prompt this type of questioning and self-reflection, and depending on other people's feedback, we can feel hopeful and galvanized by the possibility of change, or we can feel demoralized and dismayed by our failings.

A client told us the balance shifted for her when she took her six-year-old for a playdate at the home of another first grader. As she sat having coffee with the other mom, she overheard her son say to his friend, "Your house is really fun because your mom plays games with us." While it was a passing comment to everyone else, the woman was mortified; since she had been taking painkillers for her back pain she hadn't had the energy to do much with her son, and she felt terribly guilty about this. Her back seemed to be hurting more frequently, and she wondered if it had anything to do with the added stress she was under since they had let go of the babysitter and she'd cut back her job. For days she thought about what her son said, reeling from her embarrassment. She felt almost too ashamed to bring it up with her husband, but when she did he gave her a hug and joked that at least their son hadn't mentioned her fondness for reruns of *Dallas*. In seriousness, he asked what *she* thought about the pill use and her back pain, and offered to help in any way he could. As they talked she relaxed and felt more comfortable, and changing her behavior seemed more doable knowing he was on her side. She attended one of our skills groups to learn how to handle the issues—boredom, restlessness, worries about her career—that all seemed to be adding to her stress. Eventually, she decided to start physical therapy to strengthen her back and learn mindfulness meditation skills to address her stress. The pills no longer seemed like an acceptable coping strategy to her, as she didn't want her son to feel she was unavailable or "out of it." That was not the mom she wanted to be.

Ambivalence is a normal part of motivation and the change process.

Motivation waxes and wanes. We need not panic in the face of ambivalence when we know that fluctuating is just what motivation does; it's in its nature, and we can work *with* it. When we waver in our own resolutions to "exercise more" or "eat less fried food" or "read poetry" or "stop smoking," we feel this to be frustrating but normal. When our teenager was convinced last week that he wanted to give up pot, but now seems not so sure, it may seem intolerable. But ambivalence is normal, and learning to roll with it is the best way through. One of the great insights of the motivational therapies developed for substance problems has been just this: that ambivalence is *integral* to change, not an unfortunate feeling to be quashed or avoided, or a failure to "get with the program."

If using substances were like putting a hand on a hot stove, all downside and no upside, you wouldn't be reading this book, because your loved one wouldn't need help. There would be no ambivalence; he would have stopped a long time ago.

But we're not dealing with burning-hot metal; we're dealing with behavior that has an upside, often multiple upsides, at least for the people doing it and often for others as well. "I drink because it lets me relax with my friends"; "I am funnier when I'm tipsy"; "I lose weight with cocaine"; "I focus better for my SATs with lots of Adderall"; "I am less depressed about my arthritis when I use OxyContin"; and so on. There is a counterargument to every one of these reasons, but that is precisely the point: ambivalence is the pull in two directions at the same time, both of which can seem like good directions. The more this can be accepted as normal, the less people have to cling to the unrealistic idea that there's no looking back, and the more openly and effectively they can deal with their ambivalence.

When clients tell us what they think we want to hear—their unswerving commitment to change—we're wary. We actually want to hear all about their ambivalence, the reasons pro and con for continuing the status quo or for changing. We know that if we are only hearing the cons of their behavior we are only hearing half the story, and unacknowledged pros have a way of ambushing people. Similarly, if you can't tolerate ambivalence in the change process, your loved one will sense this and probably tell you only what he knows you want to hear, if he tells you anything at all. If he knows you won't go berserk, on the other hand, he'll be more likely to tell you when he's wavering. When you know about it, ambivalence can be a huge opportunity for you to help.

This is important because holding to a black-and-white notion of unwavering commitment to change is often a setup for excessive disappointment and destroyed confidence about lapsing. Many people (and their loved ones) believe that if a person returns to old behavior patterns, he must not really want to change, or even worse, is just an "addict" who can't change. A lapse is in fact much more productively understood as the benefits of using outweighing the costs at that time. By understanding the benefits we can help find competing beneficial behaviors, or ways to reduce the benefit's pull. It may also be that there is a cost to *changing* that is exerting more influence than the benefits of changing at that time. Perhaps the loss of contact with familiar friends and a mild depression are outweighing the value of stopping cocaine use. If you can tolerate thinking about his perception of the *downside* to changing, you will be better equipped to help alter the environment and your behavior to counter this downside. If you know he is struggling with newfound loneliness, you could plan social events that bring him together with supportive friends and family or new peers whom he does not associate with using.

Allowing for people's ambivalence does not mean biding our time until they snap out of it. Understanding and appreciating why your loved one does what she does will help you have more empathy and identify how you can modify your behavior, your relationship, and her environment so you can help to support long-term change.

A forty-five-year-old construction manager came to us to follow up a twenty-eight-day rehab stay. Sol was committed to abstinence, and as part of his plan he attended three AA meetings a week, as well as working with his AA sponsor (a more senior member of the group who acts as a kind of mentor). Sol liked many aspects of his AA group, but he noticed over time that when someone discussed a lapse to drinking, the elders, as he referred to them (people with many years of sobriety), would invariably question the person's level of commitment. Sol realized that if he were to lapse, he would not feel comfortable disclosing it in this group. His uneasiness grew over time until he felt he could not bring up even his intermittent cravings to drink. He feared "letting the guys down," as he put it, thinking that they wouldn't accept his ambivalence. In this case, the group became useless to him, as he was presenting an incomplete and thus unhelpable version of himself: *What's to help? Everything's fine.*

Motivation is interactive, affected by the environment, and YOU are the environment!

Motivation is, in a word, *malleable*. Interactions with other people affect our motivation. In social psychology, Deci and Ryan's self-determination theory shows us that our interpersonal environment has a huge impact on how much we feel like starting, end up sticking with, and enjoy a particular action along the way. In parenting, teaching, managing employees, and many other arenas, what we do (and don't do) deeply affects other people's motivation to act or change.

In Sol's case, his therapist helped him find a different AA meeting, one where for a variety of reasons—members his own age, a warmer feel, and most particularly a group where people spoke openly about lapses and cravings—he felt he could be completely honest, and where Sol felt supported and encouraged even when he'd slipped, which is of course when he needed it the most. (We helped alter his environment—trying a different meeting—in an effort to keep his motivation high for going to meetings. We encourage clients looking to join a support group to try several for the best fit. Many people benefit from 12-step involvement, but ultimately this model isn't for everyone, and there are other options. Even within AA, groups vary from one to the next, and multiple groups in any given area can accommodate many people.)

One big thing in your loved one's environment that you can change is, very specifically, YOU. You are malleable too! If you've been told a thousand times that you're supposed to stay out of it, because it's up to your loved one to change, then it may sound like we're saying it's all up to you. It may even sound like the job of changing is your job or that your loved one's resistance to change is your fault.

It is not your job or your fault. We can't make other people change. What we can do is learn to provide an environment that lets them be less reactive to what we're doing (such as yelling or judging) and more concerned with their own behavior and its consequences. You can't make someone want to change, but you can help him realize that he wants to change, and help reduce his need to defend his current behavior, which can get him stuck there. You'll be in a position to do this if you stay connected. You won't if you detach.

Good News: No matter how stuck things seem to be, motivation can change. You don't have to be a therapist to encourage your loved one's motivation in a positive direction.

The Things That Can Change Motivation

In practical terms, how can you positively impact another person's motivation to change? Here's what enhances people's motivation to do something, and *keep* doing it, according to the evidence:

- Feeling acknowledged, understood, and accepted as you are (*not* contingent on doing something or not doing something)
- Getting information without pressure
- Having options
- Having reasons that make sense for a particular choice
- Having a sense of competence about how to change/steps to take
- Getting positive feedback for positive change

Conversely, here's what tends to crush our motivation to do something:

- Feeling misunderstood and judged
- Other people pushing you to do it
- Having only one option

- Not having reasons for change that make sense to you (the person doing it)
- Not believing you can do it
- Getting yelled at

Acknowledging someone's point of view, truly listening to her perspective, and being as empathic as possible are what cultivate motivation. Telling her she's wrong (or crazy or lazy or fill in the blank), because all we can see is how we're right, tends to drive motivation straight down. We can say *I can't believe you would do this. Can't you see how irresponsible you are?!* Or we can say *You're not a terrible person for drinking too much. You drink that way because you get depressed and drinking makes you feel better, helps you sleep, and that makes sense to me. It doesn't mean this is how you want things to stay, but it does make sense to me.* The former undermines motivation; the latter promotes it.

Providing information about choices, with a minimum of pressure to have to act on that information, helps people hear and be open enough to take in what we are saying. Trying to force someone tends to increase push-back. Easier said than done in a fraught or scary situation, but—counterintuitively—the less pressure, the more likely action will occur. That is, the difference between this: *If you don't admit you're an addict and go to Narcotics Anonymous, you're going to die or I'm going to leave you.* And this: *I'm going to start taking a meditation class because I think it could help me with my stress. It seems like you've been drinking more than usual lately, since that disappointment about the promotion, and I'm scared about what could happen now that we know you have the beginnings of pancreatitis. I know that I worry a lot, but maybe it would help us both to talk about it? I also want to show you this website I found . . .*

Exploring options and letting any and all reasonable paths be part of the discussion are ways to engage motivation. Giving ultimatums makes people defensive, angry, and skeptical. Allowing choice lowers defensiveness and gets people invested in the process. On the one hand there's something to be resisted; on the other, choices to be made. And choice depends on having options. *You're going to rehab or I'm kicking you out of the house* is much less helpful in the short and long runs than, say, *There are a variety of options. These two seem to me to be the best, but there are other things you could do too. What do you think?*

Suggesting a rationale based on the other person's perspective also promotes motivation, because we know that when people are considering doing something different, it's useful for them to have reasons that make sense to them. In contrast, assuming someone should do something and assuming no explanation is needed because the reasons should be obvious tends to leave people feeling more skeptical. These are fighting words: *You shouldn't party every Friday and Saturday night; I won't allow it.* These words invite someone into a conversation: *It seems to me that when you party every Friday and Saturday night you're hungover the entire weekend, and that doesn't leave you any time to do schoolwork. You said you've been really worried lately about falling behind in math.*

Bolstering someone's sense of competence, giving him positive feedback, and helping figure out doable, "bite-size" changes that feel accomplishable enhances motivation. People really don't like to (and then don't) embark on new behaviors if they think they can't do them. Suggesting an AA meeting to someone with bad social anxiety, and then being upset that they repeatedly don't go, would not be so helpful. Suggesting that AA could be helpful, and offering to find someone to go with for the first three meetings, could really help. We spend a lot of time helping people gauge what is accomplishable and starting there; when people present us with a laundry list of the things they are going to change, we tell them to slow down, consider how much they can actually chew, and give themselves time to chew it. And we make sure they know how to do something, not just that they "should" do it.

Last, "yelling" versus "not yelling" (concretely and metaphorically) may be one of the biggest variables in your control for facilitating internal and positive motivation for change. Tone matters. Volume matters. In fact, these may matter more than anything else. Our families tell us that not yelling is the hardest change to make because they are often so upset. But when we yell, people don't hear us. They become defensive and flooded with emotion. The conversation becomes a fight; the fight escalates. Also, when we yell we model yelling, that is, we "teach" other people to yell back. The only upside to yelling is letting off steam. While we might feel better for an instant, there are other ways to let off steam (or cool down before we come to a boil) that don't sabotage communication and damage relationships. In addition to all the things we've discussed so far about motivation, there is one other thing we know from research studies and clinical experience: confrontation is the archenemy of motivation.

Confrontation: The Biggest Motivation Killer

The evidence gathered in almost every study of therapeutic techniques is that resistance to change *increases* with confrontation. Confrontation undermines motivation. It's fascinating and sad that for decades, traditional treatment for substance abuse enacted a self-fulfilling prophecy with harsh approaches like interventions (and boot camps and "hot seats" and so on) that induced and strengthened the very defenses (denial) they intended to break through. (Some treatment providers still take this approach—we will help you ask the right questions to avoid them.) Confrontation in therapy leads to client resistance, which leads to more confrontation. Only recently, this flawed strategy has been challenged by the fundamental insight of motivational thinking and all the evidence for it that research has provided. Treat people with respect and present them with a range of options, and their resistance will decrease. Nobody likes to be bossed around.

Why does it seem to work on TV? Because it's TV. Confrontation doesn't work on shows like *Intervention* and *Celebrity Rehab* either, but it does make for great drama because it meets all the criteria for a reality TV show (secrets, betrayals, tears, confessions, redemption, and so on). In reality (*real* reality), this version of helping people is ineffective and at times harmful. Respectful, collaborative approaches like CRAFT have a *64 percent* or greater success rate for getting reluctant people into treatment, while confrontational interventions succeed about *30 percent* of the time. Some evidence indicates that even when successful—defined as getting the person into rehab—the aftereffects of some confrontational interventions linger on in a damaging way; those who have been subjected to an intervention are more likely to relapse after their initial treatment episode. Anecdotally, this is our experience as well, as we are often left with angry, resentful, and betrayed clients who no longer want to allow their families or friends to be involved.

Choosing to be nonconfrontational does not mean doing nothing. Nor does it mean you approve of the problematic behavior or tiptoe around it. By understanding and working with your loved one's motivations, you can be a collaborative helper, and there are specific strategies that we will teach you to instigate change in yourself, your loved one, and often the whole family system. Staying involved has the power to help your loved one change course. Remember what the evidence says: your skillful involvement has a positive impact on your loved one's motivation and is usually more influential than any other factor. At the same time, specific, temporary, *strategic* detachment when your loved one is intoxicated or hung-over is something you can do to influence your loved one's motivation. Recall the husband earlier in this chapter who, *when his wife was drinking*, stopped making dinner for her and secluded himself with a book.

Remember that there is a sweet spot of engagement that keeps us connected but at the same time gives the other person room to consider information, make decisions, and learn from mistakes, as opposed to us being on his back all the time and nagging. Ultimately, we can help people change, though we can't do it for them.

What's hard about this . . . It may seem counterintuitive, especially when the stakes are high and emotions deep, that it helps people to change if they feel understood and accepted as they are. It will become easier to hold the paradoxical truth in your mind as you practice and see it working, but for now just try to be inquisitive and aware. The more aware you are, the more choice you will have to respond in motivation-enhancing ways, and the better you will become at promoting motivation for change. Remember that you are learning, so please try to be patient and kind to yourself if you lapse and find yourself yelling, or if empathy doesn't come easily. You deserve to feel acknowledged, understood, and accepted too.

The way you understand motivation profoundly affects how you think and feel about your situation. Other people's behavior is more comprehensible when you realize that the same principles of motivation apply to all of us, in whatever we're trying to do. Before you learn to use the specific skills and strategies that come later, before any changes in behavior on the part of you or your loved one, you can feel more hopeful and in control, for good reason. In fact, you may find yourself acting differently already, because you are seeing things differently, and your loved one may respond differently in turn.

Behavior Analysis

Behavior analysis involves systematically thinking through the specifics of how and why your loved one uses a substance or engages in other compulsive behaviors. It is a relatively simple exercise, but the benefits are many.

A behavior analysis does several things: first, it provides an estimate of your loved one's current use against which to measure future changes. Second, it will help you see the predictability of the situation. You may feel like things are out of control, senseless, and random, but in fact substance use is one of the more rote and boring behavior patterns in which people engage (although those patterns are different for each individual). Seeing how predictable substance use can be may help you take back your life from the grip of fear that you could be ambushed at any moment. Third, identifying behavior patterns gives you what psychologist Robert Meyers (the creator of CRAFT) likes to call a "road map" for going forward. It puts your loved one's "triggers"—the who-what-where-whys of his behavior— in plain sight. It lets you consider (from your loved one's perspective) the negative consequences of the behavior along with the positive, helping you to analyze the costs and benefits so you can pinpoint specifically what you can do to help change the balance. Fourth, behavior analysis helps generate empathy in you because it's an exercise in understanding your loved one's use from her perspective.

What's hard about this . . . Going over substance problems with a fine-tooth comb like this requires fortitude, but we think you'll find it's worth it. Your behavior analysis will inform much of the rest of what you do to help. The process of doing it usually gives people a greater sense of control, a better sense of direction, and a boost in optimism. Insofar as it cultivates empathy, it will make you a more effective communicator and positive influence on your loved one's motivation, and you may find empathy a great relief from anger and resentment.

To help you understand exactly how the behavior analysis works, we're providing an example in addition to an exercise you can do. As you read the example below from Janie, whom you met at the beginning of the chapter, keep in mind that *the reasons why people engage in a given behavior are the keys to helping them stop*, and see if you get an idea of how this principle could apply in Janie and Oscar's case.

Janie's Behavior Analysis of Oscar's Substance Use

BEHAVIOR	TRIGGERS		CONSEQUENCES	
	External	Internal	Short-term Positive	Long-term Negative
What does he usually use? Alcohol (beers, followed by bourbon). Sometimes also cocaine.	Who is he usually with when he drinks? Jack and Alex, his best friends and coworkers (and other coworkers) or extended family (his or mine)	What do you think he is thinking about right before he drinks? "Thank God it's the end of the (work) day." "Work is such bullshit. This is what really matters." "What am I going to tell Janie? She's still mad about last time." For family events, "I need to loosen up to enjoy talking to these people."	What do you think he likes about the people with whom he drinks? He feels understood and accepted by his guy friends. Jack and Alex make him laugh. I think sometimes he thinks his drinking is actually helping his work because he's "bonding" with coworkers.	What do you think are the negative results of his drinking in each of the areas below? (Asterisk the ones he would agree with.)
How much does he usually drink? 5–6 beers plus 5–6 bourbons. (No idea how much cocaine.)	Where does he usually drink? Bars, especially karaoke bars. Family events (never cocaine at family events).	What do you think he is feeling right before he drinks? Giddy, celebratory, relieved to be done with work, hopeful that something "great" will happen (as in, "what a great night!"), guilty, distant from me (less so at family events, b/c I'm there).	What do you think he likes about the places where he drinks? The bars are festive and "insiderey." For the karaoke part, a total distraction from normal life.	Relationships: Distance and fighting between us.* Forgets things people say to him, even whole conversations.* Alienates people who aren't as intoxicated as he is, especially at family events. Passed out on the porch twice. Don't know if neighbors saw before I found him.* We want to have kids, but I won't do it while this is going on.

BEHAVIOR	TRIGGERS		CONSEQUENCES	
	External	Internal	Short-term Positive	Long-term Negative
Over how long a period of time does he usually drink? 7–9 hours. Less at family events, though he usually tries to get people to go out after.	When does he usually drink? After work, three or more times a week. Cocaine once or twice a week. Family events several times a year.		What do you think he likes about the time of day at which he drinks? It's a way to forget work, or at least not worry about work. It's more exciting than his other option—dinner at home and a quiet night with me.	Physical health: Bad hang-overs.* Doesn't exercise when he's hungover.*
			What pleasant thoughts do you think he has while drinking? "I love these guys." "People like me when I come out of my shell." "This isn't escaping, this is the most real thing of all." "What a great night!" With family: "Now I can say what I really think and feel." "Everything's more fun with a buzz going."	Emotional health: Feeling guilty and distant from me, but also affectionate toward me (texts sweet things when he's out at night, things he doesn't say otherwise).* Doesn't get excited about doing things that don't in-volve drinking.

BEHAVIOR	TRIGGERS		CONSEQUENCES	
	External	Internal	Short-term Positive	Long-term Negative
			What pleasant feelings do you think he has while drink-ing? Playful (especially at karaoke), carefree, funny, fearless, good at something (he's a good singer), interesting (not like boring people who stay home).	Legal problems: Nothing (yet).* Could get bust-ed for cocaine. (Doubt he's very careful b/c he's drunk.)
			Are there any positive consequences for you? Sends me sweet texts when he's been drinking.	Job: Goes to work late the mornings after, smelling of alcohol, tired. Nobody's said anything (yet).*
				Financial: Money he/we don't have for other things. (Probably $75+ a night when he goes out, not including cocaine.)*

Note that Oscar may use cocaine for different reasons than he uses alcohol. Janie may want to do a separate behavior analysis for his cocaine use, but for now she has chosen to focus on his drinking, since it's more frequent and always comes first.

Throughout the book, we'll refer to the behavior analysis as a resource for change. For now, did looking at this one allow you to see the situation from Oscar's perspective as well as Janie's? Can you imagine how the knowledge that he drinks to forget his problems at work, to elevate life to something more than ordinary, to connect with people, and to feel more confident in social situations could help Janie feel like she understands her husband better? Can you see how the facts might inform strategies to help Oscar learn other ways to get these benefits? And how Janie might play a role in these strategies? She might think of friends he likes whom they haven't seen in a while, who are fun without getting intoxicated, and have them over for dinner. She might learn communication skills to help her broach the painful issue of not wanting to bring children into their situation, in a way that would minimize the chances that her husband would take it as an attack. She might suggest a pact that they go to the gym together, knowing that this would encourage earlier, healthier nights. Behavior analysis helps you identify the specifics of the problem so you can begin to customize realistic solutions.

Exercise: Behavior Analysis of Your Loved One's Substance Use or Other Compulsive Behavior

Use the chart below to map out the whens, wheres, whys, and with whoms of your loved one's substance use and its short- and long-term consequences, including the oft-neglected *positive* consequences (for your loved one *and* for you) that need to be addressed for lasting change. If you find you're getting bogged down, reread the benefits, above, of doing this exercise to remind yourself why you're doing it. If it's still too upsetting, take a break and come back to it. In the meantime, you might skip ahead to the "How to Cope" section (Part Two) for ideas and exercises to help you feel better.

BEHAVIOR	TRIGGERS		CONSEQUENCES	
	External	Internal	Short-term Positive	Long-term Negative
What does your loved one usually use?	Who is your loved one usually with when s/he uses?	What do you think your loved one is thinking about right before using?	What do you think your loved one likes about the people with whom s/he uses?	What do you think are the negative results of your loved one's behavior in each of these areas? (Asterisk the ones s/he would agree with.)
How much does your loved one usually use?	Where does your loved one usually use?	What do you think your loved one is feeling right before using?	What do you think your loved one likes about the place(s) s/he uses?	Relationships:
Over how long a period of time does your loved one usually use?	When does your loved one usually use?		What do you think your loved one likes about the time(s) of day at which s/he uses?	Physical health:
			What pleasant thoughts do you think your loved one has while using?	Emotional health:

BEHAVIOR	TRIGGERS		CONSEQUENCES	
	External	Internal	Short-term Positive	Long-term Negative
			What pleasant feelings do you think your loved one has while using?	Legal problems:
			Are there any positive consequences for you?	Job:
				Financial:
				Other:

CHAPTER 3.

Change:
How Do People Change?

Over time. With stops and starts, along a crooked line. With practice. With ambivalence. More often than not, without formal help. When the trade-offs seem worth it. With a little help—sometimes a lot of help—from friends and family. With anguish. With effort. With joy.

And, of course, with exceptions to every rule. Again, the process is different for each person. When you impose preconceived notions of what change should look like and how it's supposed to go, it is a setup for unnecessary stress. Rigid expectations tend to backfire, making others *more* reluctant to change while you wind up more anxious and dissatisfied if change doesn't happen the way you think it should. Meanwhile, stress undermines your ability to help.

Conversely, when you learn to recognize change in its many forms, you can appreciate when it is actually happening—you'll know it when you see it, and more readily trust the process as it unfolds. A better understanding of change can bolster your patience and perseverance. For example, if you know that people can change without formal treatment, maybe you won't panic when your loved one refuses treatment but decides instead to start exercising and speak to your pastor. You could appreciate his willingness to take action, and feel optimistic knowing that this could be the path to change for him. Similarly, if you know that slips and ambivalence are normal (though painful), you might be less likely to despair when your loved one commits to change one day, only to revert to old behaviors the next.

The behavior analysis hopefully gave you a better sense of your loved one's specific motivations and some beginning insights into the potential reasons why she might change. In this chapter we explain "reinforcement"—that is, the variables that influence a person to choose a particular action as well as how the world around her supports or discourages that choice. Changing the way you think about change can make you a more effective collaborator.

• • •

Think about a change you've tried to make in your life, especially a big one. Maybe you had the goal of getting more exercise, and you tried repeatedly and struggled every time to stick with your plan. Maybe each time you didn't reach your goal, or struggled to sustain the change, it became harder to feel optimistic.

Perhaps you have had the experience of ending a long relationship; you managed to go through with it but can still remember agonizing for months, maybe years, before you did it. Afterward, it seemed like everything reminded you of your ex and made you question your decision. Maybe you remember how lonely you were at first and how long it took before you figured out what to do with the time you used to spend together.

Maybe you've tried to change the way you relate to people, to "be more outgoing," or "not lose your temper so much." Did you feel shy and awkward at the office holiday party even though you knew everyone and they were all smiling and being nice? Did you find yourself snapping at a family member despite your sincere intention not to?

The point is that change is hard for everyone. It takes learning—learning new ways of thinking about ourselves and the world, learning new behaviors, learning to tolerate the pace of change, and learning to live without the old routine. Keeping this in mind in a matter-of-fact rather than a pessimistic way can help you stay calm and patient and go on living your life through the ups, downs, and unexpected parts of change.

Stages of Change

Thirty years ago, psychologists James Prochaska and Carlo DiClemente had a brilliant idea: instead of *telling* clients how they could change based on one or another established theory, they would listen to what people said about changing their own behavior and examine how they thought about it from beginning to end. They would look for the common denominators of the change process that were independent of the *kinds* of behaviors people were attempting to change. From their analysis of the data they collected, Prochaska and DiClemente constructed the now widely recognized "Stages of Change" model, which in addition to identifying particular stages through which people progress, also describes how one might best help a person in each stage, so as to facilitate further change. The model describes five stages that hold true for many behaviors, from smoking to eating Frito-Lays and guacamole at 3:00 a.m.

1. Precontemplation/Not Thinking about Change

In this stage, the idea of changing a behavior is not on the table. The problem has not yet been defined and, though there may be some minimal awareness of the drawbacks of the behavior, there is no intention to change. Why is having no intention of changing considered a part of change? Because the very beginnings of ambivalence can emerge in this stage and, as you know, ambivalence is an important element in the change process. How you respond to someone in this stage of change can influence where they go from here. Most important, at this stage, a head-on, straightforward discussion about the need to change is going to fall on deaf or muffled ears. Persuading or arguing in this stage will tend to provoke defensiveness.

Not arguing for change doesn't mean idly standing by. Remember, you can help even if your loved one doesn't think he wants to change. In this Precontemplation stage, that means validating any nascent perceptions he has of the downsides of his behavior and helping him to reflect on how things are going and whether he is happy with the status quo.

2. Contemplation/Getting Ready

In this stage, a person recognizes the negative impacts of her behavior, while typically also feeling pronounced ambivalence about taking any action. As she adds up the positive and negative consequences of the behavior day to day, she may be aware that there is a problem and feel equally overwhelmed by the prospect of doing something about it. It can be helpful to people in this stage to feel supported in examining the costs and benefits of change, openly and without the need to defend either side. For example, when your loved one says, "I know I'm often hungover and sleep late on Saturdays, but I do enjoy my time with my friends on Friday nights," you might simply reflect back: "Yeah, you were really sick last weekend, but I guess to you it felt worth it." If you can manage to say this with empathy for her dilemma and *without* sarcasm, you may find her voluntarily taking up the argument for change. Defenses down, she might wonder whether it is in fact worth it, rather than argue that it is.

3. Preparation/Readiness

At this stage, a person is preparing to make imminent changes based on her evaluation of the impact of the behavior in her life. She may not yet have fully determined how to accomplish these changes, or exactly what her goals are going to be, but she is considering a plan of action. In the preparation stage someone may, for example, plan to join a support group but may not have decided which group is right for her. It can be useful as a helper to the person in this stage to identify possible other ways of coping and behaving, and to encourage positive expectations. For the person looking for a support group, you might do some research on local options. You might also mention the meditation group a colleague swears by as an alternative to a support group.

4. Action

When a person reaches this stage, she is ready to undertake change and begin to do things differently. Action takes time, effort, and strategy. It is important in the Action stage to have a sense that you are on a path you feel good about. Helpers can facilitate this stage by acknowledging the effort and actively supporting their loved one's efforts. You might offer to make dinner if it makes it easier for her to get to a support group after work, and make a point of communicating that you feel good about this new path too.

5. Maintenance

In the maintenance stage, a person works to prevent a return to old behaviors and continue the gains of the action phase. Dedication, effort, time, and energy are still required. During this period, you can help troubleshoot when obstacles come up and work with her to reassess the costs and benefits of change as she goes. For long-term maintenance of any new behavior, the benefits must outweigh the costs. In other words, the person doing the changing must like her new life at least as much as her old one. The strategies in this book will help you create a positive reinforcement system around the changer, to encourage and support ongoing change.

The Stages of Change model defines change as a *process* rather than an event, through which people can be at different stages at different times. People fresh out of twenty-eight-day rehab are typically highly motivated, excited about their prospects, and in full Action stage. These people want tools and strategies, new ways to communicate, and ways to not get bored—action, action, action! They do not want to ponder whether they are ready to change; they *are* changing. We need to get out of their way and help them develop more tools and strategies to use day-to-day.

The same tools and strategies sought by someone coming out of rehab would not only be lost on, but usually raise the hackles of, someone in the Precontemplation stage. Engaging people in ways that don't match what stage they're in is not so helpful, even if it seems clear to us that they should change and what steps they could take to do so. There are more and less helpful ways to interact with your loved one, depending on his stage. Instead of wishing he was in a different stage, you can understand and respond based on where he is and help him go from there.

Another very important thing to remember about stages: people move back and forth through them, not just forward in one direction. Change, and a person's readiness for it, very seldom proceeds in a straight line. It goes in fits and starts as people learn along the way. We say this as an anxiety preventative for you. Your loved one may start to think about the issues, start to think about changing, start to make plans; then drop them, return to the old behavior, figure out again it's not working so well, start to think about changing again—all fodder for learning. Keep in mind that people learn things at different paces: some people pick up certain things quickly, while others have to go through many rounds of trial and error. For each individual, it depends on what he is trying to learn—he may get the hang of managing emotions but take a long time to make new friends, or learn to enjoy parties without drinking, or fall asleep without medication.

It is important to try to resist comparing your loved one's, or your own, pace and style of changing with others'. Preconceived notions of how the change process should go will only set you up for disappointment, as change seldom follows a predictable path. By understanding the nonlinear nature of change, you can more readily relate to attitudes and behavior that don't fall neatly in line with a forward-march-of-progress fantasy of change.

Behavioral Principles of Change

At the most basic level, using mood-altering substances (e.g., alcohol) is a choice that people make, and they make it from among a variety of options: not drinking, going running instead of drinking, talking to friends instead of drinking, drinking with a spouse or drinking alone, and so on. As you have seen, the decision to use a substance or do anything else is a learned behavior based on the rewards (or reinforcement) of that choice, and as such it is goal-directed and motivated, not irrational and accidental, based on the same principles of learning that apply to many behaviors. We learn how to do a thing (and all the behaviors that support it), we anticipate and experience the rewards of doing that thing, we do it often enough for it to become a habit, and it takes up our time and attention at the expense of other activities.

Behavioral approaches to substance use concentrate on these two ideas: choice and reinforcement. Certainly many factors affect your loved one's choices, and what is reinforcing about those choices, but a behavioral lens is one powerful aid for clearly seeing the issues at hand—that other people have reasons for doing what they do (just as you have reasons for doing everything you do), reasons based on what they get out of doing it, or what is "reinforcing" about it. If we understand people's choices in this way, and understand that reinforcement coming from other behaviors, through other channels, can promote an alternative choice, then we have a lot to work with. And when we understand that all behavior is learned behavior—because change *is* learning—we can do more to help.

When researchers rank evidence-based treatments for substance problems in order of effectiveness, behavioral approaches consistently come out on top. But before we get to the nitty-gritty of specific reinforcement strategies, we want to share what we now know about how behavior changes.

Habits are learned behavior. A good deal of what is loosely referred to as someone's "personality" is learned behavior. Likewise, much of what happens in relationships is learned behavior. Since the day you met, you and your loved one have been learning and relearning how to respond to each other, with certain emotional reactions, cognitive habits, conversational bents, and orbits of action in the give-and-take of your daily routines. It's like ballroom dancing, or maybe sometimes more like heavyweight boxing. In other words, it takes two. If you don't like the tango (maybe because you keep getting dropped on the floor), you have to put on different music and put in the effort it takes to learn another dance.

Behavioral scientists see potential for change in everything humans do. Human beings are built to learn from their environment from the moment they enter the world, and we are learning all the time (even in sleep, as dreaming helps commit experience to memory). Through our every interaction with the world we learn: *how* to do things, that we *can* do things, and how we *feel* about things. Researchers of human behavior take into account internal thoughts and feelings as well as the social and material contexts of life. From this perspective, thoughts and feelings—including motivation—*are* behaviors, called "covert" behaviors. These covert behaviors directly influence "overt" behaviors, the ones observable to the outside world. Our thoughts, feelings, and overt behaviors are influenced by the environment. As the scientists say, they are or are not *reinforced*— that is, supported or discouraged—by the environment.

Joe was a client who often felt angry and irritable, even when he was a kid. He was a hothead without always knowing why. He had discovered in high school that smoking a little pot cooled him off and made him less judgmental and irritated with people. The reinforcing effect of feeling more relaxed and having people like him better was huge. When he had to consider quitting because of a new job that required drug testing, he worried he would go back to being an angry guy with few friends. In fact, if he didn't learn new ways to stay calm and enjoy people, he likely *would* go back to being angry and lonely. He knew that if that happened, he would be susceptible to resorting to pot as a known (learned) and reinforced solution.

With some understanding of how people learn and how behaviors are reinforced, you can create strategies that point learning in new directions. In Joe's case, he found that breathing exercises and a harder cardio workout were viable alternatives to smoking pot.

"Nature versus nurture" is a false dichotomy. Human behavior springs from both our biological presets and our experiences in the world. Learning and biology interact continuously for different people in different ways and produce different results. Two people in the same circumstances—say, terrible commuter traffic every day—may experience it differently, which may in turn affect whether and how they use substances. Say one of them had a parent with a severe anxiety disorder (so, both a genetic predisposition as well as the life experience of being raised by a severely anxious parent), had been fearful since he was a child, and had also been in a serious car accident as a teenager. The relief this person finds in three drinks when he gets home may represent a more potent reinforcer of drinking behavior than it would for the person without that mix of genetic background and life experience. For some, substance use is superfluous. They can take it or leave it. For others, because of a combination of genetics and life experiences, substance use satisfies deep needs.

Here are some other important lessons behavioral science has taught us about change.

Change requires learning, and learning involves risks.
Research has demonstrated that in order to change, we don't unlearn behaviors; we have to learn alternatives. Any attempt to do something new is a risk—we might not be able to do it, or it might not work.

If a person wants to stop relying on alcohol to feel relaxed and confident at parties, he will need a) another way to feel relaxed and confident at parties and/or b) something else to do besides go to parties. Take away the substance and there's a gaping hole to fill. Appreciating the challenge and scariness of new learning puts us in a better position to help someone fill the holes (with alternatives) and bridge the gaps (with competing behaviors).

Change includes failure.

To learn to play an instrument, sink a free throw, be a doctor—to learn anything, we must be willing to sound awful, feel awkward, miss shots, and not know much in the beginning. Quite simply, when we are learning something new, we typically suck at it at first. To expect otherwise is a setup for frustration and discouragement.

Many people have the expectation of themselves, or of others, that one bad day, decision, or incident puts them back at square one. This way of thinking is particularly strong in dealing with substance problems, where some people believe that one episode of old behavior (a slip or a lapse) resets the clock to day one. People tend to be more forgiving when it comes to other areas of learning. A bad day at the foul line is just a bad day. If they do poorly on a midterm exam, we know that it doesn't mean they have forgotten everything they learned. When we understand change—including change in substance use—as a learning process, an incremental approach makes sense.

When a person has a lapse back into drinking, although she has been working hard to learn skills and new behaviors that will help her to not drink, it doesn't mean all is lost. More likely she has learned many things, but they were not enough to hold her in that moment when she decided to have a drink. Believing that any slip to old behaviors requires starting over from the beginning piles on discouragement she probably already feels. Alan Marlatt, PhD, called this the "abstinence violation effect" (AVE) and described this process as one of black-and-white thinking, where a misstep results in the person's thinking that everything is now out of their control. This way of processing the event is associated with a *greater likelihood of relapse*. It is most helpful (and protective) to understand change as an incremental, stepwise process that requires practice and patience.

Kevin, a fifty-year-old father of three, had been a heavy drinker since college, and always had a good time after a few beers. After his third son was born, however, his wife did not think his drinking was so much fun. His reluctance to get up Saturday mornings after Friday nights out with his work friends irked her. He saw her point and agreed to reduce his drinking.

Working with his CMC therapist, Kevin discovered that drinking served many purposes for him. It helped him manage his shyness (which did not jibe with his sales job) and helped him feel alive, even though he was often tired. Stopping drinking was harder than he thought, but he was motivated to be more available to his sons and his wife. He went to some support groups and tried a medication that reduced cravings. His wife was thrilled. A couple months into these changes, Kevin decided to try going out with a few friends and came home drunk and unable to get out of bed in the morning. He was so upset that he continued to drink through the weekend. His wife was upset, too, but didn't lose sight of the positive changes so far. Instead of yelling at him for not trying or caring about her feelings, she asked how she could help him get back on track.

Recognizing that for most people change is more like learning to read than getting hit on the head with an apple, you'll be less likely to blame a loved one for being "bad at it" in the beginning or despair when he has bad days later on.

Insight is not enough.

Because our choices to behave one way or another are not always carefully considered, merely acknowledging the existence of a problem behavior doesn't make it go away (if you hadn't noticed). Understanding is critical, but not sufficient.

Substances are rewarding to brains at a fairly primitive level; they affect parts of the brain involved in deep emotions. Because these brain structures—collectively called the limbic system or "primitive" or "lizard" brain—are nonverbal and nonintellectual, people can appreciate intellectually how problematic their substance use or behavior is, but still have little or no ability to change. For example, "I know cigarettes are killing me; I am just going to finish this pack." To an outside observer, this person might seem to be lying or ill-intentioned when he says one thing but does another. In fact, underneath his plan (and maybe desperate wish to change), his primitive brain is churning away, motivating him toward using—in some cases feeling like life depends on the continued use. Insight and a desire to change are important, but you cannot always rely on them if you expect to go to battle with the limbic system and win. If your loved one's lizard brain seems to be winning the battle, the strategies we give you later in this book will help you fortify the rational parts of his brain—send in the *reinforcements*, as it were—that may truly want to change.

Practicing works; practicing in context really works.

Our brains, bodies, thoughts, feelings, and behavior develop *through experience*, and continue to do so as long as we live. People need to experience change to know that it can be done, to get some feedback about what happens when it's done, to feel differently after doing it. Through this process we learn that we *can* do something differently; we *prove* to ourselves that we can do it differently; we get feedback that it is rewarding to us to do it differently; and we create a different habitual behavior.

Clearly, this can't all unfold in a therapist's office, though it may be a safe place to start. People need to practice in the real world. A therapist can role-play how to say no to a drink, but in order for the behavior to take hold, the client must go to a restaurant and practice saying no to waiters offering drinks. She may get it on the first try, or she may have a harder time than she anticipated. If we treat a stumble as a catastrophe or a sign that a person was not really serious about change, it's not likely that she will keep trying. If we encourage her to learn from the experience and problem-solve how to do it differently next time, she will more likely try again. Trying again, or practicing, will be the only way she can learn to enjoy being in a restaurant while meeting her goal of not drinking. To be motivated to change, people need to experience the positive effects of the behavior itself, in context, perhaps many times over, before it feels worthwhile to keep doing. Repeated reinforcement is another reason to practice.

This goes for you too. Just as your loved one's process includes identifying behaviors to change and then practicing change until it feels more natural and becomes habit, you will need to practice collaborating and learn how to support him in new ways.

Learning alone is not enough. We can tell people what is bad for them and watch with amazement as they do it anyway. Learning new behavior often unfolds in a cycle of planning, trial, error, observation, more planning, more trial, more error. People typically try and err many times over before they get comfortable enough to call a new behavior "learned," and many more times after that before they would say they've "mastered" it. With mastery, a behavior is solid, learned so deeply that it is automatic and will reliably win out over the older competing behaviors that may be underneath—for example, "I used to start every day with a cigarette; now I put my shoes on and go for a run." Mastery takes practice—Malcolm Gladwell famously wrote in *Outliers: The Story of Success* that experts believe it takes around ten thousand hours to achieve.

When she first came to CMC, Maryanna was unable to talk to her husband about his cocaine use without becoming furious. This pattern had been going on for ten years. She agreed with her therapist, in theory, that positive communication (see chapter 9, which is all about positive communication) would be more helpful to him and feel better to her. But even when she was only practicing with her therapist, she would lose her temper. "I'M NOT THE PROBLEM HERE," she wanted to scream. She was angry about the whole mess, angry with her husband for using in spite of how she felt, and angry with herself for not controlling her temper.

Maryanna practiced in her therapist's office for weeks until she could get her words out calmly, sounding like she meant them—and she found that part of her really did. She stuck with it because she could no longer stand the alternative, which was fighting with her husband and feeling mad all the time. For weeks more, she tried what she had practiced on her husband and more often than not reverted to her old hostile position mid-try. Eventually, though, she mastered her new positive communication skills enough to be rewarded by seeing his defensiveness decrease. The less she shouted and criticized, the more her husband talked about his cocaine use instead of shutting down. This, in turn, defused her anger, making it easier to communicate positively, and so on.

We're asking you to learn new approaches, and then to practice them, because that's how change happens in the real world. It is not always easy, but it works.

Change often feels worse before it feels better.
Building a happy life takes time. Before new behaviors (including the ways you think and feel) become habits, they usually feel awkward and uncomfortable—this goes for everyone, and it applies especially to using substances because of their direct and powerful impact on the brain.

Before a brain that has become accustomed to taking joy in cocaine can take joy in a sunset, there may be an unpleasant gap while it "relearns," in neurochemical and structural terms, how to process joy without cocaine. It takes time—weeks, months, even years—to recover from the physical effects of substances on the brain. This is a significant factor in relapse: brain functioning hasn't readjusted yet. Feeling temporarily lousy doesn't mean you or your loved one is on the wrong path (in fact, it may mean the opposite).

Jon had been drinking all day long every day for a few years without his wife, Ada, knowing. When they came to CMC, he had recently gone through a detox and she found out a few weeks later that he had gone back to drinking; this was, ironically, why he seemed so much better.

In the first year of Jon's struggle to quit drinking, while their trust was still shaky, Ada learned that the most reliable sign that her husband was sober was when he was being a jerk. In that early stage, not drinking made him irritable. Change felt worse for both of them before it felt better. Knowing that this was part of the process got her through that first difficult year. She learned not to take his mood swings personally. She developed a thicker skin, distraction techniques, patience, and even a sense of humor about it. She "picked her battles" and kept her "eye on the prize." Eventually, as Jon spent more time away from alcohol, his moods no longer depended on it. Ada got back the man she had married—*this* was the prize—but it took longer than she would have guessed, including setbacks along the way as he relapsed and she sometimes wanted to strangle him.

You don't have to be a neuroscientist to help your loved one. In our experience, however, some understanding of the physiological impact of substances helps our clients have compassion for poor, battered brains recovering from substance abuse, and for the people who have to live with these brains until they feel better.

And for that reason, joy helps.

Willpower gets a lot of play in popular culture when it comes to change, but joy takes people much, much further. People are unlikely to persist in a change that does not have its own pleasures. Research has underscored the importance of building a happy life as critical to reducing substance use or other problematic behaviors.

Consider Max. There were few things he liked doing more than sitting on the back porch smoking after his wife, Charmaine, and their three kids were in bed. He bristled when Charmaine insisted that this was driving a wedge between them, as she couldn't stand the smell and worried about his health. Charmaine knew, because Max had said as much, that his late nights were about quiet, solitude, and freedom to do what he liked. She and her CMC therapist brainstormed ways to discourage Max from smoking and encourage their spending time together, while also preserving time for Max to be by himself.

Max jumped on his wife's idea that she take charge of the kids three mornings a week, giving him uninterrupted time to write computer code— another favorite solitary pursuit. He started going to bed at the same time as Charmaine the previous nights in order to wake up early for coding (he realized later that the nicotine had been wrecking his sleep). For his part of the bargain, Max agreed to do something Charmaine wanted to do, after the kids went to bed, two evenings a week. He discovered that he liked the TV series *Friday Night Lights* as much as she did, and they enjoyed dissecting it together afterward. Or sometimes they would just sit in the same room and read. Within six months, his smoking was down to once a week, a change made possible by the inherent joy, for Max, of writing computer programs and feeling closer to his wife than he had in years.

A behavior analysis is the first step to making a change.

When we engage someone in treatment, we don't just get his life story and what his understanding of it is. We dig into what he has actually been doing, how he actually conducts his life day to day, hour to hour. What happens on Friday nights? He gets home from work and starts getting ready to go out? What exactly does getting ready entail? It starts with a series of phone calls? Whom does he actually call? His friends and his dealer? Which friends? When does he start to think about these friends, really—in that moment or earlier in the day, or even two weeks before? What is the internal process once he starts to think about them? And so on. In the cyclical patterns of behavior that emerge from a thorough assessment, we can, with our clients, find access points for intervention. We help them become aware of the effect of each action, and in doing so help them identify the skills they need to learn to make real change. The behavior analysis you did in the previous chapter will be the cornerstone of your helping strategies just as it is for ours.

Change isn't magic. It does not take a miracle. Change takes thought, planning, and work, and reasons to do something different. You can help make it worth it for your loved one, by helping to create an environment in which positive behavior is rewarded by your affection, presence, collaboration, and other forms of reinforcement, while negative behavior is shut out in the cold. You can tip a loved one's scales on the side of change.

Change and the Brain

Other people's brains may seem out of reach, but brains really can change, and they are affected by other people.

In an astonishing collection of stories, *The Brain That Changes Itself,* Canadian psychiatrist, psychoanalyst, and researcher Norman Doidge, MD, describes how a fiftysomething eye surgeon in Alabama recovered from a stroke. At the end of the standard six weeks of rehabilitation the man was still considerably impaired, walking with a cane, and managing with a barely functioning left hand.

Until recently, that would have been it, end of story, his deficits chalked up to permanent brain damage from the stroke. Enter the new findings of the "capacity of neurons and neural networks in the brain to change their connections and behavior in response to new information, sensory stimulation, development, damage, or dysfunction." Doidge describes how the eye surgeon persevered in his rehabilitation, eventually returning to work (though not to surgery), tennis, and his Porsche. Remember "joy helps"? If you don't share this man's enthusiasm for racket sports or fast cars, you can still appreciate how *his* joy in these things helped motivate him to put in the painstaking effort necessary for change. For you it would be different things. For your loved one, different things still.

The point is that the brain is capable of changing and adapting. Recovering the ability to enjoy life after substance abuse may be less straightforward to achieve and measure than recovering the ability to write legibly after a stroke, but the neurophysiological principles are the same.

Of course, you don't have to be a neuroscientist to help someone with a substance problem. You too can apply some of these amazing findings about change in the brain. First, know that changing the way we think and act changes the brain's structure over time. With the effort and concentrated attention the eye surgeon devoted to relearning the functioning he had lost from the stroke, he literally changed his neural circuitry. Second, it takes *repeated* thought and action to fully form new brain connections. Habits—healthy ones as well as not so healthy ones—develop out of repetition. In the beginning of learning, the brain is straining as new connections are made. This is one of the reasons change often feels uncomfortable, sometimes onerous—even though the eye surgeon had previously loved tennis, he had lost those neural connections and it was hard work to retrain his brain. The "rewiring" of the brain, as it learns one behavior pattern over another, takes practice, repetition, and time.

Knowing the brain can change will help you tap into the corresponding 1) optimism, 2) patience, and 3) determination for your loved one and yourself. The behavioral patterns associated with substance use and other compulsive behaviors often correspond to deeply grooved pathways in the brain that don't change overnight, but they can change with effort and over time. And this applies to you too: your responses to your loved one's behavior may well be deeply grooved. Even though you know you shouldn't yell or panic, your brain may be sending you very different cues. Across this whole spectrum, from reinforcing experiences to understanding changes in the brain, we encourage you to be flexible, patient, and open to new perspectives as you approach the problem of your loved one's substance use.

In addition to our work at CMC, we have worked for many years with professional baseball players. Remarkably, the same processes of motivation, change, and mastery are as true for being a better hitter as they are for changing your drinking, or helping someone else consider changing his.

Baseball players typically ask for help only after things have been going badly for a while (sound familiar?), and need to be invited, encouraged, and shown why it makes sense to consider doing something different. They need to be taught new steps in a new process, praised for the progress they make, and encouraged when they stumble. They too take risks to try something new, practice a new behavior they're no good at yet, and must tolerate their stumbles (still sound familiar?).

When they are in a 2-for-23 batting slump, they need to understand that they can still trust the process they are involved in and they don't have to go back to square one. They need to know that their current predicament is not fundamental to their character, and they *can* get back on track. Under this duress, they (and you) need not resort to random superstitious behavior when change doesn't immediately happen. Change is hard, yet mastery is possible.

What kind of coach do you want to be? You can scream frustrations from the sideline or you can help your players learn from mistakes. You can blame them for losses or share in the responsibility to win. You can ignore the evidence of what works or you can learn and let it guide you. You can resign in disgust or you can keep doing your job to the best of your ability.

You can keep your perspective.

You are on the same team.

What's hard about this . . . The speed of change in your loved one's process may be much slower than you would like. In fact, if you're reading this book, we can assume that it is slower than you would like. You might notice that his periods of abstinence are getting longer and longer before lapses occur; you might even see clearly that your life together is significantly better than it used to be. And still, you might experience the next lapse as the last straw and feel you can take no more. If so, be compassionate with yourself by taking those feelings seriously and attending to them. Your feelings may mean you should be doing something different. Or they might simply mean you need to find somewhere to blow off steam so you can return to the current plan. The next section will help you decide where along that continuum you are at a given time, and give you some constructive ideas for managing your emotions and taking care of yourself.

Exercise: Stages of Change

It's helpful for you to consider a significant change that *you* made at some point in your life in light of what you have learned in this section. Framing your change in stages will help you understand change as a process, and build empathy with your loved one, whatever stage he or she is in.

1. Describe the change you made.

_____

_____

_____

Not ready—What do you remember about the time before it occurred to you to make this change? Why do you think you hadn't thought about it?

_____

_____

Getting ready—When did you start thinking about making this change? Did something happen to prompt you? Were you ambivalent about it? (If so, what did you perceive to be the drawbacks of changing?)

_____

_____

_____

Ready—When did you feel ready? What made you feel ready? (For example, how did you deal with your ambivalence?)

_____

_____

_____

Action—Did you take sudden or gradual action? Was it a lot of effort? Did you ever doubt yourself? What new behaviors did you have to learn?

_____

_____

_____

Maintenance—What does maintenance mean to you? Does it still feel like an effort? If you slipped back to old behavior at any point and then recommitted to the change, how did you do this?

_____

_____

_____

2. Describe the process overall: Did change happen in a straight line? Were there setbacks? On a scale of 1 (easy) to 10 (hardest thing you've ever done), how would you rate making this change?

Now, do the same exercise as you think about your loved one and a change you hope he will make.

1. Describe the change you hope he will make.

_____

_____

_____

2. What stage do you think your loved one is in right now?

_____

_____

_____

3. What are the new things he will have to learn in order to make the change?

_____

_____

_____

4. Depending on the stage, what do you think you could do to support him?

_____

_____

_____

PART TWO

How to Cope

Things do not change; we change.
—HENRY DAVID THOREAU,
WALDEN

CHAPTER 4.

Start Where You Are

These three short chapters that come before the "How to Help" section (Part Three) are your oxygen mask dropping down from its compartment above your head. We know you are anxious to get on with the business of helping, so remember, this *is* the business of helping. It starts with you, right where you are. Ignoring this section would be like jumping out of your airplane seat in a panic to help a person twenty rows behind you when you hear the announcement of depressurization. Chances are, you'll collapse before you get there. In order to help someone else, you need to make sure you're okay first, so this section is about how to fasten your oxygen mask firmly over your nose and mouth before you try to help someone else.

At CMC, we introduce every client to three skills we call ACT: Awareness, Coping, and Tolerating. We help them realize that it takes *awareness* (of problems, goals, their ambivalence about changing) to start down a path of change. It takes learning to *cope* differently to make actual changes and it takes the skill of *tolerance* to handle distress in the process and bide the time, whatever it takes. The same principles apply to your side of the equation.

In the previous chapters, we aimed to increase your awareness by giving you new ways to understand addiction, motivation, and how people change. In this chapter you'll see how change starts, paradoxically, with awareness—and acceptance—of the way things are right now. We'll explain what we mean by awareness and acceptance, and we think you'll be glad to learn that they're not as ethereal as they sound. You'll find exercises to guide you in developing awareness and acceptance—and good reasons to bother. Perhaps most important, we want to validate the pain of your position. In some of those darker moments, it can certainly not feel "fair" that you have to deal with your loved one's problems while other families seem well adjusted and substance free. In fact, you are not alone. In a given year, 22.2 million Americans, or nearly one in twelve, have substance problems severe enough to be classified as dependence or abuse. Over *30 percent* of adults abuse alcohol at some point in their lives. Everyone else's loved ones aren't well adjusted and substance free. Opening your awareness to others in similar circumstances can help you feel less alone, adrift, and hopeless.

Loving someone with a substance problem can be agony. Awareness and acceptance are tools you can use to cope with the pain while you work at change. Chapters 5 and 6 introduce specific skills for tolerating things you can't change, at least not immediately, and setting limits to cope with situations you cannot tolerate, not even with your new tolerating skills.

How are you?

Many of us hear this question several times a day and don't think twice about answering "fine." Often there's an unspoken agreement that the person asking the question doesn't really want to know the answer. But what if the person truly seemed to care and had time to listen?

How are you, really, right now?

Sometimes people say "fine" because they don't really know themselves or want to know. When people are dealing with substance problems, whether it's a single incident (their daughter was caught with pot at school) or a longer-term problem (their husband has struggled with alcohol for three years since he lost his last good job), they may go on autopilot to avoid distress. Clinical studies show that caring for a person with a substance problem increases rates of depression, anxiety, physical illness, and low self-esteem in the people doing the caring. Over time, these emotional reactions can become somewhat automatic and continue without your thinking about them—you feel that "this is just the way things are."

But your reading this book suggests that you would rather not be where you are. This is understandable when frustration, arguing, isolation, guilt, blame, worry, hopelessness, fury—in a word, suffering—have eclipsed normal life and everyday enjoyment. Of course you want things to change when someone you care about seems to be choosing substances over normal life, everyday enjoyment, and you. We hope that reading our book also indicates your willingness to go off autopilot, be aware, engage, and have hope. Naturally your stamina will fluctuate over time, but take a moment now to notice the optimism inherent in opening this book and remember what it feels like, so you can find it again if you lose it along the way.

Awareness

In baseball, a batter may be standing at the plate, but he is not ready for the next pitch if he is thinking about the last pitch, or the booing he might endure if he misses the next one, or how unfair the umpire is, or how it would feel to hit a double. The batter is ready for the next pitch when he is present in the moment, paying attention to the pitcher, his own body, sense of balance, and others' positions on the field. It is human nature to get caught up in what has happened, how you wished it had been different, how you still wish it will be different, instead of being present in this moment and seeing what is. But in readiness or "presentness," baseball players find a palpable sense of calm, relief, and confidence. This doesn't guarantee that they'll hit the next pitch! However, it is the state in which their natural and learned abilities are most available to them.

As we say in sports psychology, we have to be "NATO," or Not Attached To the Outcome, a mnemonic we can all use to focus on the present moment and engage in a process of learning, rather than fixate on the possible outcomes of the process. Taking care of yourself is new; it won't necessarily make your loved one change, but you can trust that the process itself is constructive and deserves your attention. Which is to say, *you* deserve your attention.

Living "in the moment" picked up some unfortunate associations in the late 1960s with hedonism and, ironically from our perspective, recreational drug culture. But long before the 1960s, being present had been a core practice of many ancient wisdom traditions. Modern science is now reaffirming that mindful awareness (sometimes called "mindfulness," to distinguish its intentional, nonjudgmental qualities from automatic, ordinary waking consciousness) is a practical skill that applies to business decisions, spiritual awakening, solving interpersonal problems, making changes in our lives—and playing baseball.

Faced with substance problems in your family, and feeling that you know all too well the mess you're in, you might ask, "Why would I want to become *more* aware of this painful situation?" Good question. The answer lies in a particular kind of awareness—awareness with acceptance—that reduces avoidable suffering even as it acknowledges unavoidable pain. Awareness is necessary to instigate purposeful change; we must recognize the facts of our situation in order to change them. We acknowledge what is real, take its measure, and act from there.

Awareness allows for something different to happen.
You may feel more comfortable not knowing what you would rather not know, but—and we say this to our clients who are using substances—navigating intentional, lasting change takes awareness. It takes awareness to be proactive instead of reactive, to try something different instead of going back to the same old dysfunctional routine. Without awareness,

someone or something other than you will always be directing the action, usually according to forces of habit and the rote negative patterns you can only wish would change. Without awareness, you can only react. There is plenty to react to when someone you care about uses substances in destructive ways—you may be angry, scared, and sad, and justifiably so—but awareness can take you in a *new* direction. With awareness you can ask, "Could I try something different?"

Learning depends on it.

On autopilot there's no learning, only repeating. To learn from what hasn't worked—say, yelling—you'll need to know what exactly hasn't worked. To plan a more effective strategy, you'll need awareness of alternatives, of your goal so you can direct yourself toward it, and of your loved one's perspective so you can anticipate the strategy most likely to bring you both closer to the goal. You can read more about positive communication in chapter 9, but for now, understand that you will need to be aware in order to actually change the way you interact with someone, to practice speaking differently than you usually do—aware of your original intentions, of emotions that can throw you off, and of your loved one's reactions. With awareness you can adapt to what is happening as it is happening and incorporate new information as it comes.

It guides strategic action.

To execute a new strategy, you'll need to stay aware through each step. You may begin a communication knowing that it usually goes better when you don't yell, for example. But in a hot moment, when every pathway of your brain and every particle of your being seems geared toward yelling as you usually do, you'll need even more awareness to remember an alternative and do it. Being aware of yourself, your loved one, and the reality of your situation as it evolves is critical to sticking with a new plan and resisting the pull of habit.

It counters natural mistakes.

Making changes often requires us to act *counter* to what comes automatically. It's counterintuitive to stay calm when you're angry, and logical in a certain way to think that if you yell, you'll be heard and taken seriously. But how often has yelling worked? How do you feel afterward? Is there a chance that yelling actually makes things worse? The answers to these questions come only through awareness. It is counterhabitual to not yell when you're angry if yelling is what you usually do. It is countercultural to treat your loved one with kindness and empathy when popular opinion dictates hostile confrontation or detachment. And we can't counter anything without being aware.

Perspective requires it.

Keeping your perspective—taking a deep breath, taking a step back, taking in the forest view as well as seeing the trees—requires a broad, nuanced view of the scope and complexity of your situation. It takes awareness to see that things aren't all bad, that you're not alone, or on the other hand to notice that you're becoming depressed. It takes awareness to be patient and flexible when change doesn't come as quickly as you'd wish or exactly as you expected. Through awareness you can take things less personally, with the understanding that what is happening is just happening, not conspiring against you. You can take that deep breath, see that you have options, and find out what your options are. You can choose not to yell. You can be disappointed but choose not to nurse a grudge. You can recognize if you're despairing and choose to get help. There's no perspective on autopilot. Perspective is freedom. And power.

It promotes flexibility.

The world is not static (no matter how stuck you may feel), and it's even less so as you start to implement strategies for change. You can prepare a plan to help, based on your awareness of your loved one's situation, other people involved, and your feelings about it all, even though you can't predict exactly how it's going to go. Awareness in the moment, in real time, allows you to adapt to what is happening as it is happening and incorporate new information as it comes.

What's hard about this . . . In a classic exercise from the mindfulness training program of Jon Kabat-Zinn at the University of Massachusetts, the trainee attempts to give a raisin his full attention, noticing how it looks in his hand, how it smells before he puts it in his mouth, the texture of it on the first chew, the texture of it on the fourth chew . . . For thousands of years, Buddhist meditators have done this through paying attention to their breath. (After all, we don't always have a raisin handy.) It sounds simple—just stay with the raisin! But as Kabat-Zinn, and Buddhist practitioners, and everyone who tries some version of focused awareness discovers, it is and it isn't so simple. We practice with something like a raisin, or our breathing, because it seems simple, but also in order to learn about our mind's tendency to make things more compli-cated than they need to be. There's no better way to see how unsettled our mind is than to attempt to settle it, and there's nothing like trying to focus on a raisin to raise awareness of all the non-raisin places our mind wants to go. And when we see this, we see the choice: which way shall we go?

Thus, awareness is the basis of choosing which thoughts and actions we will pursue. It takes practice to train our minds to make a particular choice—to stay with this raisin, this breath, this moment, or this conversation rather than let an interruption distract us or even derail us and ruin our evening—and there's more to it than we can cover here. To learn more ways to practice and more reasons why it's worth it, you can consult the writings and record-ings of Kabat-Zinn, Dan Siegel, Jack Kornfield, Pema Chodron, Sharon Salz-berg, Thich Nhat Hanh, and others who have devoted their lives to practicing and teaching awareness. You can also listen to and download mindfulness practices from the Mindfulness tab on our Facebook page (www.facebook.com/CenterForMotivationAndChange.)

Acceptance

Awareness is *paying attention* to what is actually happening. Acceptance is *being willing to stay with it* while you sort out what you can change and what you can't. Acceptance leads the way to making changes out of the raw material of how things actually are. Acceptance puts you in a stronger position to change the things you can. It is also how you come to terms with the things you cannot change.

As you become more aware, it is natural to want to know what you can *do* about reality—particularly painful reality. Acceptance is an action. It is something you can *do* that leads to less suffering and, again paradoxically, to positive change.

Acceptance does not mean approving, giving up, or detaching; it means recognizing things for what they are, no better but no worse either. We may not like the truth, but it's true anyway. This is not meant to sound harsh. It's to give you permission to stop fighting so much and show you to a calm place in the eye of the storm: acceptance is a little bit of peace within us no matter what else is going on. Consider how differently your blood pressure reacts to "So, this is what's happening . . . " as opposed to "I CAN'T BELIEVE IT, WHY IS THIS HAPPENING TO ME?!"

And this is a skill you can learn. The alternative—not accepting painful reality—adds avoidable suffering—hostility, resentment, and alienation—to unavoidable pain.

Rebecca was a twenty-one-year-old who had been in treatment several times for abusing multiple substances. In early treatment her underlying psychiatric issues were not adequately addressed; as a result she struggled to stay sober and frequently relapsed. At the time, Rebecca lived with her mother, Maggie.

When the two of them first came to CMC, Maggie appeared ragged. She described crying every day and staying up at nights praying for her daughter. She was miserable when her daughter talked to her about her life, and terrified when she didn't. She frequently pleaded and shouted, while her daughter retreated behind closed doors. In her attempt to be heard and understood, Maggie pleaded and shouted more.

In discussion with her therapist, Maggie acknowledged that she had so desperately wanted things to be different that she hadn't noticed she'd abandoned many of the activities she used to enjoy; the same activities she required if she was going to manage her anxiety. With her life on hold, she hadn't been riding her bike or talking to her sister, who had previously been a source of support. Maggie had been unaware, too, that venting her worries to her daughter was pushing her away.

Rebecca told her own therapist that she felt overwhelmed by her mother's feelings. She knew quite well that her mother was disappointed in her. Hearing it more didn't help her know it better. Maggie agreed to try for one month not to talk to her daughter about how she wished things would be. Instead, she would focus on what she could do for herself.

She committed to getting back on her bike for daily rides and to calling her sister to catch up at least once a week. She tracked these activities as well as her moods and energy levels and over the month she found that the exercise of riding her bike helped her to sleep instead of worry and cry. Talking to her sister, Maggie noticed, helped keep things in perspective, and given her sister's understanding, she didn't feel so desperate to get it from Rebecca.

Maggie told her therapist that she hadn't so much gotten her life back as realized that this *was* her life. She still worried about Rebecca and wanted to help as much as she could, but she was increasingly accepting that this was a part of her life—though not everything. Indeed, as Maggie paid attention to her own changes and gave her daughter more space, her daughter began to spend more time outside her room and volunteer more information when they were together.

• • •

Wishful thinking, avoidance, hostility, resentment, and other forms of nonacceptance are like quicksand from which you, and change, cannot move forward; the more you try, the more you sink in. Reality is the ground for change.

Good News: When we accept what is hard, we don't make it harder than it is.

Let's take an even closer look at awareness and acceptance in action.

Imagine you're driving in the rain with your intoxicated wife beside you and sleeping kids in the backseat. You are often the one to drive, but tonight you *must* because your wife drank too much. The first step of awareness in this situation is to investigate how you feel, what you're thinking, and what is happening. Instead of, say, thinking about your work schedule the next day, you choose to attend to the present moment. You become aware of several things happening internally:

To start with, there's probably anger toward your wife for drinking too much, again; toward yourself for being "duped" into thinking this night would go differently; for the life you feel stuck in; and so on.

Perhaps there's also rumination: how many times this has happened before, what different combinations of insults you'd like to scream at her, cascading thoughts connected to the present and the past . . .

And then there are your physical or bodily experiences: driving, hearing the rainfall, feeling tired. Paying more attention to these sensory elements of what is happening, you become aware of how much you love the sound of rainfall, how you feel energized by the challenge of driving in the rain, and how sweet the sound of faint snoring is from your youngest child, who has a stuffed-up nose.

Awareness means making a purposeful effort to be aware of all of these things, not missing several parts inadvertently by ceding precedence to one thing, and then making a choice about where to put your attention. It could be the difference between spending the rest of the drive stewing in anger and ruminating on how much you hate your life and spending the same amount of time choosing to focus on the rain and the experience of driving and the sounds of your sleeping children. The second way is more likely to improve your sense of connection to the good things in your life.

Your choice has real consequences in the moment and in the longer run: for your physical and mental well-being, for your confidence in your ability to have some control over your well-being independent of your spouse's drinking, not to mention for the quality of your driving. It is one car ride, but imagine multiplying these effects by, say, ten experiences in a week, and you can start to appreciate the potential impact of awareness.

Acceptance in this situation means acknowledging that your wife is drunk and perhaps wishing she hadn't drunk so much, but instead of devolving into a stew of indignation about the selfishness of your wife and general unfairness of life, you feel some compassion for yourself and take the half hour to breathe more slowly. With acceptance, you choose not to fight with your wife (you always can later). At its most basic level, acceptance allows that your wife has drunk too much to drive—it's too late to change that—and so you keep your family safe by driving yourself.

The Power of Powerlessness

If you or your loved one has encountered the Twelve Steps in AA or Al-Anon (or NA—Nar-Anon), you know that Step One calls for acceptance, specifically accepting or admitting powerlessness over compulsions to use substances. This step is meant to be empowering, and for many people it is. Others find the concepts of "self-empowerment" and "willpower" the real driving forces of change. The reality is that both are true: a person can be both powerful and powerless at the same time. Similarly, a person can accept what is and want things to change at the same time.

We're not waxing philosophical here: you have a family member with a problem, and you are in pain. Everything we know about motivation and change suggests that power and powerlessness come with the territory of caring about someone with a substance problem. You have the power to *help* someone change, and the power to make changes yourself that will improve your situation, yet you are powerless to *make* another person change or do the changing for him. In the next section, you will learn helping strategies that are proven to be effective, but in any given interaction, you will not be able to control the outcome. Positive communication does not guarantee that the other person will respond the way you had hoped—it only improves the odds. For your part, as you attempt to change your behavior, you may fully intend to stay calm in a difficult conversation, and still lose your cool in the moment.

The reinforcement strategies in chapter 10 are not a magic bullet. You might stop giving your teenager cash, but he can still find ways to buy drugs. You could have good reasons for optimism, use smart strategies and powerful tools for helping, consistently show patience and persistence, and yet you will never completely eradicate the uncontrollable variables of life and other people. You need awareness and acceptance because you can only do so much. They are skills that will help you know what needs to change, what you can do to support change, what you can change within yourself to have an impact, and what might be blocking change. Still, all of your skillful efforts may not result in the change you want, in the way that you want it. Accepting that only so much of the situation is in your control will help make the frustration and fear that come with awareness manageable.

Everything that hasn't changed, everything you hate, everything you want, everything you're not sure about, and the hating and wanting themselves, along with ambivalence and confusion—acceptance puts the whole world in your hand. Openly assessing reality as it is right now can empower you to be humble about the complexity of life and free you from the burden of having to figure everything out. Acceptance is the way to *live through* something instead of being stuck in a constant fight against it. It's a powerful first step indeed.

If accepting that you're "powerless" feels empowering to you, go for it. Just take care not to wield this as an ironclad truth over anyone else. It is not the only truth. It is not a magic password to a club. It is not the key to everyone's salvation. If someone feels powerful, if someone takes more inspiration and reassurance from the idea of willpower than from power-lessness, it doesn't mean she's deluded. Remember that the change process is different for different people, at different times. There are as many legitimate, promising first steps in change as there are people trying to change. We suggest awareness and acceptance, but we don't force them on anyone. People change on their own terms, in their own words.

Exercises: You Are Here

Awareness is the "you are here" on the map of your life. You're reading this book because you're worried about someone else, and because you want things to be different, but these exercises will help you realize that helping starts here, with you, just as you are. First, they will help you to develop a habit of awareness, the starting point of acceptance and change, by prompting you to pause and check in with reality in specific ways.

Second, these exercises record the bigger picture of change so that when the present moment is not what you want it to be, instead of feeling hopeless or useless, you can refer to a memory bank of past successes, and a track record of longer-term progress. One bad day does not cancel out six previous good days, though that's not how it feels when you're in the middle of the bad day. Looking at a record of the good days can remind you they are just as real.

Third, these exercises collect data for you to analyze. When you've been tracking your exercise and sleep and make a connection between not exercising and lying awake at night worrying, you can do something about it.

The Happiness Scale

This exercise, developed for CRAFT, will help you gauge your satisfaction in a variety of areas, not only in terms of your loved one and his problems. It directs you to areas of your life you may have been neglecting or forgotten even existed—areas you may want to target for change. We suggest redoing the Happiness Scale every so often (monthly, perhaps) to compare your new ratings with the past.

Emotional states will never perfectly translate into numbers, but there's value in trying, and we only ask that you compare yourself to yourself.

As you rate each area, ask yourself: *How happy am I today with this area of my life?*

Try not to let your feelings in one area influence your ratings in another.

	Completely Unhappy						Completely Happy		
Drinking	1	2	3	4	5	6	7	8	9	10
Drug Use	1	2	3	4	5	6	7	8	9	10
Job or Education	1	2	3	4	5	6	7	8	9	10
Finances	1	2	3	4	5	6	7	8	9	10
Friendship	1	2	3	4	5	6	7	8	9	10

	Completely Unhappy						Completely Happy		
Health	1	2	3	4	5	6	7	8	9	10
Exercise	1	2	3	4	5	6	7	8	9	10
Nutrition	1	2	3	4	5	6	7	8	9	10
Sleep	1	2	3	4	5	6	7	8	9	10
Family Relationships	1	2	3	4	5	6	7	8	9	10
Significant-other Relation-ship(s)	1	2	3	4	5	6	7	8	9	10
Sex Life	1	2	3	4	5	6	7	8	9	10
Community	1	2	3	4	5	6	7	8	9	10
Legal Issues	1	2	3	4	5	6	7	8	9	10
Emotional Life (e.g., Depression, Anxiety)	1	2	3	4	5	6	7	8	9	10
Communication	1	2	3	4	5	6	7	8	9	10
Spirituality	1	2	3	4	5	6	7	8	9	10
Pleasurable Activities (How You Spend Your Free Time)	1	2	3	4	5	6	7	8	9	10
Other:	1	2	3	4	5	6	7	8	9	10
General Happiness	**1**	**2**	**3**	**4**	**5**	**6**	**7**	**8**	**9**	**10**

You can add any other areas that are meaningful to you, like parenting, household responsibilities, planning for the future (financial savings, vacation, retirement planning), and so on.

Tracking

Using a calendar with plenty of room to write, a tracking app, or a spreadsheet of your own design, take daily note of activities, moods, sleep, exercise, interpersonal encounters, and any other behavior for which you want to build awareness of patterns and progress over time. But don't track *all* of these things . . . start small, with one or a couple that matter to you. The objective is not to drive yourself crazy (people tend to quit this exercise when they take on too much), but to slowly *keep track of yourself*. Tracking is always a work in progress, and you can add or subtract items at any time. We'll make suggestions throughout the book as well—in the chapter on positive communication, for example, we'll suggest tracking any fighting between you and your loved one. Some of the other exercises, such as the "Self-Care Checklist" (page 116) and the "Daily Reminder to Be Nice" (page 141), are specific instances of tracking.

Journaling

Journaling is another way of tracking, if you prefer to write in full sentences and paragraphs.

Borrowing Perspective

Sometimes awareness evolves backward—when someone asks if there is anything bothering you, or when someone else notices that you're slamming the dishes into the dishwasher or that there's an edge to your voice. If you are open to the feedback, you can use it to bring your own awareness around to the realization that, yes, something is bothering you. Identify people who could give you supportive, honest, relatively objective feedback on where you are, and commit to checking in with them on a regular basis. Theirs should not be the last word, of course, but sometimes, when you are too close to something, others have the distance to see things more clearly. You might ask how you seem to this other person lately. Your demeanor, moods, attitudes, or behavior? The answer may be meaningful to you.

CHAPTER 5.

Self-Care I:
Damage Control

How can you accept your loved one until she stops doing what she's doing? One way is to have your well-being not wholly depend on her, and by devoting energy to something outside of your concerns for her. When you take care of yourself, you build strength to both tolerate what you can't change and change what you can. At the same time, as a calmer, happier person, you will be contributing to an atmosphere that is conducive to the change you hope to see in your loved one, and you will be modeling healthy behaviors you wish for in your loved one.

This chapter and chapter 15 are about self-care. You will find lots of suggestions and exercises to help you take care of yourself and create a life that will support you as a calmer, happier person no matter what your loved one is doing.

Fire safety rule number one: stay calm. Everyone knows this, but being told to "calm down" when you're upset is often counterproductive. So we won't tell you to calm down. We will, however, emphasize the benefits of feeling calmer and more grounded: you'll help better, feel better, and be less likely to unintentionally make things worse. If your life is not actually on fire but you feel as though it is, you can learn to control the emotional flames until they burn out. This chapter also includes precautionary strategies to make you more resilient and less flammable in the first place.

We all have a hard time squeezing in optimal amounts of sleep, exercise, nutritious food, quiet time, and doing-things-we-like-to-do time. Prolonged worry about someone you love makes it seem even harder to attend to your own needs. You may think that your ability to enjoy life hardly matters in the face of your loved one's self-destructive behavior or that you can't possibly enjoy life until your loved one changes. If you're a parent with a child using substances, you may feel strongly that "you're only as happy as your unhappiest child." Family members (not only parents) and friends usually come to us believing that they can only be as happy as their unhappiest loved one. There is real emotional truth in that, but it is only partly true—self-care is about the other parts.

Have you ever thought that if you could just make him see how much he's hurting you and ruining your life, he would surely want to stop? It is understandable logic. But in fact, pain and tension in the relationship can act as triggers for use. Again: this does not mean that it is your fault! You are not *the* trigger. Most likely your loved one knows that his behavior is distressing to you and he feels terrible about it. He may feel so terrible that he naturally wants to avoid feeling that way. He may avoid the feelings by avoiding you or by using substances to distract himself or numb out, or he may lash back in self-defense . . . sometimes all of the above. It's a vicious circle: the more emotionally wrecked you are, the more terrible he feels and the more he wants to avoid feeling terrible. Taking care of yourself and feeling better is the first thing you can do to reverse this negative cycle.

We are not asking you to pretend to be amenable to his using. Self-care shifts the focus from what you don't like and can't ultimately control to what you *do* like: your physical and emotional health, for starters, and ultimately your hobbies, work, relationships, and other interests, and the times when he is not using.

When your ultimate goal is a healthier, happier life for your loved one, being miserable and neglecting your own basic needs send the wrong message. Modeling, as psychologists call setting an example, is a staple of modern (post "because I said so" era) parenting. We expect our children to learn from our behavior. We try to curse less, observe Don't Walk signs, and generally do the right thing when they're around. More surprising is research on the influence of modeling among grown-ups: diet, smoking, and other behaviors, including happiness itself, are contagious. We are less independent than we realize. We have an impact on each other without saying a word.

Good News: Reducing your own suffering is good for everyone involved. You start to feel better and put some distance between you and the end of your rope; you gain energy and patience for dealing with problems; there will be less tension and pain in your relationship that may act as a trigger to substance use; and you'll set a good example for your loved one.

The bottom line: You don't have to suffer so much. It's not good for anybody. We cannot overemphasize the importance of self-care: strengthening your *resilience*, building your *distress tolerance*, increasing your capacity for *perspective*, and developing your awareness of your own *emotional triggers*.

Resilience

Good days and bad days, good moods and bad moods: people tend to see these states as ruled by chance—whether you woke up on the right side of bed, as the saying goes. Though you cannot mood-proof yourself completely, you can systematically reduce your vulnerability to bad moods, lost tempers, and meltdowns by tending to a few of your most basic needs. You can develop resilience—your ability to maintain equanimity, health, strength, and happiness or to bounce back, even (or especially) after a setback or a disappointment. Resilience helps people bend without breaking in the face of a challenge. Since setbacks, disappointments, and challenges are par for the course in attempting change, resilience is helpful for the long haul. If this were a sprint, we might be less concerned with resilience, but helping someone change behavioral patterns is more often like an Iron Man triathlon.

The most basic—and critical—self-care strategies are:

1. Eating well
2. Sleeping well
3. Exercising enough
4. Avoiding mood-altering drugs
5. Treating illness (taking medications as prescribed, staying home and resting when sick, and so on)

This list may seem too obvious to print. Of course you should do these things! Yet, when people are stressed or worried, they tend to push their own self-care needs into the future, pledging to eat better after this bad patch at work is over or go to the gym when they have more time. Taking care of yourself happens in some idealized future scenario where time, energy, support, and other resources await. You don't consider that these *are* the resources you need to get to that future in one piece. You say you'll sleep more when work is not so demanding, but enough sleep is precisely what you need when work is demanding. Zumba class is not a luxury to be deferred until your loved one is better; it is something you can do *now* to make things better.

We make an appeal to you here with these basic suggestions not in order to haunt you with old New Year's resolutions, but for three reasons that may inspire you, especially now: First, *the connection between physical and mental well-being is real and cannot be overstated.* Perhaps you dismissed the "mind-body connection" as a philosophical choice or New Agey myth that's not for you, but it's a scientific fact and a critical factor in developing greater resilience. Sleep, food, exercise, and friends all affect your physiology and your mental state. Second, *recognizing the extraordinary stressors in your life right now may give you a motivational boost to follow through on taking basic care of your-self.* If maintaining your ideal weight or feeling rested haven't been enough to motivate you in the past to change your diet or deal with your insomnia, consider this: diet and sleep can make the difference between unhelpfully losing your temper with your loved one and coping with grace and improving your odds of influencing change. Third, *these are all things you can control,* at least to some extent, when other parts of your life are out of control.

What's hard about this . . . Doing it. Actually doing it. Knowing we should typically isn't enough. What you learned about motivation and change in the last section applies to you as much as to your loved one. Tap into your motivations, problem-solve the obstacles, get support as needed, and be kind and patient with yourself when it's hard.

Distress Tolerance

Change takes time and is rarely—if ever—straightforward, especially where substances are involved, so your job as helper and self-helper requires tolerating the way things are now, to some extent—however distressing they may be. Tolerance is acceptance over time, and it is a cornerstone of self-care. All the scented candles and lavender bath salts in the world won't help you feel better without some degree of tolerance for what's going on in your life outside the bathtub. By tolerating what you can't change right this second, you can avoid adding suffering to what is already painful (the more you fight with a painful reality, the more you suffer) and take in the benefits of self-care. It takes practice to get comfortable using these tools, but with alternatives like insomnia, uncontrollable weeping, or exploding in rage, we think you'll agree it's worth it.

Sometimes mistaken for a personality trait—as in "she's a tolerant person; he's not"—tolerance, like awareness and acceptance, is a learned skill.

Here we offer a set of tools, adapted from the evidence-based behavioral treatment protocol known as Dialectical Behavior Therapy (DBT). These are skills you can use to balance your urge to change things with tolerance for the way things are. You can use them to help you feel better and not make things worse: distraction, relaxation, self-soothing, taking a break, and making the moment better. They may not all work for you and they won't all work all the time, but the idea is to load up your toolbox and have it ready. The more you practice with the different tools, the more you'll get a feel for your favorites and which one to reach for in which moment.

Distract Yourself

Take your mind off what is distressing by putting it on something else.

1. **Switch the focus of your thoughts.** Do something that requires your attention. You can make a list of distracting activities and keep it handy. Be sure to include small things that you can do on the spot, such as watering the plants or stopping by to chat with a coworker who always makes you laugh, but have on hand some bigger wrenches too, for bigger jobs. At the end of an especially hard week, what would take your mind off the problem? Rock climbing? Deep-fat frying? How about a few uninterrupted hours reading in bed?

2. **Switch the focus of your emotions.** You can steer your emotions in a happier direction with a mantra, a poem, a bit of nonsense verse, a funny YouTube video—any material you can call up that reliably engages your mind enough to shift the direction of your emotions. A single phrase can make the world seem more hopeful; a favorite lyric may make you feel less alone. Can you think of a joke that never gets old, or a memory that reminds you why life is worth living? Make a "distract me!" bookmark file for your Internet browser, add to it often, and refer to it as needed.

3. **Switch the focus of your senses.** Take a cool shower on a hot day; step outside on a freezing day. Go to an art museum. Stop, close your eyes (sight tends to dominate the other senses), and just listen to the sounds around you. A woman we worked with occasionally would snap a rubber band on her wrist to jar herself out of painful thoughts—to "snap out of it." Finally, don't underestimate the power of simply removing yourself physically from a distressing situation, also known as just walking away.

4. **Do something generous**, to redirect your attention away from yourself. This skill is helpful for people who tend to ruminate and would

feel better directing that energy toward positive goals. You can brainstorm in advance, being sure to include specific, immediately doable activities. For example, to volunteer you have to go through several steps (finding a place, signing up) whereas other distractions are more accessible in the moment, like calling, e-mailing, or texting a friend to let her know you're thinking about her.

Relax

You may be thinking, If only! Of course you would prefer to relax if you could. Like "calm down," being told to relax can have the opposite effect. But appealing directly to your body with specific relaxation techniques will a) relax your body, b) put your mind on relaxing your body instead of on what was upsetting, and c) relax your mind, because when your body is relaxed, your mind tends to follow suit. This threefold effect of relaxation reverses the spiral of distress. It helps counter the process where the tense body and stressed mind feed off each other's cues that something is wrong and requires your immediate attention. Something may in fact be wrong, but whether or not it requires your immediate, drop-everything-else attention is worth questioning. By learning, with practice, to relax occasionally, you can give yourself an important break.

Body tells mind tells body . . . this feedback loop goes both ways. Panic disorder (commonly called panic "attack") is a condition that is intensely distressing to the person experiencing it, often accompanied by rapid shallow breathing, tunnel vision, rapid heartbeat, terror, and the feeling you are going to die. "Panic" is a mind-body feedback loop. As breathing becomes more rapid and shallow, less oxygen gets to the brain, which the brain registers as something to panic about. The brain tells the body to panic, breathing gets even shallower, and so on. Breathing strategies in the moment, or medications that reduce these reactions allow the brain to tell the body "No need to panic." If you find yourself getting lost in a negative cycle of worry, anxiety, or outright panic, pausing to breathe will help you cope better with situations that feel like or are emergencies.

Soothe Yourself

Self-soothing involves making a gentle, comforting appeal to any of your five senses. Brew some tea (herbal if you're anxious, iced if it's hot out, coffee if you don't like tea). Pet the dog. Wear a cozy sweater. Get your hair done or treat yourself to a shave. Listen to music you love. Go to the health club and take a sauna. Again, it helps to make a list in advance. Then, in the moment, try to focus your attention on what you're doing. When you catch your mind wandering to worrisome thoughts, gently bring it back to the self-soothing moment: the warmth of the mug, the rise and fall of your dog's soft belly, the shampooer's fingers at your temples, or the sauna heat on your skin.*

What's hard about this . . . You might be put off because *your life is going to pieces and someone's telling you to put on a cozy sweater.* True, these tools aren't surefire or ultimate solutions, just small ways to calm down, be good to yourself, and exercise some control. If you keep at them, these techniques can make you more comfortable in your life and reduce your overall feeling that things are falling apart. They represent a choice between, say, a 3:00 a.m. habit of sleepless worrying and a 3:00 a.m. habit of sitting quietly with tea and a blanket and the dog and the rustling leaves. You may not feel exactly blissful as you sit there, but that doesn't mean it isn't working, if it is helping you exercise some control in a world that can feel pretty out of your control. Self-soothing can help you improve a situation a little or a lot, and can keep you from inadvertently making it worse.

Take a Break

The difference between running away from a problem and taking a healthy break lies in awareness. With awareness you can plan to tune out for twenty minutes of shopping or a week's vacation, with the intention of facing your problem from a rested and revitalized perspective upon return. With awareness you can recognize when you most need a break and when it is okay to take one. If you don't take breaks, the emergency sense you carry around when a loved one is having problems can suck the life from you. You want to keep plowing through to the other side, but you need to play for the long term, and taking breaks along the way is part of the long-term strategy.

Make It Better

Here, "better" does not mean fixed, and "it" is not your loved one. You can make the moment better by creating a positive experience out of a negative one in any number of ways.

---

*In a calmer moment, you might reflect on your existing patterns of self-soothing. How much do you rely on alcohol or other intoxicants? Is eating, or watching television, or some other once-soothing behavior tinged with excess and/or compulsivity?

1. **Half-smile.** Here too, the body-mind connection goes both ways. As with relaxing, forcing a smile when you don't feel like smiling can make you want to smile even less. The trick to avoiding that fakey feeling can be in the *partial* smile, or half-smile—just a slight upward turn in the corners of your mouth as you relax your facial muscles, especially in your jaw and around your eyes. The half-smile has an uncanny way of slipping under the mind's defenses and making you feel better *because* you're smiling. It may sound like a silly trick, but some people feel profoundly empowered by choosing how they will face the world.

2. **Meditate or pray.** This is an option, not an order, of course. You might try experimenting if meditation or prayer isn't something you already do. On your feet or on your knees, silently or out loud, in private, in church, in nature, you can meditate or pray in whatever form feels comfortable to you. For many, meditation or prayer is another word for—and effective channel to—awareness and acceptance. Either one can open doors to different states of mind and act as an emotional or spiritual salve in trying moments. Tapping into a spiritual practice can also lead you into a community of fellow meditators or worshippers.

3. **Move.** Sometimes when the mind is in overdrive with worry or anger, it helps to orchestrate a physical release. Going for a power walk, hitting the tennis court, or standing on your hands, jumping up and down, or stretching for just a few minutes—all these can shift you out of your head and into another, better state of being. Most people find that physical exertion feels better than mental tension. With practice, getting your body in shape can leave you feeling strong and competent, too.

4. **Find meaning.** Suffering can make people more compassionate toward others. Having lived through pain, sometimes people are better able to appreciate moments of peace and joy. Suffering can motivate people to take positive action—to work for a cause, for example, or to create art. The story of CRAFT, as Bob Meyers tells it, starts with the pain Bob and his mother experienced from his father's alcohol problems, and the realizations that came out of growing up with it. If looking at something one way is driving you crazy, can you look at it another way? Can you think of another way to tell the story? "Being philosophical" involves looking beyond our immediate suffering for a bigger or at least different view.

5. **Borrow some perspective.** Invite another perspective in, especially

if yours is getting claustrophobic. Concepts and beliefs you take for granted might be getting in your way or making you suffer more. Imagine (or better yet, ask!) what your good friend would say about assumptions like, "Only a bad parent would try to have fun while their child was still struggling with addiction" or "What happens in a family stays in a family" or "Other people don't want to be bothered." Good friends tend to be more compassionate than you are to yourself, and can lend you a helpful perspective shift.

As with all self-care advice, you may need to experiment to find what works for you. Know yourself, but also keep an open mind. If you have forgotten what distracts, soothes, or improves a moment for you, try to remember a time when you felt peaceful and what made it peaceful. Or try something new. Ask others what they do. (For more encouragement to try new self-care techniques, see chapter 15.) If one thing doesn't resonate, find something else that does. Use your best problem-solving skills (chapter 8) to brainstorm and plan how you'll go about it.

Other people can be instrumental in helping you stay accountable to your self-care goals. Perhaps you know someone who would help support your efforts to take care of yourself—call her your self-care buddy (or don't, if that sounds too dorky), and keep her apprised of your new self-care strategies so she can hold you accountable. Your mom might like to hear about those lavender bath salts. A friend could join you for a walk.

Perspective

Often, family members or friends first contact CMC in a burst of urgency. They may think it's a crisis—whether, due to the cumulative effects of stress, they just can't take any more, or because they perceive their loved one to be in danger—or both. Tolerating distress when it is not really an emergency (and staying calm even when it is) creates time and space to consider options and act in ways that are more likely to help. Panicked reactions, on the other hand, usually make things worse. In fact, every strategy we recommend calls for patience and a certain amount of equanimity.

Another word for this is *perspective*—an understanding of a situation and your reactions to it that allows you to step back and keep your options open. With perspective, you know that when your husband is drunk and belligerent, you could try to have a conversation with him, you could leave the house, you could call the police, you could call your brother for advice. You recognize these choices and you also remember this is how he always acts when he's feeling down and drinking. Perspective is seeing patterns, options, and a path forward. It is a critical part of resilience. If you cannot wrangle perspective from a situation, it's like driving without shock absorbers: you feel every pothole and bump. Without perspective there is no separation or space between you and the unfolding events, no way to catch your breath, no way to see options.

Katie had become dependent on opiates in her early twenties. A year and a half into a daily heroin habit, she had had enough and was for the first time considering treatment. Katie's parents made an appointment for the three of them to meet with someone at a rehab facility their family doctor had recommended. In their desperation, the parents hung all their hopes for their daughter's recovery on this one meeting, which turned out to feel like more of a hard sell for the facility's rehab program than an unbiased assessment of what Katie needed. When Katie told them she hadn't gotten a good feeling about the place, that the man hadn't really been listening to her, they were crestfallen and furious. They wondered: Should they try to force her to go? Should they even listen to their daughter's opinion, since she was so obviously not well? Was she just stalling? Was she in denial? When they told the receptionist at the rehab that they were going to have to call back because Katie wasn't ready, she rolled her eyes and said, "That's what they all say."

In an initial phone assessment with a psychologist at CMC, Katie's parents reflected on the variety of options they faced. Since Katie was sniffing heroin, not injecting, the risk of overdose was lower, and they realized they had time to do some research. They also realized that she *was* willing to consider other treatment options, and that *they* hadn't been impressed with the salesman at the rehab either. They decided they could tolerate the situation long enough to help Katie identify other programs. A couple of weeks later, Katie entered an inpatient program of her choosing and participated wholeheartedly for six weeks. She found a place where she felt respected, including her choice (and our recommendation) that she stay on medication that would allay her cravings while she learned skills and built a social network that would help support her new life without drugs.

Katie's parents endured a tough month of uncertainty while Katie decided where to go. They discovered that it helped them to help Katie research different treatment options, because it focused their attention on something more constructive than grinding their teeth. The hardest part was stepping back and letting Katie make the decisions, but they had to admit that it was deeply satisfying to see her take responsibility for helping herself—which they would not have seen had they tried to do it for her. They realized that Katie's initiating change wasn't the only positive thing happening. With perspective, where their daughter had seemed alien to them before, they felt a new sense of connection and compassion.

You Have Triggers Too

It's both a bio-psycho-social reality and a cliché of addiction that people trying to change substance use or other compulsive behaviors can be triggered to use even though they don't want to. What is not so commonly acknowledged is that *your* anxiety or anger about your loved one's use can be triggered even when you know he is trying to change. When your own anxiety is triggered beyond your awareness, it is a surefire way to lose perspective and the ability to cope and plan.

Lydia's younger brother had problems with crystal meth and in his twenties got treatment for the first time. About six months after leaving rehab, he came to spend a week with Lydia, staying at her apartment in Brooklyn. She hadn't seen him since he was in treatment and was relieved to see he'd kept on the weight he'd gained back and his skin was clear—two telltale signs that he wasn't using. He told her he had been sober since treatment, and Lydia thought, *I want to believe him.* She took time off work to tour the city with her brother, and the first day they enjoyed each other's company more than they had in years.

But Lydia didn't know what to make of another sign: she could hear her brother padding around the apartment long after she had gone to bed. If she managed to fall asleep, she would wake up, hours later, to find he was still up. She could tell he was trying to be quiet but he was not very good at it. Having learned something about awareness from her sessions at CMC, however, Lydia realized after a couple of nights that it was more than noise that was keeping her up (she had been known to sleep through the loudest thunderstorms). Aware of her pounding heart and racing thoughts, she wondered whether they, more than her brother's clatter, could be preventing her sleep. She realized that she was lying in bed straining to hear, to categorize his every move as benign or drug-related.

In a quiet moment, Lydia recognized that she had developed hair-trigger anxiety when it came to her brother and any behavior she associated with his using, like staying up late or taking a long time in the bathroom. She also noticed how sleep-deprived and irritated she felt and decided her vigils weren't helping either of them. Instead of yelling at him for being loud and insensitive—her first impulse—she told him what the nights had been like for her since he arrived, how it helped to understand her reactions in terms of triggers. She told her brother that she had a habit of worrying and sometimes felt anxious even when she told herself there was no reason to be. He in turn talked about his sleep issues and how they related to his moods and other things going on in his life. It was the first time since leaving treatment that her brother had spoken to her about his experience of the last six months beyond "Don't worry, I'm fine."

When Lydia woke the following night to clinking sounds in the bathroom, she used breathing and muscle relaxation to help her tolerate the distress and get back to sleep. Once she started sleeping again, they both noticed that her daytime humor improved.

With perspective, emotional resilience, and distress-tolerance skills, you can enjoy the time when your loved one isn't using instead of dwelling on the last time he did—or waiting for the other shoe to drop. Distressing thoughts and painful feelings will come up, but with awareness you can see them for what they are (habits of mind) and choose a healthier alternative to obsessing or acting out. As you build emotional resilience, such thoughts and feelings won't bother you as much.

When triggers are predictable, it helps to plan ahead. The next time Lydia expects a visit from her brother, she might have earplugs on hand to wear at night, when she knows her anxiety is most likely to be triggered. She might plan to exercise more and drink less coffee during the day to help her sleep. She could be ready with appropriate strategies for tolerating anxiety, if it came up—going for a walk might not be feasible at three o'clock in the morning, so instead she could warn her husband that she might need him to hold her. She could design some household rules, such as no cooking after ten o'clock, and communicate them in advance, to keep her brother and her out of each other's way at night in her small apartment. She could practice her communication skills in advance, too, but we're getting ahead of ourselves. ("Positive Communication" is chapter 9.)

Therapy (and Other Therapeutic Options)

If you are not getting the support you need from other family members or friends, you may want to seek outside help from your doctor, a therapist, marriage counselor, mentor, spiritual adviser, and/or a support group. Fellow family members may be too caught up in their own reactions to hear your concerns, help you feel calm and optimistic, or strategize constructively. It is not weak or selfish to ask for help. Loving someone with a substance problem can be traumatic—literally. We have family member clients who meet diagnostic criteria for post-traumatic stress disorder. Out of fear, pride, stoicism, or an understandable urge to place blame, some refuse help on the grounds that they're "not the one with the problem." Our suggestion would be to try to let go of the fear, pride, stoicism, or blame, long enough to get some support.

On the other hand, it is not necessarily helpful to let loose willy-nilly to anyone who will listen. Sometimes the knee-jerk reaction is to reach out indiscriminately for support. We suggest that you pause long enough to think about what kind of support you want and from whom you can get it. Consider who is actually in a position to help you. Consider what kind of support you want—do you want someone asking "How *is* it with Tom?" every time you meet, or would you prefer more logistical support such as babysitting the kids on a Saturday night? Or both?

If you have a loved one in trouble with substances, Al-Anon is the family corollary to AA, a far-reaching network of support groups for family and friends. As it happened, Bill Wilson, the founder of AA, had a wife who became aware of his problems with alcohol in the context of their relationship. That is, she saw that his problems were their problems. As writer Susan Cheever tells it in her biography of Wilson, "One night, when he asked her to hurry so that they wouldn't be late for [a meeting], she threw a shoe at his head. . . . In this flying shoe was the idea that later became Al-Anon, a program for people who are bothered by others' addictive or recovering behavior."

Support groups create a stigma-free zone for venting and solidarity. Twelve-Step support groups offer a particular philosophical, even spiritual, approach to managing the chaos of substance abuse. Al-Anon (and Nar-Anon) attendees refer to the same steps for guidance as their loved ones in AA (and NA). A great thing about Al-Anon is that you will probably find a meeting near you. And if one meeting doesn't feel right, for some reason, chances are you can try another not too far away. (The "steps" are the same, but as with AA, the vibe and other specifics can vary significantly from group to group.) All these groups are free.

Al-Anon emphasizes self-care and solidarity. You can read in a book that you are not alone, that many people experience these problems, but actually being with others and feeling that camaraderie and support is different. Families Anonymous is another 12-step option that caters especially to parents.

What's hard about this . . . If you take the evidence-based principles in this book to an Al-Anon meeting, you will probably hear conflicting opinions. They may say that your loved one can't be helped until he "hits bottom" and that you too have the "disease" of codependence. These concepts are not a part of evidence-based practices, but since Al-Anon groups have been a source of solace and support for many people, they could be for you. One of the 12-step slogans says "Take what you need and leave the rest." This is good advice.

As for your loved one, so for you: you may not resonate with the 12-step philosophy. If you don't, there are other options, though not yet as many as we'd wish. Some organizations offer guidance for starting a group if one doesn't already exist in your area. The Partnership at Drugfree.org (which you may know by its old name, Partnership for a Drug-Free America) puts parents in touch with experienced parent-coaches for peer support over the phone, and is generally a rich resource for parents. SMART Recovery, an alternative to 12-step, offers some local groups as well as online meetings for families and friends.

You might not want to attend any support group, 12-step or otherwise, and that's okay too. For some people, listening to other people's stories and complaints about substance abuse is the last thing they want to do. But make sure you do have someone you can talk to, someone who will empathize with you—even if it's empathizing with your need to talk about something else.

This chapter asks you to take responsibility for your part in your own health and happiness, for yourself and the benefit of your loved one. This does not mean there is something you could have done differently to prevent your loved one's behavior, or anything you could do now to make him behave a certain way. The power to influence someone, no matter how great the influence, is not the same as responsibility for another person's choices. Our loved ones' problems become our problems—that's a price we pay for love—but our loved ones' problems are not our fault.

And, to be clear: self-caring is not about trying to be perfect (perfectly calm, perfectly happy, perfectly well rested, and so on). It's about bringing intentionality to what you do at every level—self-kindness and self-understanding as much as healthy eating and exercise, patience as much as effort, acceptance as much as change. In short, it is about doing your best, allowing that your best may look different from one day to the next.

Exercise: Self-Care Checklist

Ask yourself the following questions each week. If you took up tracking or journaling from the previous chapter, record your answers in your tracking log or journal. You may track or journal any number of these areas daily, especially areas in which you are focused on change.

1. Am I eating a healthy, balanced diet? (Am I making an effort to eat five servings of fruit or veggies a day? How much of what I eat are prepared foods, e.g., processed or fast foods, or frozen dinners?)
2. Am I using alcohol or other substances—including caffeine and nicotine—to cope, and/or consuming more of any substance(s) than I want to be?
3. Have I had trouble getting to sleep or staying asleep in the past week? Am I getting the amount of sleep I need?
4. Am I treating any mental or physical health problems? (For example, following through with appointments? Taking medication as prescribed? Slowing down/taking time off when I'm sick?)
5. Am I getting enough exercise?
6. Do I have enough energy to do the things I need and want to do?
7. Have I tried using at least one new tolerance tool in the past week? Did I practice with any I've already tried?
8. Am I keeping track of my progress in at least one area that is important to me?

Exercise: Tolerance Tool Kit

With this open-ended set of exercises, we suggest you start assembling some tools and practicing with them. The more specific examples are meant to prime the pump, not to tell you what to do.

Distract yourself.
Brainstorm ideas that could work to distract you in any of the four ways below. Be sure to include a range, from small, easy, and immediately doable to bigger activities that require more time and commitment. Make a short list, and keep it somewhere accessible.

- Switch the focus of your thoughts. It may be arbitrary, like counting backward from 300 by sevens, or it may be something you'd mean to do anyway, like making soup, but whatever it is, make sure you keep a list of ideas so you're not at a loss for something to do when you're in a moment of distress.

- Switch the focus of your emotions: gather favorite mottoes, e-mails, videos, quotes, lyrics, limericks, and so on where you can find them when you need to turn your mood in another direction.
- Switch the focus of your senses. Brainstorm compelling ways to appeal to each of your five senses. Get a massage. Take a hot shower. Stop and smell the roses. Page through a coffee table book of beautiful pictures.
- Do something generous, to redirect your attention away from yourself. You may not want to do this if you already feel stretched too thin in the caretaking department. On the other hand, reallocating your energy to a friend you've been neglecting or a cause that is meaningful to you could be just the thing to help you feel more balanced.

Relax.

Do an Internet search for relaxation techniques and learn about slow, deep breathing, progressive muscle relaxation, body scanning, and more. Download a "breathing app" or "meditation app" on your phone and use it daily.

Soothe yourself.

Create a self-soothing kit of comforting items and activities.

Take a break.

This could be as simple as shutting the door to your office and closing your eyes for five minutes, or it could be using your remaining vacation days. Whatever it is, make sure it's a break for *you*. (Some vacations are stressful!)

Make it better.

You're never alone when you're having a hard time, even though you may feel lonely. From longstanding experience with pain and suffering, humankind has invented a range of approaches to finding meaning and carrying on. You don't have to reinvent the wheel.

- Practice half-smiling in different situations and notice any effects.
- Consider taking up a meditation or spiritual practice if you don't have one.

- Read stories about people coping with adversity.
- Write down three nice things that happened today, or three things for which you are grateful (as a daily habit, this can be transformative).
- Think of someone you know or know of—friend, relative, philosopher, teacher, singer-songwriter, world leader—whose perspective you admire, and investigate where it comes from. Listen to a TED Talk. When you come across words of wisdom, take note. Take part in something bigger than yourself.

Exercise: Cognitive Awareness Building

In the midst of a complicated problem, rumination (excessive and repetitive thoughts) may take over our mental life. This is a normal, human tendency, and while it can be constructive to give a problem abundant attention in your thoughts, overthinking can also create anxiety.

Ask yourself, "Am I ruminating or am I problem-solving?" If you have new ideas, by all means pull out a pen and paper, brainstorm, and record them; give the matter your attention. But if you see that you are replaying the same event or running through the same string of frightening possibilities in a loop, then use that awareness to consciously move your thoughts in a different direction. This can feel like a grueling effort. Try using the distracting or soothing skills in this chapter, as it's easier to move your thoughts to another focus than to *just stop thinking* about something.

CHAPTER 6

Have Your Limits

Sometimes too much is too much. As you practice using your new aware-ness, coping, and tolerating skills and take better care of yourself, in com-bination with a more optimistic understanding of how people change, you may be surprised at the extent of your resilience. You're not expected to skip around the room singing "Que Sera, Sera," but hopefully, your feel-ings seem more manageable, a sense of calm more accessible, and your life more in your control. You can begin to have more moments when at least some of the facts of the matter don't bother you as much as they did before, and the limits of what you can stand turn out to be more flexible than you had thought.

In theory, you can handle anything. In the real world, everyone has limits— to what they can tolerate and what they can do. Coping does not mean lying to yourself or anyone else about what's okay and how much you can take. Sometimes you can't and shouldn't put up with one more disappointment. Sometimes you need to take time out and collect your-self, for your own sake and no one else's. This chapter is about knowing what your limits are and what you can do about them, independent of your loved one's behavior—how you react to the stressors in your life, when you're pushed too far, and how to avoid going over the edge.

Knowing Your Limits

You can think of your limits as boundaries, personal thresholds, life rules, or expectations (whichever rings true for you) that demarcate your physi-cal and emotional well-being in your interactions with other people. They are the lines between what is acceptable and unacceptable, between what you can and cannot handle. How do you know what you can handle? Lim-its can be shifty. You might surprise yourself by rising to an occasion you thought would be too much. On the other hand, sometimes your limits will turn out to be closer than they appeared. What you can handle without losing your temper, dissolving into tears, or panicking may fluctuate from day to day. Nonetheless, with awareness, careful self-assessment, and practice, you can learn to see your limits from a safe distance and even use them as guides. Consider the following questions:

- Do you find yourself doing or saying things in the moment that you later regret?
- Are you acting in ways that do not match your internal image of yourself and the person you would like to be?
- Do you notice tension, resentment, or frustration building up within when dealing with your loved one?
- Do you feel mentally and/or physically not okay?

If you answered yes to any of these questions, you may be living beyond your limits, telling yourself you can handle more than you reasonably can. Dealing with another person's substance problems can stretch you until you've completely lost sight of what a reasonable limit really is. Not only is this a desperate, miserable place to be, it is not solid ground for the helping work ahead. Taking a step back and looking at things with your new-found perspective, equanimity, and resilience will let you examine your boundaries from a safe distance.

Knowing your limits is part of being aware and having reasonable expectations; you can work with them instead of being surprised and shattered by them. If you expect to have limitless patience for your loved one, you'll be more vulnerable to becoming overwhelmed when you run out of it. You may wish you had more tolerance, patience, or goodwill, but it also takes strength to recognize when you've had enough.

The conscious act of recognizing how much you can stand makes your situation more predictable—no small comfort to people who have been trying to live with chaos. Awareness won't change your circumstances, but it does allow you to anticipate what's coming and plan for it as best you can. Foresight gives you time to avoid situations that you know will push you over the edge, where you lose your temper and say things you regret, or cry so much you feel out of control, or otherwise don't recognize yourself.

Good News: Knowing your limits *increases* your flexibility as well as your ability to help.

Catherine's husband often drank too much. Before she started with her CMC therapist, she wasn't sure why her reactions swung so much. Sometimes she raged and argued with him and took it as a sign they should divorce, sometimes she felt they would get through it. As she paid more attention to the limits of her temper and optimism, she discovered two major variables: 1) when she was already more stressed out than usual, typically from a combination of not exercising or sleeping well, and 2) when his drinking (and the related hurtful things he sometimes said to her) happened in front of their friends. Seeing these, she prioritized her efforts to protect herself from avoidable stress by focusing on her self-care. She also minimized her time with him when she anticipated that he would be drinking around their friends, by coming and leaving early from the gathering or planning ahead with one of the friends to spend time together in another part of the house.

What's hard about this . . . It might occur to you that if he stopped behaving this way, your limits wouldn't get crossed. True. We're not excusing bad behavior or implying that your reactions are the problem; we're encouraging you to honestly assess your limits rather than feel bad when you run into them.

We've mentioned a variety of factors, including moods and past experiences, that can influence what any one person can handle without harm to his or her well-being. Some of these—moods, for example—fluctuate only partially under our control. Others, like childhood experiences, may have happened quite outside our control. By developing awareness of your own limits, you will begin to see what you can handle in certain situations, with certain people, in a variety of emotional states. Catherine could shrug off her husband's arrogance more easily when she was alone, but when he was disrespectful around friends, she couldn't stand to be with him. A mother we worked with found her teenage son's messy room annoying but tolerable, while his neglected schoolwork typically provoked her to nag him until they ended up in a screaming fight. Another client told us that she obsessed over her partner's hangovers on weekends because it affected the kids, but she didn't think much about them on weekdays when he went to work.

Reading the Signs

Your own experience is the best teacher. Since most people spend the majority of their lives in fairly familiar territory, limits tend to follow certain patterns. If you can pause and examine how you respond to events and interactions with your loved one, you can begin to understand your limits. Ask yourself the questions below to help you recognize the signs:

- Are there types or topics of discussion you've had with your loved one that always go badly?
- In what situations have you felt pushed over the edge?
- Has your loved one spoken or acted in ways that you find intolerable?
- Has your loved one gotten into emotional states that you felt you couldn't handle?
- Do you extend yourself in ways that you later regret, such as lending money, giving time, or doing chores?
- Do you find yourself ruminating or fixating on particular interactions with your loved one?

Such reflections on the past can inform your approach to the future. Generally, you can look to the following four aspects of experience to increase your awareness of your limits: *emotions, physical sensations, thoughts,* and *actions.* These four types of signs will help you navigate safely away from emotional flooding and existential cliffs. The territory may change, but you can always read the signs.

Emotions

Most people can identify certain emotional states that contribute to their feeling on or over the edge. Fear, rage, hurt, or despair can lead to larger emotional and physical problems when they are sustained too long. However, with awareness, they can also serve as helpful alerts that you are approaching the edge, if you catch them before they have gone too far. Feelings don't usually strike like a bolt of lightning; instead, they tend to build gradually and to progress in an arc. Noticing the signs when you start to feel afraid (perhaps you fidget or feel a tightness in your chest) or when you first feel the heat of anger (maybe your neck gets flushed), you can choose a coping strategy and change course before it is too late. If you decide to call a friend before anxiety overwhelms you, you might distract yourself enough to go to sleep that night instead of lying in bed listening to the ticking clock. Most people have a hard time leaving an argument when their temper is fully inflamed. Seeing your anger in an early stage, before the conversation goes too far, you can choose to end the conversation or change the tone before you reach your edge.

Physical Sensations

Our bodies can reveal our emotions, but most adults are experts at ignoring their bodies. Despite backaches, twitchy eyes, or knots in their stomachs, people tell themselves they are "fine." When you pay attention, your body's signals can warn you as you approach a limit. Do you feel a headache coming on when you don't know where she is? Feel sick to your stomach when he shouts at you? Are you too tired to go to the gym after you have stayed up all night worrying about what she's doing? A physical symptom that threatens to keep you from your routine—or any physical symptom of distress that you notice when you stop to think about it—might be a sign of an approaching limit. As with emotions, learning to read the signs can save you from repeating the pattern.

Thoughts

The content of your thoughts, when you notice it, can also be a red flag. "He takes me for granted," "Why does this always happen to *me*?" "She'll *never* change," "I can't take this anymore" are just a few examples of the dramatic, exaggerated things people say to themselves before they hit the wall. Psychologists call this "catastrophizing." In another common way of thinking, people disregard their own limits because their loved one needs them too much. But you need to remind yourself that it is not sustainable to be on call around the clock, 365 days a year.

Actions

You can take your own behavior as a hint. Maybe you know that right before you completely lose control of your anxiety, you tend to make impulsive spending decisions. Perhaps you choose to have a drink too many yourself. Maybe you stop talking and avoid your loved one because you don't think you can stand how he'll react. Perhaps you become physically reckless because you think you have nothing to lose.

Harvey had been trying to manage his wife's drinking for several years, mainly by coming home early on weeknights to monitor her, as well as to help the kids with their homework. As a result, he felt he was short-changing his job and vexing his boss, to whom he couldn't explain such a personal matter. Late afternoons when he arrived home, he was already fuming and resentful, his stomach upset.

Tracing his path to this unhappy place, he noticed that he spent much of his time on the drive home berating his wife in his head for being so insensitive to him and the kids. He saw how he went over in his mind the "evidence" of her selfishness. Recognizing rumination as a sign of an impending limit, he made plans that protected his physical, emotional, and financial well-being. He asked his mother to sit with the kids two nights a week so he could stay at work without worrying about his family. These two nights significantly reduced his stress about work, even if they didn't match his ideal of how he thought his life was supposed to be. To keep from ruminating all the way home, he had two alternatives ready: he would think about the kids' school projects or sing along to music whenever he noticed resentful thoughts creeping in.

Harvey did not assent to his wife's drinking with these changes. He did make his life better for himself and less dependent on her behavior, in turn putting himself in a better position to influence her behavior.

Braking Before You Break: Setting Your Limits

Ignore the signs to your limits and you may be on your way to a breaking point. Hitting that point can set you or your loved one back by adding to hurt feelings, confusion, and a variety of other unhelpful emotional states. In the moment that you break, your reaction feels justified—that's the nature of being overwhelmed and not thinking straight. If you can see your breaking point a half mile down the road, however, you can slow down, pull over, adjust your expectations, and set a limit. You can tell yourself *don't go there*, and find a safer way around. You can brake before you break.

Here are some examples to help you get a feel for the difference between braking and breaking.

> Breaking point: *This is the third night in a row he's going to come home late and disappoint the kids, and I'm going to hand him his head!*
> Braking point: *I've been stewing all day and I need some time off. I'm going to take the kids to a movie so we can have fun.*
> Breaking point: *I'm tired and cranky, but I can't stand letting him get away with going to bed early again. I'm going to insist he clean the kitchen even though he has been drinking.*
> Braking point: *I'm so tired and cranky that I am going to order takeout so I don't have a mess to clean up. I will talk to him about cleaning up tomorrow when he is sober and I am rested.*
> Breaking point: *He spends so much money on cocaine, I can't stop worrying about our finances, and I have a stomachache all the time.*
> Braking point: *If I got a separate bank account, I could at least protect my income from going toward his habit.*

Notice how breaking tends to happen *to* you, in reaction to something you can't control. In order to brake, you will need to be at the controls: your hands on the steering wheel, your feet on the pedals. Knowing the difference depends on awareness. To build awareness and acceptance of your limits, you can ask yourself these questions:

What exactly is it that I dread?
How can I prepare myself for the best and worst outcome?
What can I do with this anger (or other emotion) before it gets out of control?
How can I settle my anxiety/other emotions enough to think straight and make good decisions?
What parts of this situation *can* I control?

Any of the awareness exercises from chapter 4 can help bring the signs of your limits into view. The "Self-Care Checklist" in chapter 5 is meant to encourage you to take care of yourself, but it can also help you respect your limits and breaking points, since they partly depend on tolerance and resilience.

Living Your Limits

Determining a limit and living with it are not the same thing. You may be hugely relieved by your decision not to pick him up at the train when he has been drinking; he can walk or find a ride home. You may celebrate the prospect of no more good-night phone calls when she's drunk. But actually following through can bring on a new, challenging mix of anxiety and guilt. Living with the limits you set requires conviction in their validity, plus tolerating your loved one's reaction when you stand by them.

This chapter introduces limits as guidelines for self-care. In the next part of the book, we'll present the goal-setting, communication, and reinforcement strategies you can use to solve more complicated problems with limits, when it isn't as simple as turning on the stereo in your car. This chapter is meant simply to give you permission to have limits, to help you see the value in knowing where they are, and to encourage you to pay attention to the relationship between your limits and how you take care of yourself. If you're not sure how to talk to your loved one or anyone else affected by your limits, you can keep them to yourself for now.

Be patient while you get the hang of your limits. If you are used to losing your temper when he chooses that glass of wine over you, it might be enough for now to just notice that and take care of yourself. Practice setting and communicating lower-stakes limits in situations that are less charged—ordering in instead of cooking, having your mom babysit so you can stay later at work—where your boundaries will more likely be honored. Start smaller, set out a plan, and practice getting comfortable with your limits. Pick the lower-hanging fruit.

What's hard about this . . . Family systems are like any organic system that tends toward a homeostatic state. When one person in a family (or couple or friendship) changes, everyone around him may try, consciously or unconsciously, to pull him back to the old routine (because that's where they still are). As we'll see in chapter 11 ("Consequences"), a "burst" of reaction is natural from others when we set new limits and their behavior doesn't elicit the result they have come to expect. However, if you can tolerate an unpleasant reaction a few times in a row, the behavior will likely burn out.

Evie's husband was trying to stop drinking by checking in with his addiction psychiatrist a couple times a month while he powered through long days at his all-consuming job. Evie took care of their three kids and cooked everything from scratch while she tried to run a small business. When her husband wasn't relapsing, Evie was pretty happy with the fullness of their life. When he decided to drink for a weekend, she was devastated. She knew her husband and their household were doing better on the whole, but she was always ready to snap, and snap she did when she found out he had been drinking.

As she educated herself on how people make behavioral changes, she came to understand that lapses were a likely part of the process for her husband. So, she decided to focus on minimizing the effects of his lapses on her, so that she wouldn't break. She served leftovers more often. Her husband helped by getting up with the kids one morning each weekend. She made a point of taking five quiet, uninterrupted minutes each day to just breathe. She trained her nine-year-old daughter to ask her how she was doing as they drove home from school—not that Evie would unload everything on her daughter, but because it helped to remind her to ask the question to herself. Paying more attention to her own limits and reactions, she noticed that not only did she keep her temper in check on more occasions, but when she did lose it, she was able to get her equilibrium back more quickly than she used to.

. . .

Living life always at the edge of your breaking point is like a game of Jenga. The players take turns pulling out blocks one by one from the tower of blocks, hoping at each turn that this will not be the block that makes the whole thing collapse. We try to help families dealing with substance problems stack the blocks of their lives differently, so that a single block does not make the difference between a standing tower and a pile of rubble. The elements of self-care in this part—awareness, acceptance, distress tolerance, rest, nourishment, exercise, getting help when you are physically or psychologically ill, and setting limits—are the materials for a stable foundation and earthquake-proof building. *Stability doesn't depend on nothing going wrong.* Rather, it depends on your ability to weather problems and mistakes, making sure the regular demands of life do not wear on the whole system too much, and repairing damages when they occur.

Take our suggestions with your own limits in mind. The research is clear about the power of family involvement, but there is no master checklist of things every family should do. The quality of your involvement matters, as you will see, and a big factor in quality is whether you are involved in ways that make sense to you. Let your limits guide you in deciding what you will do and when you will do it.

IN CASE OF VIOLENCE:
A SPECIAL CASE OF LIMITS

It's a sad and well-documented fact that when domestic violence occurs, alcohol and other substances are often involved. If you think you are at risk for violence in your relationship, the principles in this chapter apply all the more urgently, with some additional considerations specific to domestic abuse. Please take your feelings seriously if you are worried that your loved one may become violent—either in general or specifically in response to a change you plan to make. When we recommend making changes, our hope is for things to improve, but if you feel you are in danger or physically at risk, please get more information on how to protect yourself. **This section is not meant to be a complete resource on this matter.** We suggest where you might turn for more information and help and a few steps you can take toward greater safety:

If you are in immediate danger, call 911.

When you have time:

Get informed. If you haven't already, call or go online and learn about domestic abuse. The National Domestic Violence Hotline has a website at www .thehotline.org including detailed information to help you assess risk, take precautions, and make plans for action; or call them at 800-799-7233.

The Behavior Analysis exercise in chapter 2 (page 67) can help you trace patterns of violence and pick out risky situations so that you can better anticipate danger and make plans to avoid harm or minimize it and escape. Redo the exercise with the focus on your loved one's violent behavior (instead of his substance use, which will come up under "triggers").

Get support. Between trusted friends and family and public organizations dedicated to helping people in danger of domestic abuse, identify people you can call for help and safe places you can go for refuge.

Pack a bag. Be ready to leave. Pack an overnight bag with items you would need if you had to stay away, and keep it in a safe, accessible place. The National Domestic Hotline provides a checklist of items you might want to pack, from personal toiletries to legal documents to house keys.

Plan your exit. Know how you will leave, especially if you have to leave in a hurry, where you will go, and how you will get there.

If you have children, depending on their age, you may want to talk to them about safety and exit strategies, both for when they are with you and if you think they could be in danger when you aren't together.

Protect yourself (and any other family members at risk). Organizations like the National Domestic Violence Hotline can help you stay safe or minimize harm with specific strategies for protecting yourself in the moment (for example, staying out of the kitchen to keep your distance from knives, glass, and other potential weapons) and the long term (protecting your privacy, for example, and securing your finances).

If you leave, consider not returning. If your loved one leaves and you don't want him to come back, a restraining order establishes a line of legal defense. (You can get a restraining order before violence has occurred if a serious threat exists.)

Exercise: Know Your Limits

Use the questions below to reflect on your limits. Remember, they may be different from day to day depending on your internal and external resources. Consider interactions with your loved one that leave you feeling you've "lost it," when your emotions have spiraled into states of abnormal distress, you have said or done things you regret, or a conversation stayed in your head and left you ruminating over every word. These are clues you are "over the limit."

1. Investigate how you feel before, during, and after these interactions: hurt, disappointed, exhausted, scared, hopeless, betrayed, angry, terrified . . . ? It might be painful to clarify your feelings if you have become accustomed to ignoring or actively suppressing those feelings. In fact, it would be understandable if you disengaged from your feelings when you felt there was nothing you could do to change your situation. But this book is about what you can change! Clarifying the degree and type of your feelings can give you important information to decide where and when your limits are being broken and the action you may want to take to reset them.

2. Assess whether you need some distance from the problem. When you think about getting some distance, do you think *I'd just prefer to get away, I'd really like to, I think I should, I think I need to, it feels imperative, it's the only option* . . . ? These are different spots on a continuum of emotional experience. Consider, in a calm moment, what action seems to fit best: *I need to talk to a friend and get a different perspective, I need to do something to get my mind off all this, I should take a long shower to feel better, I need to spend the night elsewhere, I have to get away for the weekend, I should speak with a lawyer to see what my separation/divorce options are, I'm moving out for a week/month, I'm taking all my stuff and leaving now.* Looking at that continuum of actions can help clarify what you actually want to do, given all the important variables of your individual situation.

3. If you've read all this and are thinking, *This whole situation is beyond my limits!*, we understand. Exploring your feelings, noting when things feel out of control or beyond what you can handle—all of it is designed to establish how and when you should be intervening to protect yourself more and in what way. Start with something small, something you can change, a positive impact that you will feel. And keep reading.

PART THREE

How to Help

Thirty years ago my older brother, who was ten years old at the time, was trying to get a report on birds written that he'd had three months to write, which was due the next day. We were out at our family cabin in Bolinas, and he was at the kitchen table close to tears, surrounded by binder paper and pencils and unopened books on birds, immobilized by the hugeness of the task ahead. Then my father sat down beside him, put his arm around my brother's shoulder, and said, "Bird by bird, buddy. Just take it bird by bird."

—ANNE LAMOTT, *BIRD BY BIRD:*
SOME INSTRUCTIONS ON
WRITING AND LIFE

CHAPTER 7.

Start Where They Are

With a better understanding of the problem your loved one faces and how motivation works, you likely feel more connected to him and empowered to help. With more attention to self-care, you may be sleeping better, panicking less, and feeling more optimistic than you have in some time. Perhaps seeing things from his perspective has helped you feel warmer toward him. Hopefully all of the above are true, because in this section you will take your empathy, energy, and optimism and run with them.

But don't worry if all that hasn't yet fallen into place. You can continue to learn as you work with the helping strategies in this section. Meanwhile, just knowing that change often follows a zigzag course should help you to keep your balance, worry less, and remain willing to stay engaged.

This section, "How to Help," concerns direct CRAFT helping strategies and treatment options. Helping starts with empathy and stops with fighting. In this first chapter, you will learn skills to set the empathic stage and stop the fighting. In "Goals and Problems," you will learn to divide "the problem" into smaller, solvable problems; for example, "She's ruining my life" becomes "She has stopped doing certain chores, is frequently late for school, has refused to consider treatment, and doesn't go on bike rides anymore." Similarly, "Positive Communication" helps you to fix the communication breakdowns that are virtually ubiquitous in relationships affected by substance abuse, in specific steps from "We're not communicating" to exactly what you want to say and how to say it with the best possible chance of being heard.

In "Reinforcement" you will learn specific strategies to reward behavior that you want to support and discourage behavior that is harmful to your loved one or your family. Reinforcement creates a positive feedback loop in which the more things change, the more everyone will want to keep changing. Using the skills in this section, you can find your way to enjoying each other again.

"Consequences" are the flip side of reinforcement. Chapter 11 will help you leverage the negative consequences that naturally result from negative behavior in order to discourage that behavior—sleeping through her alarm after using the night before, getting kicked off the basketball team because he was caught with a joint, missing dinner with you when he stayed too late at the bar. Simply allowing "natural" consequences to happen creates another powerful feedback loop. People learn from the direct consequences of their actions. When it comes to negative consequences, you have only to step out of the way.

In the second half of this section, we explore treatment from three angles. First, we will describe the full range of options along with key questions to help you assess the best fit for your loved one—and for you. Next, we will guide you through a plan to broach the subject of treatment with your loved one, because how, when, and where you suggest treatment options will affect how your suggestion is received.

Then, we'll help you navigate the treatment system while your loved one is in it. Some programs and providers will encourage your involvement, others not so much. Some kinds of participation are more effective than others. We'll help you decide how to be involved and give you skills to advocate for your needs. In short, beyond *you can help* is you can *keep* helping. (You can also take breaks from helping when you need them.)

Try the helping strategies as you feel ready. Meanwhile, don't forget that by reading, understanding, and taking care of yourself as you've been doing, *you're already helping*.

Start Where Your Loved One Is

No matter how ugly your current situation appears to you, the beauty is that it contains all the information you need to go forward. Maybe you wish your loved one would acknowledge how remote and empty she seems in the morning after a night of heavy partying (not to mention that you hate that stale cigarette smell). Maybe you wish he knew he is funny without smoking pot, and how your stomach churns when he doesn't come home after work. While we appreciate your wishes (they are reasonable, after all), change starts by recognizing what matters to you, what matters to your loved one, and the differences.

Before you completed the Behavior Analysis in chapter 2 (page 67), you may not have understood your loved one very well. The chasm between you can be scary to peer into, but we hope by now you have more reason to believe that over time, your wishes and her wishes can come together, especially as you learn more skills to help this process along. For now, all we ask you to do is appreciate that while you may not be in the same place, change starts where each of you is.

Jennifer came to us for an evaluation and spent most of it talking about her domineering husband. She resented his judgments about the three drinks she had each night. She had mental health issues that included insomnia and obsessive-compulsive disorder—as she put it, "I have much bigger fish to fry than my supposed drinking problem." The problem, as she described it, was that her husband wouldn't stop criticizing her. He wasn't in the room with her, but she argued with him fiercely, defended herself against him, and all but directly asked the therapist for the understanding that she wasn't getting at home. The therapist tried several times to reorient her by asking what *she* thought about her drinking. Did the wine help her fall asleep? Did it help her break out of her obsessive thoughts? Were there any effects of the drinking that *she* didn't like? Eventually, Jennifer mentioned that she didn't like the possibility that her drinking could be acting at cross-purposes with her Prozac, which was helping with her OCD.

This was her "motivational hook" into changing her drinking, something she could work with instead of argue with, but it took almost two hours to find it because her husband's voice in her head was so loud she couldn't hear her own. We didn't meet Jennifer's husband, but this book is for him and other readers like him who don't realize that criticism and anger can be counterproductive to the discussions they desperately want to have with their loved ones.

An Invitation to Change

Have you ever tried to force someone to dance? It usually doesn't go well. Stiff, awkward, and unsmiling, the prospective partner tends to pull away, and the next thing you know, you're wrestling or playing tug-of-war when you just wanted to dance. You *can't* force a person to dance; you have to ask. CRAFT was designed to help you make change as inviting as possible to your loved one. Over time, as you practice these helping strategies, it will become clearer that change is good for everyone. You will create an environment for yourself and your loved one where the appeal of change is mutual and palpable, in which she will recognize better options and find both freedom and encouragement to choose for herself. This chapter sets the stage for inviting rather than demanding change.

The same invitation to change goes for you. We know these strategies ask a lot of you and it's up to you whether and how much you choose to use them. You don't have to do this. The evidence for CRAFT won't mean much if you personally run out of the will to do it; as with dancing, it tends to work better when you volunteer. Most people feel *more* vital and happy from helping in this way. But we also know it takes energy and willingness to start. You are welcome to stay with self-care until your reserves of willingness build.

Setting the Stage

(An Invitation to) Stop Yelling

The tone you take with your loved one has an impact, often more than the words you use. Our number-one recommendation: Stop yelling. It is our version of the Hippocratic Oath—"First, do no harm"—a deceptively simple instruction but one that our clients often say is the hardest thing to change even when they understand why they should.

You may find yourself yelling with the hope of discouraging your partner from coming home late and intoxicated, or any number of other reasons. What may not be so obvious is that yelling may undercut his motivation to come home sober, if to him it means "This is what I come home to." Similarly, yelling may be your desperate effort to communicate your despair and pain ("You always do this; you never change") but what you may be inadvertently communicating is that you don't believe your partner is capable of change, which he may take as a reason not to bother. While yelling may sometimes achieve your goals, it almost always makes you the bad guy, the one with the yelling problem. The takeaway of an interaction in which you yelled will most likely be how mean and out of control *you* are rather than what your loved one could do differently.

In a fascinating study, researchers discovered that a single act of confrontation by a therapist resulted in increased alcohol consumption by patients *twelve months later*. You are not a therapist, but the reasons harsh words don't work are the same at home. Let us teach you the skills to avoid this motivational trap.

For several years Hannah had been going out and getting drunk with friends at least two or three times a week. When her husband, who often worked late, was home when she got home, he would usually explode with pent-up worry and anger. They didn't really fight, because Hannah felt too guilty and incoherent to yell back, but they would both go to bed feeling terrible and she would lie awake arguing with him in her head.

Hannah's behavior started to change when she and her husband decided to learn to meditate. He suggested it because he thought it could help him with his anger—which he knew, from losing his temper at work, wasn't all about her—and they were both looking for something they could do together. They joined a group that met weekly, and Hannah found encouragement for enjoying life without alcohol in the culture of the group, something she'd never experienced in the wining and dining circles of her social and work life. Plus, she discovered that meditating with a hangover was hell. Still, every few weeks she would go out with her old friends and get drunk like old times. The Saturday she realized she didn't want to do this anymore was the Saturday she woke up bruised from a drunken fall the night before.

As she explained it to her therapist, the difference was not only that she realized she was putting herself in danger; it was that her husband hadn't yelled at her that night or the next morning. This had given her room to reflect on her behavior rather than feeling trapped between the rock of having to defend herself and the hard place of letting her husband tell her what to do. After that weekend, motivated by her own conviction, she *chose* not to drink.

It is a lot to ask of you to be nice, flexible, and collaborative at times like this. It may seem like too much, until you see how it works. We're not asking you to stuff your real feelings about your loved one's substance use. We *want* you to express your feelings—your true feelings, and your whole feelings. But we want to teach you to express your feelings in ways and places that will be constructive for you. Ask yourself if yelling (or cold-shouldering, belittling, hectoring, and any other expression of hostility) has worked in the past—to change anything or to make you feel better beyond that moment. If you've run that experiment and seen the results, it might be time to try something different.

We don't expect that you'll never yell again. We present this as an absolute because we hope that having a clear, simple intention will help anchor you when the water gets choppy. The chapter on positive communication to come will show you in detail what you can do instead of yell. The point here is that positive communication *depends* on your trying not to yell, and on being able to stop once you've started. Yelling less is better than yelling more. We invite you to approach each interaction as a fresh opportunity to not yell, regardless of what came before it.

Avoid Arguing

Get ready to "roll with resistance," as some motivation experts say. Arguing, with or without yelling and even with the best of intentions, provokes defensiveness, and as you know, defensiveness undermines motivation for change. In the following chapters, you will learn a communication strategy that is much more effective than arguing.

In the meantime, if you find you are in the habit of arguing, notice the habit. Awareness will let you see that you are arguing and give you a moment to release your jaw. Similarly, you can notice the clenched jaw or crossed arms of your loved one, or any other signs of defensiveness, and use it as a cue to change your approach. Backing off, rather than upping your attack, will give your loved one room to recognize his own ambivalence and argue with himself instead of having to defend against you.

One powerful way to avoid arguing and defuse defensiveness is to acknowledge the other person's mixed feelings, and "roll" with them. Ambivalence can look like defensiveness, especially when you force your loved one to take one side of the argument by arguing the other side. For example, as his parents try to convince him he will feel better in the morning if he gets home early, a teenager may have twenty ferocious justifications for why it makes sense for him to stay out past midnight. He might be less adversarial if they told him they know it's hard to leave his friends, but they also know he wants to go to the car show with them in the morning. A husband might fight with his wife when she tells him his drinking friend Sam is a loser. There's less to fight about if instead she says that she knows he likes to blow off steam with Sam, but she misses him and wishes he would go with her to the kickboxing class at the gym. By approaching the situation as a dilemma rather than an argument in which we represent only one side, we invite the other person to acknowledge both sides of his ambivalence and help him to see the consequences of his behavior more fully (in these examples, sleeping through the car show or the gym).

We know from research and practice that people feel relieved when they are allowed to put mixed feelings on the table. Often, people pretend that they have no ambivalence, because they are too busy trying to convince us that they are doing the right thing. They may, in their current stage of change, believe that the benefits of their behavior outweigh the costs. They may be more than one conversation away from change. If we label this "denial," call it foolish or selfish and don't take seriously what they have to say, we'll get stuck on the opposite side of an argument that is not likely to go our way.

What's hard about this . . . What about *your* feelings?! You think that he started it, and you may be right! But even if it feels justified, and you're angry, and he's being a jerk, we assure you that if you fight with him, you're reinforcing the fighting. In contrast, when you refuse to get into it, refuse to yell and refuse to argue, you help "extinguish" that behavioral dynamic. If you don't engage with your loved one in an argument, if he yells at you and you manage to not yell back, then he's just howling in the woods by himself. While it may take a few exchanges where he gets no response before he stops trying to fight, he will eventually stop. He will realize there's nothing in it for him.

Life can be messy and ambiguous. If you're not sure whether something you're doing, or saying, or even some way you're thinking about a problem involving your loved one is conducive to helping, see if it meets the criteria for enhancing motivation from chapter 2:

- Do your actions or communications express empathy? Are you trying to acknowledge, understand, and accept your loved one as she is, not how you wish she was?
- Are you offering information, or are you pushing it on him or arguing your opinion?
- Do you recognize more than one good option?
- Do you respect your loved one's freedom—and responsibility—to choose?
- Have you considered her point of view? Are you taking into account what makes sense to her?
- Do you believe in him? Do you recognize his abilities and see that he is capable of change?
- Are you giving her positive feedback for positive behavior?

The Voice in Your Head

We're convinced by the research that supports motivational approaches and CRAFT strategies; we see that they are effective in our own work with clients every day. Despite our best efforts to be convincing, however, you may hear a voice in your head that says "That won't work." It may pose as the voice of "healthy skepticism," or "reason" or "common knowledge," when our suggestions seem counterintuitive. It may be a habit to think that way. With awareness and practice, you can stand up to this voice. We hope reading this book has sloughed off some of your old assumptions, or that you feel ready to put them aside, at least temporarily, in order to try something different. You don't know whether it will work until you try, and you certainly don't know that it won't.

The voice in your head may blame you if change doesn't happen (or doesn't happen as fast as you want it to). It may even accuse you of not doing enough to prevent the problem in the first place. We'll say again: it's not your fault. Antibiotics have a helpful effect on strep throat, but they didn't cause it. You can help, but you're not to blame for the problem and you're not responsible for the outcome. You're only responsible for trying in the ways that you choose to try.

After you try the CRAFT helping strategies, we invite you to try again, and again, and again. In science, we don't put much stock in a particular outcome unless it can be repeated. If what you tried didn't work, consider what went wrong and adjust your approach. If it worked once, but not the second time, don't give up. Don't blame your loved one and don't blame yourself; do keep trying. We're not saying "Don't worry, everything will turn out fine." We're recommending informed, proactive engagement, plus patience. Change usually takes time and practice.

Good News (with a little bad news): First the bad news: these are not quick fixes. But this is also the good news! The changes we suggest making now in the way you relate to your loved one will support positive change on his part over the long run. Once you get the hang of this approach, you can keep doing what you're doing and keep on helping. You're learning a new way to relate, not merely a way to "get him into rehab." Rehab may be a part of it, but this is so much more.

You can only do your best. Thankfully, in clinical trials, it has been proven that your best is enough to help your situation change. You're in a position to help, on the one hand, but you're also unhappy with the relationship the way it is. Try to take on the helping strategies in the following chapters in the spirit of making yourself happier and inviting your loved one to join you, rather than making your loved one change. Start where she is. Start where you are. Go from there. Remember, you're in this together—that's why it works.

Exercise: Daily Reminder to Be Nice

You don't have to wait for your loved one to make changes to start being nice. This exercise will help you start to set the stage for change, starting with less distance, tension, and anger between you. Being nice doesn't mean you condone everything that is happening; it is an invitation to live a better way. And when you time it right, when your loved one is abstinent or otherwise not engaged in behavior you want to change, being nice rewards the behavior you hope to encourage.

Also, it feels nice to be nice! You may feel awkward, not to mention sad, contemplating this list if it reminds you that there aren't many niceties in your relationship these days, but you can bring them back, and you will get the hang of it, and most likely it will feel good. Plus, people tend to be nice back.

Activity	Mon	Tues	Wed	Thurs	Fri	Sat	Sun
Did you express appreciation to your loved one today?							
Did you compliment your loved one today?							
Did you give your loved one any pleasant surprises today?							
Did you visibly express affection to your loved one today?							
Did you spend some time devoting your complete attention to pleasant conversation with your loved one today?							
Did you initiate pleasant conversation with your loved one today?							
Did you make any offer to help your loved one before being asked?							

CHAPTER 8.

Goals (and Problems)

Stepping-Stones

Years ago, one of us (Jeff) was hiking in the deep woods of Oregon with a friend. We came to a rushing stream that was not on our map and cut across our trail. We were several days into the hike with several more to go, so getting across without falling in and soaking ourselves was as important as not turning back. After a brief round of kvetching ("Just our luck!"), we saw that we had a problem to solve, in several literal and figurative steps. First we looked for new paths. We scouted the banks for possible crossing points—specifically jumpable rocks leading from one side to the other. Next we evaluated these paths.

Before we leapt, we scoped out our course, assessing distances between rocks, apparent slipperiness and stability, and the depth and current of the water around them. Then we considered the downside: What would happen were we to fall in? Would we be swept away and drowned? Could we get back up and cross but then be too wet and cold to continue, or would disgruntlement be the worst of it? We chose a path that looked the most doable and decided we could tolerate the remaining risk.

Then we took the first actual step. And the next . . .

In this chapter we will show you the CRAFT approach to developing reasonable, achievable, verifiable goals for yourself and your loved one. The heat is typically high in a family dealing with substance problems, with cooler heads and realistic goals often not prevailing. Setting a feasible course of change leads to trust in yourself as well as confidence in the path you're charting. Having a plan can keep you calm, organized, and positively oriented.

Specifically, CRAFT includes six guidelines for goal setting that maximize your chances of success (and minimize disappointment and conflict along the way). We'll illustrate goal setting with specific examples, but it will work in any area of your life, including every area of CRAFT in the chapters to come: communication, reinforcement, and so on. Goal setting is a way of thinking about what you have and what you want, and dividing up the difference into manageable distances.

We also offer eight steps for problem solving, which you can apply when you run into problems in the goal-setting process—obstacles on your trail—and for any other trouble that comes up. These steps will guide you from problem to solution in any situation, from communicating with your loved one to setting limits for yourself to crossing a forest stream.

Relationship Happiness Scale

How should you start to set helping goals if you feel as though you're standing in deep woods with *no* map and *no* trail? Since this is a common feeling for families dealing with substance problems, CRAFT employs two different "Happiness Scales" to help you survey the territory and feel around for your goals. The Happiness Scale, at the end of chapter 4 (pages 99–100), is designed to help you assess how you feel about different areas of your life. It's a critical first step, and is focused on your *whole* life, not just your relationship with your loved one.

In this chapter we introduce the *Relationship* Happiness Scale, to help you consider the ways you and your loved one spend time together (or don't spend time together), the things you do for each other (or don't), and how happy you are (or aren't) with different aspects of your relationship. As you rate your relationship across ten or more areas of life, try to notice where you can build on current happiness as well as work on unhappiness. If you are used to looking at your relationship solely in terms of your loved one's substance problem, we hope this exercise will broaden your view, like climbing to a high point from which you can see more than the obstacles directly in front of you. From this vantage point, you might be surprised to find some happiness already "out there" that you overlooked. The Relationship Happiness Scale prompts you to inspect whole-relationship issues, not only substance issues, for a more balanced and comprehensive picture of how things are going—including what is going right, and what has suffered from inattention while the substance problem has dominated your view.

Relationship Happiness Scale
Ask yourself the following question as you rate each area:
    How happy am I today with _____[name of your loved one] *in this area?*
    Circle the number that applies to your *current* happiness—that is, how

you feel today. Try not to let your feelings in one area influence your ratings in another.

	Completely Unhappy							Completely Happy		
Substance Use	1	2	3	4	5	6	7	8	9	10
Household Responsibilities	1	2	3	4	5	6	7	8	9	10
Social Activities	1	2	3	4	5	6	7	8	9	10
Money Management	1	2	3	4	5	6	7	8	9	10
Communication	1	2	3	4	5	6	7	8	9	10
Affection and/or Sex	1	2	3	4	5	6	7	8	9	10
Job or School	1	2	3	4	5	6	7	8	9	10
Emotional Connection/ Support	1	2	3	4	5	6	7	8	9	10
Independence	1	2	3	4	5	6	7	8	9	10
Raising the Children	1	2	3	4	5	6	7	8	9	10
Other:	1	2	3	4	5	6	7	8	9	10
General Happiness	**1**	**2**	**3**	**4**	**5**	**6**	**7**	**8**	**9**	**10**

Jake and Minnie came to see us about their eleventh-grade daughter, Emily, who seemed to be smoking pot every day. Her approach to schoolwork and college deadlines had become uncharacteristically lackadaisical, and she was apparently stoned when she came home from school.

Emily had been a shy kid. She'd had a few good friends in elementary and middle school that she'd kept in touch with, but the girls she had been having over lately made her parents uncomfortable. They seemed oblivious to anyone other than themselves and they always left Emily's room reeking of cigarettes.

Her parents were distraught by the time they came for a consultation. Jake wondered if they should send her away to a wilderness camp he had heard about, and Minnie felt confused and angry, as she bore the daily brunt of their daughter's sullenness and "bad decisions."

Using the Relationship Happiness Scale helped each parent appreciate what they thought Emily was doing "right": her old friends were still a good influence (social activities), she was fairly conscientious, for a teenager, with her chores (household responsibilities), and in coping with her shyness over the years she had developed stronger-than-average self-reliance (independence). Even the areas they rated lower, such as communication and schoolwork, seemed somewhat more approachable through the exercise of pinning them down with a number.

What's hard about this . . . Everyone has "low-scoring" areas of their relationships at one time or another. The lowest scores on your Relationship Happiness Scale will seem the most urgent, but they may not be the best place to start. These areas may have been bad for a while and accumulated heavy baggage. We recommend practicing with easier goals and problems in less fraught areas of your relationship first. By starting with items that are lighter or less complicated, you will build your skills and confidence. Small successes often have more impact than you might predict.

Doable Goals

To make big goals seem doable, it helps to break them down into intermediate goals. A colleague who works with ADHD sufferers tells her clients, "If you're having trouble getting started, it means the first step is too big." People tend to blame themselves for failing to reach their goals, and blame others for failing to reach theirs when the flaw may lie in the goals themselves, or the way they are approached. Instead of being self-critical, you can turn your critical eye on the goals you set and how you plan to reach them. Your goals should help you get somewhere you're trying to go. In short, if a goal isn't working for you, change it. Thankfully, you're not left to grope your way blindly through trial and error, because CRAFT incorporates a standard behavioral strategy for defining (and troubleshooting and revising) goals. Adaptability is built into the process; getting it right the first time is often not a reasonable goal. Nonetheless, by following these six guidelines, you will give yourself the best chance of success at every step.

A doable goal is stated simply and briefly.
A goal will be easier to remember and carry around with you if it is short and catchy. Advertisers know this when they write jingles to appeal to us with *their* goals for what they want us to buy. As you start this process, you may perceive that your initial goal is freighted with history, emotional baggage, and multiple rationales, requiring that you drag yourself through a complicated story every time you try to make a move toward your goal. However, clarity and concision are hallmarks of a doable goal.

When they came in for the assessment, Jake and Minnie's goal seemed clear to them: *We want our daughter to stop smoking pot.* It was a simple and brief statement, but deceptively so. Understanding substance prob-

lems, motivation, and change as you do now, you may recognize that this
objective was unmanageably big and complicated for a first step. Their
seemingly simple goal was actually a multiphase project, so accomplishing
it depended first on redefining a series of smaller goals.

A doable goal is put in positive terms—
what will be done rather than what won't.

Here "positive" doesn't refer to your feelings or demeanor. It doesn't mean
"cheerful." For the purposes of goal setting and, in the next chapter, communication, we define a positive goal or communication by what you *do*
want rather than what you don't want. You may wish to quit smoking or
to watch less TV; you may want your loved ones to stop doing X, Y, or Z.
The positive framing comes down to what you *will* do.

Jake and Minnie's goal started with a loop tape in their heads: "Our
daughter must stop smoking pot . . . Our daughter must stop smoking
pot." The statement was not unreasonable, but it contained no concrete
positive steps they (or she) could take toward the changes they so desperately hoped to see. On the contrary, the more they said it to themselves, the more helpless they felt, and every time their daughter smoked,
it seemed like more proof that they were powerless to stop her. When they
said it to Emily—"You must stop smoking pot"—she shut down the conversation and withdrew from them more.

As they set about redefining their goal, Jake and Minnie were uneasy
(to put it mildly) considering goals that included any amount of pot smoking. They did, however, see the logic of smaller, positive goals in a stepwise
approach. They also found that Emily showed interest in and was willing
to discuss alternatives to smoking pot, even though she still refused to
talk about quitting. Even if her ideas of how else to spend her time didn't
exactly match her parents' ultimate fantasy (singing in their church choir!
meeting new people! studying!), they still appreciated her progress away
from pot and toward her learning to set goals for herself.

The first rewrite of Jake and Minnie's goal went like this: *We want Emily*
to spend more time at home instead of smoking pot with her friends.

A doable goal is specific and measurable.

"Get my act together." "Get in shape." "Be a better parent." "Be responsible." "Be more loving." "Spend more time at home." These statements are
all brief and positive—but so vague and amorphous that as goals they are
meaningless at best; at worst they're totally overwhelming. To be specific
and measurable means to ask who, what, when, where, and how, exactly;

doable goal is one you have control over.

e emphasis being on *you*. Avoid the trap of a goal that depends on meone else's actions to achieve. You may wish that you and your loved e would not be late for trivia night anymore, but you cannot ultimately ntrol how long it takes him to get ready. A surer setup for success hinges the things you can control—how long it takes you to get ready, and ether you wait for him—with the hope that your actions will influence . Influence is not control.

Emily's parents both worked, so they could not be with her after school en she made the tough decision to leave her friends and come home. cy couldn't do her tasks for her (that was, after all, the point). Those re her goals, which she agreed to. What her parents could and did do s notice when she followed through on her part and give her their ise. Jake, who liked to make charts, made one for Emily to help her d them) track the various tasks that would earn her money. And they ld control what they did with their money, of course; they happily nded it over when Emily had earned it at the end of the week.

doable goal relies on skills you already have or are learning.

sely related to achievability and control, this point is a reminder to ke sure you have the skills to carry out your goals. Calmer communi- ion in the evenings is a fine goal, but if you know you can't control your ger when your partner comes home intoxicated, you will need to work that skill to make it doable. Thus, a prior goal would present itself— arn to manage my anger" subject to revision according to these same guidelines. Goals that depend on skills you don't have or don't have ugh of are setups for failure and discouragement.

Emily's parents proposed home activities that they knew she could . In an ideal world, they might have lobbied for three hours of study three days, but in this world they took into account her current lack interest in school while remaining optimistic that she could build up academics and abstinence with incremental gains. Early success with able goals would foster her motivation to do more. Success does in fact ed success.

It was not easy for these parents to tolerate their fears of their daugh- 's substance use and struggles in school, but they were encouraged changes they noticed in their communication with her through the al-setting process. The return of pleasant, two-way conversations h their daughter was so gratifying, they made it part of their new

to break apart a goal into a series of tasks we can put o
check off when they're done. "Be more loving" could be
kiss each other good-bye in the morning, or it could be t
bage. A doable goal specifies which.

Emily's parents discussed how much more time they c
stay home and when it might happen. They settled on he
home from school three afternoons a week, which seem
they arrived at the next guideline.

A doable goal is reasonable and achievable.
In the language of behavior modification, we call this r
bit goal attainment "successive approximation" or "sha
smaller accomplishments along the road to ultimately a
goal. Nobody learns to play Chopin in a week or roll a
Successive approximation works by making each move in
greater goal both achievable and rewarding in itself.

Emily's parents decided that coming straight home t
week seemed reasonable. It wasn't every day, but they th
enough to improve the overall balance of her life. On the
recognized that coming home meant not hanging out
(one of the benefits of her substance use, which they di
the Behavior Analysis exercise). By putting themselves
could see that it might be a bummer to come home to "r
she might be tempted to forget it and go with her frien
therapist helped them brainstorm how to make con
appealing, and encouraged them to discuss this with En

Emily talked about wanting to earn money so she coul
music in the city. Her parents judged this activity as some
ing than others she might propose, and they decided the

Together, they rewrote their goals like this: *Emily*
three days after school. On those days she can earn thi
by: 1) loading and emptying the dishwasher all three d
the downstairs (excluding her brother's room) once a wee
plants twice a week, and 4) helping her younger brother w
a week. Both parents would make a point of complin
tasks well done—a simple but meaningful reward.

Note that while the overall word count of the goal ha
interest of being positive, specific, measurable, and achi
of it is as straightforward and concise as it could be.

definition of success—that is, they made it a goal—and drew from it for patience with this more gradual course of change. They never changed their underlying message ("We want you to stop smoking pot"), but they planned to help her reach the same conclusion, step by doable step.

How Do You Solve a Problem?

In most cases, this six-step goal-setting strategy will help you turn problems into doable goals. However, not every problem will strike you as an "opportunity in disguise." Sometimes a problem is just a problem because we've had it so long, or because of its emotional content, or because we can't solve it alone. Looking for solutions, you can run into any (or all) of the following obstacles: being overwhelmed by complexity ("This has too many moving parts for me to sort out"), lacking knowledge ("I don't know how to make a budget"), lacking resources ("I can't afford to do this" or "I don't have time"), having conflicting goals ("I want him to stop, but don't like how he treats me when he's sober"), and, last but not least, fear or insecurity ("What if I screw this up? or "What if things don't change?").

For those times, CRAFT (among other behavioral approaches) sets out eight steps for solving problems systematically. This strategy will help you avoid the unreliability of quick fixes and the pain of avoidance strategies. As you practice with these steps, try to apply (and give yourself credit for) what you already do well, and take the time you need to learn what would be useful to you that you don't already know. We use the example of Kiki to illustrate these eight steps.

Kiki, thirty-two, had been married to Lyle for five years. They had met at a club and partied together in their early days, but she had figured that would slow down with time as they developed new, shared interests and friends in their marriage. She came to CMC when she realized that Lyle had been going out more, not less, in the past year. By the time of her first appointment, he had been "going missing" for two-day stretches, which left her frantic and frequently sick to her stomach. Lyle would apologize each time afterward, but he didn't seem to mean it, and with any pressing on Kiki's part, he would erupt in anger and say nasty things, claiming for example that he "didn't sign up to marry a nun" and he was just "having fun" and she should "get in control" of her "overreactions." Kiki came to us because she was tired of feeling awful and wanted us to help her get Lyle into treatment. (He had been sent away to rehab when he was seventeen, an unhappy experience that was one of his many reasons for not wanting help.)

When she came to us, Kiki suffered with a low mood and high anxiety as her "happy face" strategy had started to collapse and her sense of helplessness was mounting. After completing the Relationship Happiness Scale, she was amazed to realize how she felt about other aspects of her marriage. In fact, her husband was good at his job, and they had been saving money for a down payment on a house. It occurred to her that she could give him more credit for not partying on weeknights, too. He was helpful during the week—maybe this counted even if it was motivated by guilt? On the low end of the scale, she saw their communication in a way she hadn't before: their fights and estrangement over the past year were at least as troubling to her as his substance use. Of course they went together, but maybe not inextricably. Perhaps communication was a place for a fresh start.

1. Define the problem narrowly.

What seems to be the problem? Often what we call "the problem" is really a pileup of problems that overwhelms us with its size and complexity when we regard it as one big thing. On closer inspection, the component problems may seem less daunting when we approach them separately.

When Kiki thought about her goal, getting Lyle to treatment, she didn't know where to begin; she also figured talking to him about it was sure to turn into a fight. She decided that his weekend binges had become such a hot issue between them, she wouldn't try to touch the topic just yet. As she saw it, their fighting was the first problem at hand.

In her diary, Kiki kept a daily log of their fights. She "analyzed the data" after tracking it for a few weeks, and certain patterns and triggers emerged. Monday mornings were particularly bad. She would wake up furious with him for leaving her alone and using all weekend, and he'd be feeling guilty and defensive, all before anything was said. Starting the week off with a fight, she realized, wasn't helping; in fact, it was making a bad situation worse. She thought it would be a real improvement if they could get through Monday mornings without a fight after a weekend when he'd used. This was the problem, narrowly defined.

2. Brainstorm possible solutions.

Brainstorming is a skill that depends on suspending your disbelief and your self-censoring long enough to imagine new solutions to old problems. Write down any old solutions you may have thought of already, too, but don't rule out anything that occurs to you, no matter if it seems ridiculous or out of the blue.

Family members often come to us with rigid thinking. They've been afraid, perhaps for a long time, of what's going to happen. They're afraid to make mistakes or they feel too discouraged to try, because nothing has seemed to work in the past. But there is no such thing as a brainstorming mistake. Whatever occurs to you, write it down. You're not going to do all of it. Some of it's going to be nutty. That's okay, let it out. If you're blocked, try brainstorming with a friend.

Kiki brainstormed the following as solutions to the problem of getting through Monday mornings without a fight:

Stay in a hotel Sunday night and go straight to work from there on Monday.
Get Lyle to agree to a mutual vow of silence on Monday mornings.
Leave the room if we start to fight.
Get a divorce.
Put on music we used to listen to before all this started.

What's hard about this . . . In families with substance problems, behavior can become restricted and rigidly routine. People may avoid trying new things because the situation already feels so unstable or they may be just plain too exhausted, and so the problems get more locked in. Brainstorming lets you consider how it could be different without leaving the safety of the hypothetical until you're ready with a plan.

3. Eliminate unwanted solutions.

After you brainstorm, review your list of possible solutions and cross off any that you can't imagine doing. Don't overthink this step. You'll be more likely to act on the ideas you're drawn to for whatever reason. Don't make it too hard for yourself. Imagining new ideas is one thing; forcing yourself into a "solution" that doesn't suit you probably won't be a viable solution after all.

If you get through your list with no ideas left uncrossed, let your brain storm again.

Reviewing her list, Kiki ruled out the hotel as being too expensive. She wondered if a cheaper version could be to set her alarm so early that she could be out the door before Lyle woke up, but that didn't seem realistic or fair because she hated getting up early. Plus, she was hoping to find a solution that wasn't based on their avoiding each other altogether.

The vow of silence had seemed ridiculous to her when she wrote it down, but on second thought, it seemed so crazy it might work. Leaving the room was a good idea in theory, but it didn't seem practical for their small one-bedroom, one-bathroom apartment when they were in a rush to get ready for work. She decided she'd written "divorce" more to vent anger than as a solution. Finally, she decided that until they saw some improvement, listening to music from their good old days would just make her really sad.

4. Select one potential solution.

If you identify more than one good option, plan on using one at a time, not in rapid succession. If a solution works, great. If not, you'll have some others to try. A vow of silence? In one way it seemed rather severe, but optimistically Kiki thought they could make a sort of game of it.

Hopefully, the morning silence would let them be together without fighting, and by the time they got home from work on Monday night, the pain of the weekend wouldn't be so raw. They'd have a day's worth of events to distract them, shift their moods, and give them something new to talk about.

5. Identify potential obstacles.

This preparatory step and the next one contribute to your confidence going in and also to your chances of succeeding. Of course there will be problems—there are problems now! Meeting obstacles in the calm of planning instead of the heat of trying will put you in a better position to deal with them. You probably can think of many things that could go wrong. Don't be afraid of them. Lay them out and you will see that you have the answer to most of them. Some of them won't even be real problems, just nervousness. Absolute deal-breakers are rare when there's time to plan ahead.

Kiki realized that they might fight about the silent breakfast idea when she brought it up to Lyle. In fact, he might refuse to do it altogether. There might be something they needed to communicate about that couldn't wait. And silence isn't necessarily benign—what if it was just like giving each other the silent treatment? What if it didn't help at all?

6. Address each obstacle.

One by one, Kiki addressed the undesirable outcomes she could anticipate. Much of her problem solving centered on how and when she intro-
duced the idea to Lyle. She certainly wouldn't bring it up on one of those
Monday mornings! Late in the week it might seem like she was already
on him about the upcoming weekend. She resolved to plan what she was
going to say as an exercise in positive communication (as you'll learn in
the next chapter) and find a time midweek to say it when they were both
in pretty good moods.

She would avoid fighting with him if he didn't want to try it.

She would ask him if he had any ideas.

She would go ahead for her part in any case.

If he agreed, they could have a notepad on hand in case they needed
to communicate. They could try to establish some guidelines for written
communication. (She hoped that because of the very nature of writing,
their communication would slow down enough for them to reflect more
on what they were saying.)

They would need to stay aware of the quality of their silence to make
sure it didn't turn seething or mean. Silence would let them pay more
attention to nonverbal communication. She wasn't sure, but she thought
that nonverbal communication between them might be more direct and
honest. At least it would be different enough to disrupt their usual patterns. And it could be funny!

She would continue to track their fighting so she would know for
sure that the total amount was decreasing—if it wasn't, she would problem-solve that problem when she came to it.

What's hard about this . . . The other person may not play along. But while you
can't anticipate every obstacle, when you expect the unexpected, it probably
won't throw you off as much.

7. Assign task(s) and timelines.

Once you've gotten this far, it's time to commit to action. We recommend
that you schedule a specific time for each step of your plan, and then do it.

Kiki's first task was to write a draft of how she would suggest the silent
breakfast to Lyle. She put it on her calendar for her lunch hour the follow-

ing day. When she was fairly satisfied she'd hit the right tone, her next task would be to call her brother and try it out on him—Saturday, she decided. She would make notes if her brother gave her any useful feedback, and revise her script if necessary. Her third task would be talking to Lyle. She put this on her calendar for the following Wednesday if the time felt right. See how "do it" becomes doable with discrete steps, in order, with enough time?

8. Evaluate the outcome.

Did it work? Is it working? The CRAFT model of helping is based on understanding what works. By being aware and tracking the data, you can feed the outcome of every interaction back into your problem-solving system for modification, celebration, or a return to the grindstone if necessary.

It worked. Lyle agreed to Kiki's idea because he also wanted to start the week without a fight. Silence let them sit together peacefully and eat breakfast. Sometimes it led to pantomimes, which they found hilarious and started looking for excuses to do. Silence changed their Monday-morning-after-the-weekend-before, and began to change the whole tenor of the following week.

Silence also let Lyle reflect on his weekends instead of defending them. He remembered that he missed doing things with Kiki. Kiki realized that even though she spent the weekends wishing Lyle were home, she had dreaded Monday mornings more than she had been happy to see him. Now, in the spirit of experimentation that came with trying something new, she looked forward to their morning time together.

The Prize

Everywhere in life, there's room for improvement. You could learn to play a Chopin nocturne, roll a kayak, have better knife skills in the kitchen, and be more informed about current events. In your relationships, you could have better sex and clearer communication, more independence, more help with the garden, more savings in your joint account. More realistically, though, you can't have it all, at least not all at the same time. You must prioritize. If you don't, you'll waste precious energy feeling bad about what's not changing instead of nurturing what is.

As you work on these goal-setting and problem-solving strategies, remember what is most important to you. Breaking down your ultimate goals into doable goals and solvable problems allows you to take change one step at a time, in order of priority. A teenager's messy room and piercings won't bother her parents as much if they view them as separate and lesser problems from the pot smoking, rather than lumping them all together as one big mess. As they target the pot use, the room can stay messy and the piercings can stay in, and they don't have to feel like they are signs of everything that's wrong.

Meanwhile, keeping one eye trained on the greater goal can help you shrug off setbacks you encounter along the way. If you rank getting treatment as the most important thing your loved one can do for now, his moodiness in the early stages of abstinence will be easier to ignore. In any case, the very act of prioritizing goals and problem solving usually helps people feel more in control of their lives. Indeed, when you choose what to care about and what to work on, you *are* more in control.

Exercise: Goal Setting

This strategy is standard in behavioral treatments, and it has been proven in the context of CRAFT studies to help family members. Choose an area from your Relationship Happiness Scale and follow these guidelines to define a doable goal.

Make your goal:

1. Brief and simple.
2. Positive—that is, put it in terms of what you do want rather than what you don't.
3. Specific and measurable.
4. Reasonable and achievable.
5. Within your control.
6. Dependent on skills that you (and your loved one) have or are learning.

Exercise: Problem Solving

Pick a problem that you identified with the Relationship Happiness Scale or that emerged from your goal-setting process. Try to solve it with the following steps.

1. Define your problem. (Just one. Keep it specific. Put it in writing.)
2. Brainstorm possible solutions. (The more the better! Write them down.)
3. Eliminate unwanted ideas. (Cross out any of the above "possible solutions" that you can't imagine yourself doing.)
4. Select one potential solution. (Which one can you imagine yourself doing this week? Circle it.)
5. Anticipate possible obstacles. (What might get in the way of your solution working? Make a list.)
6. Address each obstacle. (If you can't solve each obstacle, pick a new solution and go through the steps again.)
7. Assign task(s) and timeline(s). (Describe exactly when and how you'll do it. Then do it.)
8. Evaluate the outcome. (Did it work? If some changes are needed, list them and commit to trying it again.)

CHAPTER 9.

Positive Communication

Positive communication is a critical skill for making change. It's also an *acquired* skill. One thing we know about families struggling with substance use: communication suffers. Poor communication may be long-standing or new, but substance problems usually make it worse.

And that makes sense. When one person in a family behaves in a way that harms the others despite their hopes, expectations, and previously understood norms, it causes a breach in the social fabric. Whatever the reasons for the behaviors, and even though, in their heart of hearts, most people abusing substances feel bad about these breaches, friends and family naturally react.

You, who perceive the costs of your loved one's behavior even if he or she doesn't (or at least not enough to do otherwise), will feel disappointed, hurt, or angry, and naturally you'll want to express it. "I hate you for lying to me again." "How could you do this?!" "You're a disappointment," and so on. These reactions make emotional sense. You "got it off your chest," "gave him a piece of your mind," "told it straight up." And then? The behavior continues, so you have to get it off your chest again, but each time your chest is heavier, your words are angrier or more hurtful; and the aftermath is a *deeper* hole.

There can be many reasons to communicate. You want to *express your feelings*. You want the other person to *feel a certain way* in response. You want him to *do something* in response. You want him to *care* about what you're saying. Communication often works, and you get what you want. Or you don't get what you want, but it's not a big deal—you can try again now or later, or simply move on.

But stress in a relationship raises the stakes of communication, in the amount of negative emotion people feel like communicating (more) and the importance they place on the result of their communication (much more). They say, "You missed your son's soccer game *again* today because you were hungover *again*," and it's not enough for the other person to listen and understand. They want action, retribution, apology, change, and not to feel this way right now. What they get instead, often, is none of the above. Because their pitch rose, their volume increased, and their words were more angry than measured, they got little or nothing.

It feels right to speak this way when you feel this way, when you want all these things. And you may not know what else to say. But you can learn another, more effective way. This chapter will show you the core communication strategy of CRAFT and a bundle of other techniques to significantly increase your chances of being heard and understood, and thus of influencing change.

Five Reasons for Positive Communication

Because positive communication takes effort and practice and may feel forced and awkward at first, we will start with five major reasons why we think it's worth it and we hope you'll agree.

First, a communication system or style that frequently breaks down into negativity and attack or silence only deepens wounds and rifts. This is true in families, in workplaces, in schools, in sports; everywhere. A negative communication loop makes things worse between the players and perpetuates the bind everyone is in. This is particularly true of communication in a system (family) that is fighting with substance problems. Positive communication is the way out.

Second, positive communication is "contagious." When you communicate positively, others tend to mirror it. They listen better and understand more, and in turn they feel better. Positive communication invites positive communication. It's the opposite effect of the communication breakdown process. When you reduce friction and increase amiability with the little sticky issues, like hot beverage slurping or leaving hair in the shower drain, the goodwill carries over to bigger problems and paves the way for positive communication more generally. Win, win, win.

Third, it works for you. You actually *will* get more of what you want. It's not manipulation; it is the outcome of improved communication. The other person will listen better, understand more, and at the very least be able to respond less defensively and from a more thoughtful, more collaborative position, whether he or she agrees with you, wants what you want, or not.

Fourth, it works for the other person. That is, it helps. The most helpful way to communicate with your struggling loved one is *positively. Your* communicating more effectively will help *him*, by helping him to be less defensive and more collaborative and as a reinforcer of positive change. Reinforcement for positive change, the basis of CRAFT, is accomplished at least partly through words. You may forget to say "Thank you" to your son for taking out the garbage, because he forgot the other three times this week. You may neglect to say "I love you" as your husband leaves for work because you're thinking about how he'll probably come home late. Still mad about your daughter's breaking curfew last weekend, you don't compliment her on getting right to work on her homework. It's understandable, but these are missed opportunities to use positive communication, *words*, to reward the behavior you want.

Fifth, positive communication helps everywhere. The skills apply to every interpersonal situation, from developing more satisfying friendships, to talking to your doctor about an embarrassing health problem, to settling a customer service complaint, to helping your loved one change. We promise that taking the time to learn these skills and using them will help *you* in your life.

Seven Elements of Positive Communication

Most of the time, most days, with most people, you don't need a cheat sheet to get your message across. You order coffee, cooperate with colleagues, go to the dentist, chitchat at the dog park, and e-mail your friends effectively enough, without giving much thought to *how* you're doing it. Higher stakes, however, require you to plan ahead and think about what you want to say and how you want to say it. People prepare for presentations at work or in school, and plan what they will say in a job interview. Yet when it comes to their personal lives, people tend to wing it. It's counterintuitive, when you think about it: People tend to be the least prepared for communications with the people who matter the most.

Spontaneity is great when it works, and there can be value in speaking your mind. But, if you step back, what feels "spontaneous" is sometimes better described as "pent-up." Interactions that feel "spontaneous" are often springing from old, emotionally loaded issues and fighting words that you can't wait to unload. In fact, so-called spontaneous reactions are often the least fresh, most habitual of all forms of communication. When automatic approaches and spontaneous reactions aren't getting the job done, or when they have become rutted in a negative track, you're better served by intention, strategy, and preparation.

Psychologists have developed a number of communication strategies over the years in a variety of therapeutic camps, including Cognitive

Behavioral Therapy and family therapy. This chapter compiles the greatest hits starting with seven points from the communication-training component of CRAFT. (You'll recognize the first three elements from goal setting in the last chapter.)

1. **Be positive.** "Positive" here refers to word choice, tone, and framing. Words can be harsh, pejorative, or critical; or they can be positive, complimentary, inclusive, and hopeful. Depending on tone and other nuances of delivery, the same words can sound frustrated, dismissive, anxious, or judgmental, or kind, patient, and matter-of-fact. Similarly, you can frame a statement in overly general, exaggerated, or blaming terms, or make them descriptive, specific, and neutral—to very different effect. Consider how it feels to be on the receiving end of these words, respectively: *confusing mood swings* versus *crazy*; *using OxyContin* versus *junkie*; *upsetting* versus *devastating*; *"Here's how it looks to me"* versus *"That's total bullshit"*; or *"Let's see where we can go from here"* versus *"We're back to square one."* Words matter a great deal, not as a matter of "political correctness" or quibbling over semantics; the evidence says that words matter if you want the other person to hear you.

   As with goal setting, the other meaning of "positive" is describing what you *want*, instead of what you *don't want*. This shifts the framing from critical and complaining to supportive and doable. And, as we'll discuss in the next chapter, this ties into positive reinforcement strategies, since it's easier to reward someone for doing something—a concrete, verifiable *thing*—than for not doing something.

2. **Be brief.** Most people say more than necessary when they haven't planned it in advance, especially when nervous or angry. Try to home in on your central request ahead of time, and stick to it. Script, edit, and rehearse what you want to say as concisely as possible. Extraneous words can drown out your core message. Less gets you more.

3. **Be specific.** Vague requests are easy to ignore or misunderstand, and are often difficult to translate into concrete behavior. In contrast, referring to specific behaviors makes change observable, measurable, and reinforceable. Instead of "It wouldn't kill you to help out more," specify how you would like the person to help: "It would really take some pressure off me if you emptied the dishwasher in the morning." "I loved it when you used to rub my feet while we

watched the news" is easier to understand and act upon than "You used to be a loving husband."

4. **Label your feelings.** Kept brief and in proportion, a description of your emotional reaction to the problem at hand can help elicit empathy and consideration. For best results, state your feelings in a calm, nonaccusatory manner, and try not to hyperbolize. For example, "I worry when you come home later than you said you would," as opposed to "It's totally inconsiderate of you to come home late and I'm losing my mind." Labeling positive feelings, when you mean them, also helps lower defenses and reward positive behavior: "I am so thankful when you help the kids with their science homework. I'm glad you're here."

5. **Offer an understanding statement.** Genuine understanding helps reduce defensiveness and promotes collaboration. This is the proverbial putting yourself in the other person's shoes, also known as empathy. You don't have to agree with him, don't have to like what he's doing, may even think it's crazy, but at the same time you can understand it, or some part of it. Try finishing this sentence and really meaning it: "Yeah, I can see how you would . . ." That's understanding. It's not feeding someone a smarmy line about how "I hear ya," or putting words in his mouth that you wish he would say. Using understanding statements requires that you recognize a part of the other person's emotions, actions, or reactions that you do understand, and include it in your message. For example, "I know it can be hard to leave a party earlier than your friends."

6. **Accept partial responsibility.** Ouch. This one is hard, but we encourage you to consider the payoff. Sharing in a problem, even a tiny piece of the problem, also decreases defensiveness and fosters collaboration. It shows the other person that you're interested in solving, not blaming. Accepting partial responsibility does not mean taking the blame or admitting fault; it communicates "We're in this together." Some examples: "I know sometimes I overreact," "I forgot to remind you," "I'm not the best communicator myself sometimes." Such acceptance on your part may not spring to mind in the moment when your emotions say "It's all *her* fault," but everyone can find some way that they're not perfect when they think about it. Your loved one is probably used to feeling like a screw-up and being the focal point of blame. Your willingness to share the load, even in a small way, will help bring her back to the conversations you would like to have.

7. **Offer to help.** Especially when phrased as a question, an offer to help can communicate non-judgmental, problem-solving support. Try asking, "Would it help if . . . ?" Or if you have no idea what would be a supportive gesture, simply, "How can I help?" Either way, you let your loved one know you are willing to collaborate on a solution. And chances are, your loved one does need help.

After years of alternately ignoring or lashing out at her husband's sometimes heavy social drinking, Lucy tried positive communication skills to speak directly to him about it. Ivan had grown up in a European country where heavy drinking among men was culturally acceptable, and he prided himself on drinking moderately compared to his family. Lucy had grown up with a father who drank heavily every day while her mother silently fumed or blew up in anger. Lucy's father eventually died from his drinking. It was no wonder Lucy and Ivan needed new skills to find common ground. Here's how Lucy positively communicated her desire not to spend time with Ivan when he drank too much:

I know you're just having fun with your friends, and that you drink a lot less than most of the guys around you. (Understanding statement.)
Whenever you have more than a couple of drinks, though, I feel scared and distant. And I want to feel close to you. (Labeling her feelings, being positive.)
I know I seem angry, which is confusing when you're just having a good time. I am mostly just afraid—I don't want you to lose control like my dad did. (Accepting partial responsibility, labeling her feelings.)
So that we don't fight, if I start to get upset, I am just going to go to bed early, and I would like it if you let me go without getting upset or trying to talk me into staying. (Referring to specific behaviors.)
I'm happy to explain it to our friends in whatever way feels most comfortable. (Offer to help.)

In this example, you can see that positive communication does not sugarcoat the truth or pretend something is okay when it isn't. By using these skills, you can feel awful about a situation and communicate positively and honestly nonetheless. Ultimately, since positive communication leads to less fighting and more rapport, you may end up feeling better.

Having a Conversation

In addition to the seven specific elements of positive communication, we offer some powerful techniques and suggestions to help your conversations go better.

Prepare and practice.

It may seem ridiculous to practice something you've done your whole life, but positive communication is different. It's not taught in school. We regularly role-play with smart, capable, fully grown adults to help them form one simple communication that includes all seven elements. It can take literally hours of practice to transcend negative habits that in many cases were ingrained over years. Simplicity and grace do not typically come easily. We suggest you approach positive communication as you would a public speaking engagement—minus the stage fright, hopefully. Use your therapist, your smartphone, your bathroom mirror, or your commute home as opportunities to practice. It may feel silly, but practicing will build your skills and with them your confidence.

Consider your timing.

Timing isn't everything, but it's definitely something, especially when you plan to make a request. Pick an optimal time for communication by drawing on the wealth of information you have about yourself and your loved one. Do you tend to have better conversations at the beginning of the day, after work, over dinner, in the car, on the phone . . . or can you think of any other relevant factors? Try to base your decision about timing on these variables rather than any pressure you may feel to just get it over with or get your own needs met now (though we understand both impulses). Generally, you're looking for a time when a) you're both in relatively good moods, and b) your loved one is not intoxicated (and for that matter, neither are you). This second point sounds obvious, but people fall into it easily. How many times have you exploded with pressure-cooked emotions when he shows up intoxicated? Why *wouldn't* you want to tell him everything that weighs on your heart and preys on your mind?

While we understand the impulse, we suggest that you try hard to avoid any conversation when your loved one is under the influence. It's a setup for misunderstanding. He is altered, after all, in his feelings and ability to process information. Some substances numb emotions, for example, inclining a person to underrespond, while others escalate emotions and lead to overreaction. Or he may simply forget and your efforts will have been wasted.

Pace yourself and prioritize.

Change happens gradually, and you can only communicate so much at a time. Even the most positive communications can backfire if you pile on too many requests at once, so it's useful to prioritize. This is where goal setting meets positive communication. As you consider what you're going to say (and how, when, et cetera), bear in mind the goal you hope to achieve. If you have several, rank them in order of priority and achievability. Remember too that you can revise your goals if your priorities change over time, or even in the moment depending on how an interaction is going. You can always save something for later.

Start small.

As with goals and problems, particularly at first, choose smaller, less emotionally charged communications for practice, and keep your expectations in check. With less emotional pressure on the whole interaction, you're more likely to succeed, and the more you succeed, the more confidence you'll develop to take on bigger topics. Don't try to fix the universe in one conversation; remember, change happens incrementally. Realistic initial goals are specific, skill-based, and in your control; for example, "Don't raise my voice, no matter what she says" or "Just get through what I practiced, and don't keep talking after that."

Manage your tone of voice.

Remember, tone trumps content. Tone is the sine qua non of positive communication, and it is the most frequent way that communication goes haywire. After taking the time to write a perfect script with all seven elements, if you convey it angrily, sarcastically, threateningly, or while weeping uncontrollably, it won't work. Tone is a more direct and visceral part of communication; human beings process it before words. When the tone of the person speaking to them is offensive, aggressive, or sarcastic, in the interest of self-protection most people will not typically wait around with an open mind. Most people put up defenses immediately, and this is probably true for your loved one.

People can't really fake a benign, positive, or welcoming tone. It's not enough to lower your voice if you are still so angry you are hissing through your teeth. Your angry feelings won't magically disappear, though, which is why self-care strategies to help you calm down and increase your resilience come first. Tone management requires that you put some of your feelings to the side while you compose and deliver your communication. Finding the right tone is often the hardest part of communication to master. It may help to conjure up a positive feeling or memory of your loved one to displace negative feelings. The truth is that as angry or unhappy as you may feel at any given moment about your relationship, the positive is in there too; if you can access it during conversation, the tone will come through.

Good News: Tone is a powerful tool. It's so powerful that when you use it properly, it doesn't matter so much whether you have the answers or say the right thing. It's not necessary to hit all seven points of positive communication. You can stammer and not finish sentences—if your tone is gentle, empathic, or even just neutral, you're already helping, and making it that much more likely that the other person will listen when you do find the right words.

Relax your body and take care of yourself.
Paying attention to your body during communication will help you regulate your tone, pace, and all the other factors of effective communication. Breathe. Literally. Remember, emotional tension often manifests as held breath, which increases muscle tension, which in turn increases the emotional tension. It's okay to step back and pause. If you struggle with the tone of your voice, consider smiling, or using the half-smile distress tolerance technique from chapter 5 (page 109). Smiling is a signal to the body to relax.

Take good care of your body the rest of the time too. Think of good sleep, nutrition, and other contributors to physical health as your fuel for positive communication. If you are sleep deprived or hungry, the resulting fatigue, irritability, and other symptoms will likely manifest in your communications. Exercising, meditating, getting enough rest, and eating well will help you keep your emotional balance.

Listen.
Really listen. Sometimes when people think they're listening, what they're actually doing is waiting for the other person to stop talking. They may be taking that time to think about what they're going to say next. This is

not really listening. Listening is paying attention to what the other person is saying and suspending your assumptions and opinions long enough to take it in, in good faith and a sincere effort to understand. It's a skill you can learn.

Really listening is active, not passive, and it is harder than most people think. Changing the way you communicate requires that you monitor your own reactions at the same time that you process the other person's meaning. If you come to an impasse where you don't understand or disagree, try to suspend your expectations or judgments, resist the urge to contradict, and be *inquisitive*. You may wish that you were hearing something different. Try to stay calm—breathe—and tap into your empathy to come back with a constructive response.

To be a successful listener, you may have to change your mental framework for the whole situation. A man listening to his wife with the assumption that she's irrational is probably not really listening. If he's listening at all, what he's taking in is just the evidence that "proves" him right—and justifies his next argument. What if he changed his goal, from proving his point and trying to get her to agree with him to collaborating and having something good happen? What if he listened in the spirit of wanting to walk the dog together later and enjoy the evening, rather than in order to explain what is so stupid about what she's saying? When you catch yourself thinking "Here we go again," or "That's what she always says," try to pause and ask yourself how you would like to be feeling about the relationship in an hour. *Really* listening puts the responsibility on you to find a way forward when communications start to break down. Instead of getting locked into being right and convincing the other person that you are right, try to make listening your goal for the moment. Think of listening as collaborating.

You can also try to reflect out loud what you think you've heard. Reflecting another person's words can reassure the person that you're paying attention (making him less likely to yell in an attempt to be heard) and trying to understand, which conveys that you care. Reflecting also lets you clarify his meaning and reduce misunderstanding in the process.

Validate.

Validating is the underutilized skill of listening to someone who is expressing feelings and *refraining from trying to convince the person out of those feelings.* What if your loved one says she feels too anxious or ambivalent to make any changes? Or angry with you for something you think is not warranted? Validating requires resisting the impulse to tell her she shouldn't be so anxious, or has no right to be angry with you. In these moments, you don't have to agree and you don't have to understand exactly where the other person is coming from. You don't have to say anything you don't mean. You can simply say, "I can see that you're really upset right now," to have a defusing effect.

As you practice this skill, be aware that when you want to talk people out of emotional states, it may be because whatever they're expressing makes you uncomfortable. It's natural to want to deflect negative feelings directed at you; and it's difficult to feel that someone is suffering, especially when you don't know how to help. It's normal to want to say, "It's not so bad," "You're overreacting," or "Calm down," but those usually have the opposite effect of what you intended. When people perceive that their feelings are not being heard or have been dismissed as invalid, they tend to respond by either shutting down completely or pushing harder to make sure they are understood.

You can validate your loved one's feelings without sacrificing your own limits. For example, just because you say, "I know you're really mad at me right now," does not mean you are giving your loved one permission to yell at you or throw things. There can still be consequences for *doing* X, Y, or Z. In fact, validation can help you protect your limits, because it tends to cool the whole system down.

Ask permission.
According to some theories, therapists should never give advice. We're not those therapists. It's true that intrusive or dogmatic advice can undermine a person's sense of effectiveness and options, critical factors in motivation. Studies have shown, however, that thoughtful advice carefully delivered actually promotes motivation and change. Everyone needs advice, but people tend to receive it better when it's provided with respect for their autonomy—their choice to use the information or not—rather than forced upon them. Your loved one is no different.

Simply asking permission to offer your thoughts can communicate respect for your loved one's feelings before you say another word, and set a better stage for what follows. As always, tone matters. "Can I give you some advice?" could be an innocent question, but when spoken with hostility or sarcasm, it becomes a cliché of meddling, condescension, and judgment. Ask sincerely—"Is it okay if I tell you my thoughts about this?"—and wait for an answer. It's not a rhetorical question; that is, you should be prepared to *not advise* in case the answer is no, and this might be an opportunity to build trust by respectfully not giving unwanted advice or opinions. Trust, in turn, helps pave the way for the reception of future communications, including advice. If the answer is yes, proceed with your positive communication.

"Sandwich" it.

Offer a tasty communication sandwich. "Sandwiching" in communication is when you put a request or potentially distressing message between two positive statements. For example, "I can see how hard you've been working and I know you're under a lot of stress. I would like you to come home earlier on weeknights, and I see how that might be difficult to schedule, but I have some ideas about how to help." The request "I would like you to come home earlier" is easier to swallow when it's sandwiched between understanding and an offer to help, as the first part lowers resistance, and the last part lets the person consider the tougher middle part with a sweet taste in his mouth.

Use "I" Statements.

Beginning statements with "I" (rather than "you") is a hallmark, not to say cliché, of therapy-speak, but we suggest you don't knock it until you try it and see how effectively it can decrease defensiveness in others. How different would you feel if someone said to you, "I get so frightened when you come home late. I can't stop all these terrible scenarios from running through my head," as opposed to, "You are so inconsiderate coming home this late. Do you have any idea what you're putting me through?" Even "You make me so frightened," while not explicitly insulting, is more accusatory than "I feel frightened when . . ." and therefore more likely to provoke indignation and argument (such as, "You make a big deal out of everything"). When you speak from your own experience, you can take responsibility for your own feelings and show your loved one how to do the same. "I" statements also help avoid name calling on both sides. "You're a jerk for getting drunk at that party" is more likely met with "You're such a bummer that I can't help myself," and so goes the conversation down a painful and well-grooved path of insults and misunderstandings. Instead, "I feel lonely when we're at a party and you drink that much" might get a softer response and allow the conversation to continue in a positive direction.

Use your awareness.

Monitor yourself and give yourself permission to start over if you sense the conversation going off-track. Maintain awareness as you speak and listen, and observe your tone. It's okay to catch it slipping, apologize, and try to get it back. Communication with your loved one is not a test with a panel of judges about to hold up cards on your performance. If you lose track, get flustered, or misspeak, pause and try again. You might say, "I'm struggling a bit here to be clear, and it's important to me. Let me start over." If the conversation breaks down beyond your ability to turn it around, stop. You can say, "This doesn't seem to be going in the helpful direction I was hoping to go, so I'm going to stop for now."

Try to let go of any attachment to the outcome.
Of course you care how the conversation goes, but remember NATO—Not Attached to The Outcome? In every communication, you can increase the likelihood of a positive interaction by doing your part. However, the outcome depends equally on the other person's part, which you cannot control. Positive communication skills will improve your odds of being heard and your loved one feeling understood, but for any given conversation, the outcome is not guaranteed.

Communication Traps

As we saw in chapter 2, research has demonstrated that there are ways to interact with people that increase motivation and engagement . . . and there are ways to decrease it. CRAFT research in particular has demonstrated that the following communication "strategies" don't work: nagging, pleading, accusing, threatening, yelling, and lecturing; pouring alcohol down the drain or flushing drugs down the toilet; drinking or taking drugs to show your loved one what it's like to live with someone using substances. From our own experience, though we don't know of any research evidence on this, we would add cursing and name-calling.

Some of these forms of negative communication may have happened in your family countless times. And it's okay. With the stress and worry you're under, you have probably not felt very in control yourself. Again, it's okay. People mean well when they do these things, and *not* doing them is counterintuitive until you learn why and how not to. And still, positive communication probably won't come easily. But you can take strength from the research evidence at your back that shows these variations on the theme of confrontation—opposites of positive communication—don't work. Positive communication does.

What if There Is No Communication?

On the other end of the spectrum, many people feel as though they're tip-toeing on eggshells around a very big gorilla in the room. In these cases there's no fighting—because there's no talking. If this sounds like your situation, it may be that people fear that communication will turn ugly and cause more pain and confusion than already exist. Other times, people avoid talking about facts that seem too scary to manage. It's remarkable how people living under the same roof can compartmentalize their lives.

Are you avoiding discussions that you suspect you need to have? If the problem isn't so much negative communication as no communication, ask yourself what you are avoiding at different times throughout the day to increase your awareness of when you shut down and don't say what you're thinking. The ratio of how much you're thinking about it compared to how much you're talking about it may be an indicator of silent stewing, and this might prompt you to say something. Or consider whether the anxiety of avoiding the problem threatens to approach or surpass the anxiety of looking straight at it. In any case, try starting with the Seven Elements of Positive Communication (page 159) and let them guide you through a draft of what you would say, knowing you can practice safely with a friend, counselor, family member, or with yourself in the mirror, until you're ready to bring it up with your loved one directly.

The Pain That Comes with Honesty

A common feature of substance problems is not being truthful. While lying is not something people are proud of, it is an almost inevitable part of managing compulsions. It is very hard to meet the demands of daily living—job responsibilities, family, and other relationships—while at the same time meeting the demands associated with compulsive behaviors. Usually, something has to give. Often, one of those things is being truthful. Given the choice, most people would rather tell their boss that they were "out sick" rather than "crashing from yesterday's cocaine binge." Likewise, most people find it easier and less painful to tell themselves *I'll be able to cut back* than to admit, *I thought I could stop two years ago and still haven't.*

Understanding the all too human reasons your loved one may lie (let you believe a partial truth, tell you what he thinks you want to hear, or tell you what he wishes were true) can help to bridge the gap of broken trust and encourage more honesty. Is it possible that . . . ?

1. He is afraid you will be disappointed.
2. She is afraid you will think she is weak.
3. He is afraid of real-world consequences (job loss, relationship loss, etc.).
4. She feels overwhelmed at the idea of trying to change.
5. He is afraid that he can't change.

Rather than brand someone as a liar, we can look closely at where the lying is happening in this person's life. Can you understand the reasons behind it? Is it mostly about the substance use? Does the truth come out or do the lies go on and on? Is there remorse? If the dishonesty you see does not spill over into every part of your loved one's life, and it is reasonably contained and regretted, then it is within the range of normal for a person with substance problems.

You don't have to like (or pretend to like) your loved one's dishonesty. Your understanding does not preclude consequences for it. You can, however, try to stay calm and use these communication skills to help her be increasingly honest with you over time, while you use your other skills to cope with what you hear. However scary or infuriating the truth is, including the truth of dishonesty, when you know what you're dealing with there is hope and the possibility of helping.

Have patience with yourself and the process as you learn these skills. You may be an effective communicator in other areas of your life, but changing the way you communicate with your loved one about substance problems will take practice: practice constructing sentences with the Seven Elements of Positive Communication; practice delivering your lines with someone who puts you at ease; in fact, practice with everyone everywhere you go, to see how these skills can improve just about any interaction with a human being. The exercises that follow will guide you through that practice.

Exercise: Communication Analysis

Think about the last argument you had with your loved one that began
with you trying to tell or ask him or her something. Describe the situation
in as much detail as you can.

> Example: *I was taking Chris to dinner with me, after which he planned to
> meet his friends. On the way there I told him, "Please don't drink tonight
> because it's embarrassing and you know what a bad influence those kids
> you're seeing later can be." He replied that it's not such a big deal and I really
> don't know his friends at all. I yelled something back (can't remember what
> now) and we ended up turning around to go home.*

Now rewrite your part of the argument so that it is positive, brief,
specific, names your feelings, shows understanding of your loved one's
struggles or point of view, accepts some responsibility, and offers to
help.

> Example: *Next time Chris and I have a nice dinner when he* doesn't *drink,
> I am not even going to mention drinking. I will appreciate the fact that he
> is sober and not compare it to when he is not. Also, I think I need to let him
> know how happy being with him sober makes me feel (though I don't want
> to lay it on too thick because then he shuts me down) and that I know it's not
> always easy for him.*
>   *I'll say something like, "Chris, this was so nice—it's really great to spend
> this kind of time with you (he knows I mean sober, I don't need to say it), and
> I know it's not always easy for you. I'm happy to take you to see your friends
> after spending time with you like this."*

Exercise: Role-Play

Now take your positive communication plan and enlist a partner or partners you trust to practice saying it. It's helpful to practice in both roles, to
get comfortable with your delivery and also hear what it sounds like from
the receiving end. Don't worry about getting it right the first, second, or
tenth time. It's called practice because you don't know how to do this yet.
We suggest starting with all seven elements in place even if it sounds awkward, and ticking them off ("That's accepting partial responsibility, that's

offering to help . . ."), to force yourself to think through each element. In time it will come more naturally. Role-playing can even bring some fun into humor-deprived areas of your life. In the right spirit, the sheer awkwardness of positive communication before you become fluent can be hilarious.

CHAPTER 10.

Reinforcement:
The Driver of Change

You'll recall from the first chapters of the book how the decision to use mood-altering substances is a choice that people make, even if at later stages the behavior is so automatic that it no longer looks like a choice. As you know now, this choice does not result from craziness, immorality, or bad character. It is informed by a unique combination in each person of genetics, environment, physiological and psychological variables, life experiences, and learning and habit formation.

At the crux of all these factors is a choice, conscious or unconscious, that is based on the results a person expects to get or feel by making that choice. These results—physical feelings, pleasant emotions, social ease, and, significantly, the lessening of bad things (including withdrawal symptoms), to name a few—are what behaviorists call "reinforcers."

Reinforcers affect everyone's behavior, though they're different for different people: "When I nap . . . I feel refreshed." "When I eat . . . I stop feeling hungry." "When someone thanks me for a favor . . . I feel good." "When I read . . . I feel interested." You can use your loved one's reinforcers in the service of change.

The first part of this chapter explains how reinforcement works and why it is the single most powerful tool you have. The second half of the chapter will help you first identify specifically what is reinforcing to your loved one, then strategize to reinforce alternative, positive behaviors that support health and well-being in your life together.

You may have seen a *New York Times* article that went viral in 2006, "What Shamu Taught Me about a Happy Marriage," describing a woman's success using animal training techniques on her husband. Besides being funny and cute, it illustrated the power of behavioral strategies, particularly positive reinforcement, to promote change. People aren't dogs. Or rats. Or orcas. But reinforcement is a staple of some of the most effective

174

therapeutic approaches with humans. People, as well as other animals, like treats.

Reinforcement in the Choice to Use Substances

The chain of events in reinforcement goes like this: a person takes an action and what follows either increases or decreases the likelihood that the person will repeat that action. Anything that increases the likelihood is called a reinforcer. Mood-altering substances (and some behaviors) are powerful reinforcers due to their effect on the brain. "When I drink . . . I feel relaxed" is a description of reinforcement in action, assuming relaxation is a desirable state for that person: drinking leads to relaxation, and relaxation makes drinking more likely. Reinforcers can also take the form of something negative *not* happening, or going away. "When I drink . . . I don't think about the chaos at home"—in this case drinking is reinforced by the absence of unpleasant thoughts.

In the same way, reinforcement can make any behavior that you *do* want more likely to happen again: "When I got home on time . . . my husband was delighted and cooked dinner for us." Delight and dinner are the reinforcers in this situation. Or, in a variation that hinges on the removal of something negative, the husband could allow his wife a half hour of quiet time before she joins the fray of the family and their three rambunctious kids. In this case, the reinforcer is the removal of stress. If he uses either of these reinforcement strategies when she is sober, he significantly increases the chance that she will come home sober more often. Reinforcement works on all behavior.

Reinforcing constructive, non-substance-related behavior is the core strategy of CRAFT. You can choose to respond to your loved one's positive, nonusing behaviors in a way that will *increase* the likelihood of these behaviors reoccurring. At the same time, you can choose how to respond to his negative behaviors, including but not limited to substance use, in a way that reinforces it or not.

The two most powerful things you can do to help promote change are:

1. Reward your loved one for positive behavior.
2. Ignore or withdraw a reward for negative behavior.

Remember Ivan and Lucy from the previous chapter? Lucy's father had a serious alcohol problem when she was growing up, and her husband, Ivan, was raised in a culture of heavy drinking. When Ivan kept his drinking to two or three drinks, Lucy made a point of being warm and affectionate toward him. She had identified the behavior she wanted and defined it in specific, measurable terms. She stopped paying so much attention to what she didn't want—how his voice got louder and his jokes less funny after three drinks, which she had often called "being an idiot"—and focused on what she wanted and how to encourage it.

Asking for the behavior she wanted with her new positive communication skills was one approach to her goal. In another, complementary, strategy she reinforced the behavior she wanted from her husband when he did it. She picked out two things that he found rewarding (her affection and attention), and made sure to give them to him when it counted—when he stopped after two or three drinks. Sometimes she made the link between his behavior and her response explicit, but more often it didn't need saying; they were too busy enjoying what was happening to talk about what she didn't want to happen.

In time, Ivan understood that when he drank less he felt closer to his wife. She laughed at his jokes and he loved making her laugh. He knew when they went to bed at the same time that they were more likely to have sex—and the sex was better when they had been enjoying each other's company and he didn't have as much alcohol affecting his body. While he liked drinking, he liked these times with his wife more. The balance shifted in his mind, and he changed the way he behaved.

What's hard about this . . . Some people don't want to think of themselves as a "trainer" of someone they love. If you have doubts about the virtue and authenticity of a behavioral approach, consider how Lucy and Ivan *experienced* it. Lucy's gratitude and warmth when her husband didn't drink too much were genuine; Ivan's change of priorities, heartfelt. Being deliberate doesn't mean you're scheming. There's plenty of evidence that a behavioral perspective is one of the most respectful, hopeful, even playful perspectives you can have, since it takes a fundamentally collaborative, nonjudgmental approach to learning and change.

Reinforcement is happening between people every second, consciously or unconsciously, planned or unplanned, with more and less positive results. We are social creatures and we influence each other in every interaction we have, whether we mean to or not, and whether or not we succeed in the ways we meant to. When Lucy called her husband of ten years an idiot, she was hoping to discourage the "idiotic" behavior. Until Lucy learned how positive communication and reinforcement worked, she did not know what else to do. After all, she had learned from her mother, who had been doing the best she could with the skills she had. When you understand how reinforcement works you, like Lucy, can use your influence for good in all your relationships. If reinforcement is happening all the time anyway, why not harness it to change things for the better?

Currently, you may find yourself in a cycle of punishment, nagging your loved one to stop using, giving him the silent treatment, slamming things around, yelling, and so on. Unfortunately, these (understandable) responses create a negative reinforcement loop. As you carry your distress around with you and fixate on the problem, you naturally end up nagging, withdrawing, and otherwise punishing . . . *even during the times when he is not using.* Still mad about the last time he was high, you're punishing him two days later. The situation often deteriorates to the point where people with substance problems get the same punishing reaction from those who are worried about them whether they are intoxicated or sober, using or not.

Not only does this pattern not work to decrease the substance use, it can indirectly influence your loved one's decision to continue using. Seeing that he gets yelled at when he uses and yelled at when he doesn't use, he may decide to go and use because "it doesn't make a difference anyway." Meanwhile, the substance itself continues to have a powerful reinforcing effect on your loved one and his choice to use. Reinforcement got you into this loop—and it can get you out.

Reinforcement Creates an Environment Where There Is Less Room for Using

Time, energy, and resources are limited (you've noticed?). Did you ever think that this could be a good thing? Since there is only so much time in a day, you have to choose. This is true for your loved one, too. She can't be hungover every day *and* train for a marathon. He can't get high *and* be attentive to the kids. She probably won't have a second date with the non-smoker who is turned off by the smell of her smoking. In each of these examples the person will have to choose.

In the rest of this chapter, you will learn how to identify activities that compete with your loved one's substance use. You can help reacquaint her with interests that she may have given up and reconnect her to the people and things that she values. These activities take the place of substances, and are reinforced because she enjoys them.

Identifying Rewards

Understanding behavior as a system of choices, actions, and reinforcers is relatively straightforward. It will help you identify what's relevant, focus on the things you can change, and give you something much more definite to work with than an irrational, unpredictable, overwhelming mess. The first step to creating a reinforcing environment is to identify the rewards you will put in place for the behavior you want to encourage. Here are some general guidelines for selecting and applying reinforcers.

Know what he likes.
The reward should be rewarding to your loved one. The most common mistake people make in reinforcement is choosing rewards *they* would like rather than what's most rewarding for *the person they want to reward*. You know what he likes. Take some time to think about this and write down as many ideas as you can (in other words, brainstorm). A "special" dinner of all-organic root vegetables may be your idea of a treat at the end of the week, but if he'd rather eat a porterhouse steak, that would make a more effective reward. If your daughter wants to play drums, it doesn't matter so much that you would prefer that she learn violin. Perhaps you can learn to like her drumming when you see how motivated she is to take lessons and practice rather than hang out with her drinking friends. Evaluate the rewards on your list from *her* perspective.

Keep them (mostly) free, inexpensive, and accessible.
A reward shouldn't cost a mint or take a village to produce. Do not confuse reinforcement with consumerism that depends on big gifts, new electronic gadgets, or lavish swag for impact. Choose rewards within your budget that expose your loved one to healthy activities and communities: membership to the local YMCA, a backyard barbecue with new friends, foot rubs, favorite foods, or coffee at the bedside after extra minutes to sleep in. The power of rewards to effect lasting change comes from their integration into the fabric of your lives together, so they should be affordable and sustainable. Also, don't forget the value of warm greetings, sincere thanks, or an affectionate touch. Simple appreciation goes a long way—when it is expressed. So often, under stress and on autopilot, we forget to make these gestures.

Make it easy for yourself.
The rewards you choose to give should feel comfortable to you. If a gift feels like too much, a gesture doesn't feel genuine, or words don't feel honest, keep brainstorming until you identify a reward that is both rewarding to your loved one and comfortable for you. If you feel too hurt or angry to get into the spirit of reinforcement, try scaling back. Reinforcement is not about pretending everything else is fine or cutting someone slack he has not earned. Remind yourself of what you are trying to accomplish.

Positive Communication As Reward

Positive communication is in and of itself one of the most powerful reinforcers available to you. People respond well to clear communication, kindness, understanding, and offers to help. In reinforcement terms, they are more likely to repeat behavior that was rewarded with positive communication.

I could see it wasn't easy for you to say no when your brothers wanted to do shots with you. (Specific, understanding.) *I want you to know how much I appreciated that. I feel very optimistic right now.* (Labeling feelings.)

Good morning! It's so nice to have company at breakfast. (Specific.) *I was thinking of going to the hardware store later and I could drop you off at your appointment on the way.* (Offer to help.)

Don't forget nonverbal communication. Verbal communication can seem like a minefield when you are attempting to extract yourself from entrenched negative patterns. A kiss, a hug, a pat on the arm, a touch as you walk by, a smile, a knowing expression that says you feel the same way—these are the pictures of communication, and worth a thousand words.

What's hard about this . . . People often resist rewarding their loved ones because they think they wouldn't be expressing their "real" (hostile) feelings and they expect their loved ones would "see through" their faking it. If you have to fake it, you shouldn't do it. But if you see the value of moving past anger, and feel ready, there's a good chance you have other, positive feelings as well. Remember that your "real" feelings are complicated and variable (you might love him and miss him one moment and want to wring his neck the next). Keep the objective in mind—reinforcing the change you want to see—and try to call up some genuine warmth, appreciation, and approval to reward positive behavior when you see it.

Identifying Positive Behaviors and Activities to Reinforce

The next part of the reinforcing environment you're creating involves the *specific behaviors you want to reinforce*. For this, you need to take out your Behavior Analysis form from chapter 2 (pages 67–68). If you haven't worked through it already, you should do so before you go further into this chapter. A behavior analysis will help you pinpoint the reinforcers of your loved one's substance use; in other words, what exactly he or she gets out of it. Under the heading "Short-Term Positive Consequences" you might have written things like: "to relax," "to tune out," "celebrate"; whatever is rewarding for your loved one about her use. These are the reinforcers that are already in place.

Next, brainstorm a list of alternative behaviors with benefits that can compete with the reinforcers of using. For example, if one reason she gets high is to "relax," alternative behaviors with similar benefits could include taking a nap, sitting on the sofa and reading a magazine, going for a walk . . . and you would reward this behavior *in addition to* its intrinsic, relaxation-promoting benefit because, at least for now, it's not a fair fight. Substances are powerful and change is hard. People need extra encouragement, especially at first. You're looking for activities, hobbies, or experiences that are healthy and positive, that you can reinforce, that can then compete with substance use.

Think of including friends and family and community, and brainstorm ways to help your loved one build a social life that does not include substances. You may have to dig into the past if more recently substance use has eclipsed other activities she used to enjoy. A behavior analysis will give you even more ideas—we've tailored one for healthy behaviors at the end of this chapter.

Once you have put together a list of several ideas, ask yourself the following questions for each (we recommend writing down your answers as you go along):

Would your loved one enjoy it? Would he enjoy it in general and also enjoy particular benefits that he would otherwise get out of using substances?

Jake and Minnie, the parents we met whose daughter, Emily, smoked pot every day, considered what she would be doing if not smoking pot. Were there hobbies or activities they wanted to encourage? Which of these could compete with her pot-related behaviors? They listed getting to school on time each morning, exercising three times a week, taking guitar lessons and practicing daily, and meeting with a tutor twice a week. Which of these activities would Emily enjoy? They didn't doubt that meeting with a tutor, for example, would be good for her and compete with substance use, but it would be a nonstarter if she wasn't motivated to do it. Worse, it would end up on the pile of things she "should" be doing but wasn't, adding to her (and their) sense of failure. They settled on guitar lessons and planned how they would positively communicate their offer. After months of arguing about the pot, they wanted this conversation to go differently, and it did: Emily was excited about learning guitar and readily agreed to their one condition, that she would not be high for lesson time. Finding something they could all agree on was not a small victory for them. It opened the way to discussing other goals, and the tension in their house, which they'd started to believe was permanent, noticeably eased.

You might be thinking that life is not all fun and games and guitar lessons. True, less enjoyable or less immediately enjoyable activities may eventually be necessary to further positive change. We just don't recommend *starting* with tutoring—or job hunting, or back-tax filing—as you identify alternative behaviors to reinforce. Starting with less enjoyable behaviors, no matter how good they are for your loved one, won't directly compete with the immediate gratifications of substance use. Ultimately, the environment that you create will contain a balance of shorter- and longer-term rewards, but all in due time. Believe it or not, the self-confidence and coping skills required for a successful job hunt may start with guitar lessons.

Does the alternative behavior compete with the substance-using behavior in time and function? Again, the goal is to build, bird by bird, a life that competes with substance use. If your loved one typically uses with her best friend on Friday nights, is there another activity you can support that she and her friend would enjoy together at that time? Or something that she would enjoy doing on Saturday mornings to influence her decisions about what happens Friday nights?

While it can seem chaotic from the outside looking in, decisions to use substances are usually well-grooved routines. In your original Behavior

Analysis you probably noticed that your loved one's use happens at certain times of day and on certain days (even a daily habit usually has a pattern over the course of the day). A positive behavior competes with this use pattern, then, when she can do it during the *time* she would have spent using and/or recovering from the effects of use.

For even more competitive edge, the new behavior should fulfill a similar *function* as the substance use. If drinking is the way she connects with other people, you can create other opportunities to socialize. If it's to cope with stress, you can reward activities that are healthier *and* reduce stress. Finally, consider whether the behavior is functionally incompatible with using, that is, requires fine motor skills, like a cooking class, or fine mental skills, like reading, or vigor, like exercise or getting up early. Consider settings where substance use is not allowed or readily available, such as gyms, parks, choirs, museums, or meditation groups. Try to involve people who don't use with your loved one and don't encourage use.

Would the opportunity to engage in the new behavior occur often enough, or could it occur often enough in the future? A onetime or once-every-ten-years positive behavior is certainly worth having on your bucket list, but you'll want to include mostly behaviors that are regular, routine, or at least repeated with some frequency, so that their continuation will make a difference over the long run. Think: weekly classes, regular exercise, getting up in the morning or coming home at night, or practicing a skill.

Is the new behavior or activity something that you could enjoy too? This could be an opportunity to start enjoying time together again, as the life you are building to compete with substance use includes you! If spending more time together before he stops using would seem to put the cart before the horse, remember the evidence. CRAFT studies have consistently shown a connection between enjoying time together and decreased destructive behavior on your loved one's part as well as an increased sense of well-being on yours in this order. Improvements in the quality of everyone's life can and usually do happen even before substances are fully out of the picture.

What's hard about this . . . If your strategy for reinforcement includes enjoying some activities together, try to resist the urge to talk about anything too serious during these times. The point is to have stress-free, conflict-free time together to improve your relationship in general and reward nonuse. Do not underestimate how challenging this can be. Given how much you might be holding in (currently or historically), you may be tempted to fill your loved one in on everything you've been thinking about. You may have to use self-care strategies (e.g., distraction, relaxation) to control yourself and trust that you will have opportunities in the future for more serious conversations. For the present, try to simply be together.

You don't have to enjoy doing all the same things or force yourself to do anything you don't want to do, but sharing an activity can make both of you feel better. Doing things together that you both enjoy also reduces overall tension and distance, which may inadvertently act as a reason for using. (To repeat: it's never your fault, and at the same time, an unhappy home can be a reason for using.) Generally, having fun together contributes to a collaborative atmosphere that is more conducive to change.

What's hard about this . . . You may be so burned out or angry that you can't imagine having anything to talk about together, let alone "having fun." Give yourself permission to start small. Consider activities where you don't have to talk, like watching movies, riding bikes, or throwing a Frisbee.

The Difference between Enabling and Reinforcing

While we don't use the word *enabling* much (because it confuses people about doing *anything* positive or rewarding for their loved one), you won't fully understand reinforcement until you understand the difference. "Enabling" refers to anything you do that reinforces or increases the likelihood of *your loved one's substance using behavior*, or any other behavior you don't want to support. A positive reinforcement strategy works to *reinforce your loved one's positive behaviors*. You can see enabling in the following example: you decide to cook a steak dinner on the evening that your partner plans to pick up the kids and put them to bed, behavior that you think is incompatible with using. The behavior is well targeted, the reward is well chosen, and the evening is going according to plan as he tucks in the kids while you cook. But while you are setting the table, he disappears into the basement for ten minutes and returns red-eyed and high. The sky would not fall if you served the steak, but in strict behavioral terms it would be counterproductive and "enabling," because he would get the *reward* (steak) following his *negative* (getting high) behavior. A screaming fight might also be enabling, as it could give him all the reason he needs to justify smoking more pot.

Ideally, as you problem-solved for this night, you prepared for this possibility and have a plan B. For example, you could put the food away and calmly say (as you rehearsed): "Thanks for dealing with the kids. I'm not comfortable eating dinner together when you're high, so let's try this another night." Or leave the meal and simply say, "Feel free to eat. I'm going to read instead because I'd rather have dinner with you when we can talk and you haven't been smoking."

If your loved one is intoxicated, you should use positive communication skills to remove yourself from the situation as speedily and uncontentiously as possible. This is not the time to hash out your feelings of disappointment and betrayal, however warranted. The next time your loved one is sober may not be the time either, since this could do the opposite of reinforcing that sobriety, in effect punishing it. With other outlets for unburdening your feelings (self-care, friends, family, counselors, and so on), you can stay with your plan to reinforce the behavior you want and ignore the behavior you don't want. (There's more on the power of ignoring in the next chapter.)

Ongoing Reinforcement Strategies

At this point, after understanding what new behaviors can compete with substance use, and developing strategies to reward or reinforce these behaviors, you have all the information you need to effectively reinforce positive change. The following are tips to help you in this process:

Time it right: speedy delivery. Don't wait to deliver. To forge the strongest possible association between behavior and reward, time your reward to follow immediately, or as closely as possible, after the behavior. If the target behavior is coming straight home at the end of the day, for example, the reward could be designed to happen as soon as your loved one gets there—an hour of quiet time for a spouse to unwind, or an hour of "screen time" for a teenager. You can also gear reinforcement to longer-term, cumulative goals, with weekly rewards for a week's worth of target behavior, in which case the timely delivery of the weekly reward would be key. A dual strategy could include both on-the-spot and over-time rewards: say, smiles and thanks every time a task is done, plus something bigger when it's done regularly for a month. Note that in cases involving ADHD, immediate delivery is particularly helpful.

Reward in proportion. Make a big deal out of a big thing, but scale back for more minor behaviors. To reward your loved one for getting out of bed without having to be dragged, make her coffee, and bring it to her with a smile. Save a four-day spa vacation for bigger achievements or a consistent run of smaller ones over a period of time. Base your rewards on how difficult you know the new behavior to be for your loved one, and how valuable it is to you. Don't underestimate the power of a kiss or kind word.

Switch up the reward. This will help keep her interest. Some animals never tire of the same treat day after day, year after year, for the same behavior, but humans are more easily bored. When in doubt, refer to the first point of reward selection: you *do* know what he likes, and you can think of more than one thing. Reinforce him in different ways that all mean something to him.

Make the connection. Or not. It is not always necessary to announce what you are doing. ("I will be rewarding you with affection when you don't drink.") Or you may want to make the connection very clear, depending on whether you think he can hear it without feeling defensive. Reinforcement works without discussion, but your loved one may wonder about a change in your behavior and ask you ("Why are you being so nice to me?"), in which case it would be good to be prepared. You might plan to say something like "The effort you've been making to not smoke in the mornings is not lost on me. I really appreciate it, so I just wanted to let you know that I notice!" Use your positive communication skills to make sure your loved one understands the cause and effect. There's a big difference between "You're going to have to earn this" and "This is something you could earn."

You needn't mention the substance use if that feels too "hot" or likely to provoke a defensive reaction. Just keep your focus on the behavior you want—"I'm so happy you're playing basketball again that I wanted to come and cheer," as opposed to "I'm so glad you're not too hungover to play basketball," or "I appreciate your playing basketball instead of drinking yourself to death." With practice, you'll learn to sense when it would be safer to say "I had a great time with you tonight," and when the mood can handle "Thanks for stopping after two drinks like we talked about."

Beware the competition. As you set out to reinforce nonusing behaviors, you'll be competing with everything your loved one enjoys about using. There may be other people working against you or people who have interests in her behavior staying the same, such as friends she uses with or dealers. Keep adding weights on the nonusing side of the scale, in the form of enjoyable alternatives and rewards, and hang in there—eventually it will tip.

The double-hard part about this . . . First, you'll recall from our discussions of dopamine and the brain's reward system earlier in the book that your loved one's ability to enjoy alternatives to using may be neurologically compromised. For you, dinner and a movie together might be an ideal way to spend an evening. For her, and specifically for the blunted pleasure receptors in her brain, it may pale in comparison to club hopping on amphetamines. This is why your reinforcement strategy is so important for motivation: external rewards can pick up the slack when the behavior you want isn't intrinsically rewarding enough (yet) for your loved one to do for its own sake.

Second, as your loved one's use has taken up more space, she may have forgotten what else she enjoys. Even more troublesome, she may have turned to substances to meet her needs before she discovered alternatives. You may think she's been wasting her life, while she looks at her life and can't imagine what else she would do with it. Many family members express reluctance to reward their loved ones for something they believe she should be doing— should *want* to do—anyway. But "should" is moot in behavioral learning. The issue is how: how she can do it, how she can want to do it, and how you can help.

Let Loose the Reinforcement!

Reinforcement goes far beyond changes in substance use. Other reinforcement-worthy behaviors you could consider include: your loved one's self-care efforts, his kindness or generosity to you or others, and honesty. You can reinforce your own positive behavior, too. You could reward yourself for the work you're doing in this book, for example. What could you give yourself for a week of tracking or some other exercise? Is there one you've been avoiding? You could give yourself a special treat for following through with a challenging reinforcement strategy involving your loved one.

Once you're attuned to it, you may notice reinforcement happening (or not happening) around you in the world: the person who sells you your muffin in the morning is especially friendly and you smile back at him; the bus driver stops for you when she sees you running and you thank her profusely; someone in HR helps you through a particularly thorny issue at work and you bring her flowers when it's over; your child eats all the creamed peas and corn your mother prepared for him and you sneak him an extra cookie after dinner. Behavior change with substance use is often more complicated, and it may not come easily to your loved one—or to you—but it can be helpful to remember that you have as many chances as you want to take. Try and try again. Try to appreciate the small changes—small increases in positive behavior that happen even if "the problem" isn't "fixed." Small changes build confidence and create a foundation for substantive, long-lasting change.

Exercise: Reinforcers

People like gold stars. Brainstorm rewards in the following categories. We've included some examples to get you started. For this you'll need to get inside your loved one's head, to make sure that surprise dog-sledding getaway is something he, not just you, will enjoy.

Inexpensive/Immediate Rewards/Reinforcers
- Be affectionate
- Talk about something that interests her
- Listen (really listen)
- Cheer him on
- Rub her shoulders
- Praise an accomplishment
- Give a compliment
- Give a little gift
- Offer your help
- Keep him company
- Take a walk together
- Serve a meal
- Do the dishes
- Watch TV together
- Let her be alone
- Do a chore that he doesn't like doing
- Tuck a sweet note into her lunch/briefcase/sock drawer
- Get up with the kids so he can sleep in
- Run an errand for her
- Smile at him

YOUR IDEAS:
-
-
-

More Expensive/Planned Rewards/Reinforcers
- Take a vacation together, or help her go on a vacation without you
- Prepare a special meal
- Go to a restaurant
- Give a special gift
- Meet him at the airport

- Do a big chore she doesn't like doing
- Pay for a class/set of classes

YOUR IDEAS:

-
-
-

Rewards/Reinforcers for Young Adults and Adolescents
- Allow a later curfew
- Allow friends to come over
- Help with homework or leave them alone to do homework
- Provide music lessons
- Give tickets, gift certificates, iTunes, etc.
- Serve her favorite food
- Allow extra time for screen access (TV, computer, phone)
- Provide a favorite snack
- Give a magazine subscription
- Give sports accessories
- Give a video game
- Give a ride somewhere
- Allow use of car
- Allow staying up late
- Allow to sleep in
- Pay for a special haircut/mani-pedi/dermatologist appointment
- Allow her to sit alone when the family eats at a restaurant
- Let him redecorate his own bedroom

YOUR IDEAS:

-
-
-

Exercise: Healthy (Nonusing) Behavior Analysis

Just as your loved one has triggers for use, she also has triggers for healthy behaviors, which a Behavior Analysis can help you understand. This version of the exercise will help you identify all the external and internal reasons that your loved one may or may not choose to do something healthy. Use this information to help tip the scale toward healthy behavior by helping your loved one gain access to it and by actively reinforcing it.

Enjoyable, Healthy Behavior	Triggers		Consequences	
	External	Internal	Short-Term Negative	Long-Term Positive
What is your loved one's enjoyable, healthy behavior?	Who is your loved one usually with when s/he does it?	What do you think your loved one is thinking about right before doing it?	What do you think your loved one dislikes about the people with whom s/he does it?	What do you think are the positive results of your loved one's behavior in each of these areas? (Asterisk the ones s/he would agree with.)
How often does s/he engage in it?	Where does your loved one usually do it?	What do you think your loved one is feeling right before doing it?	What do you think your loved one dislikes about the place(s) s/he does it?	Relationships:
How long does the behavior usually last?	When does your loved one usually do it?		What do you think your loved one dislikes about the time(s) of day at which s/he does it?	Physical health:
			What unpleasant thoughts do you think your loved one has while doing it?	Emotional health:
			What unpleasant feelings do you think your loved one has while doing it?	Legal benefits:
				Work or school benefits:
				Financial benefits:
				Other benefits:

CHAPTER 11.

Consequences

Reinforcement is the currency of behavior change. On one side of the coin is positive reinforcement: rewarding your loved one's healthy, connected, constructive, and sober behavior—the strategy of the previous chapter. In this chapter we look at the other side, or what to do with the behavior you *don't* want. What *can* you do when there seems to be nothing to reward—when he comes home high, or she sleeps through her alarm, or he turns loud and belligerent after too many drinks at a family dinner?

You can apply the same principles of reinforcement, but in reverse. That is, just as you paired positive behavior with positive consequences to encourage it, negative behavior paired with negative consequences will discourage it. The *combination* of these strategies is more powerful than either alone. Negative behaviors don't simply vanish by themselves; they tend to come up even during the process of positive change. It takes time to learn to stay sober instead of using, to work out instead of stressing out, to go home instead of going all night. Given a mix of behavior that you don't want and behavior that you do, it helps to learn to work with both to effect change.

This chapter will describe four strategies for discouraging behavior you don't want. First, and most directly related to the positive reinforcement strategy you just learned, you can simply hold back the reward. If you plan to reinforce your loved one coming home sober by making dinner and eating together, it follows that you would *not* make dinner for him and *not* eat together when he shows up high. Second—and these options are not mutually exclusive—you can allow the natural negative consequences that result from a negative behavior to happen and have an impact. For example, let her sleep through her alarm and be late for school. Third, you can ignore the behavior you don't want. Say, instead of taking the bait and arguing with him at a party, you talk to someone else and find another way home. Fourth, you can punish, but we don't recommend it, for reasons we'll discuss.

Families that we work with usually fall into one of two camps. Some are reluctant to let their loved one have any negative experience, while others think their loved one is "getting away" with too much, or "has it too easy," and isn't experiencing negative consequences enough. While both of these perspectives are understandable, neither is particularly accurate or helpful. People learn from negative consequences, and it's helpful to let them do so (within reason). On the other hand, even if you and others have been insulating your loved one from the negative effects of his behavior, swinging the opposite way to punishment isn't the best strategy either. You can suppress behavior with punishment, but this doesn't eliminate it; it usually just goes underground.

Withdrawing Rewards

The reinforcement strategies you formulated in the last chapter put you in a position to reward the behaviors you want. Those exercises also supply the rewards you can withdraw in response to behavior you don't want. Your loved one learns that he gets your attention, for example, when he is not drinking, *and* he learns that he misses out on your attention when he drinks. With reinforcement strategies in place, the withdrawal of reinforcers becomes a negative consequence of substance use and other unwanted behaviors. In other words, you take away something that he likes in response to a specific negative behavior.

Withdrawing a reward in response to negative behavior *strengthens* the power of the reward to reinforce positive behavior. A double-strength strategy combines the two: reward the behavior you want, and remove the reward for behavior you don't want. Here are some guidelines to help you select a negative behavior to target and a reinforcer to withdraw.

Know what he likes. The reinforcer has to matter enough to your loved one that she will miss it when it's gone.

Make it work for you. This side of the reinforcement strategy has to work for you too. The reward should feel easy, and safe enough to withdraw that you will actually follow through. Avoid picking something so charged that its removal would cause an explosion. Avoid threatening to take away something if you don't think you will actually follow through—for example, if you're not prepared to change the locks on the house, don't tell him you are kicking him out.

Make it work fast. Pick something you can withdraw during or immediately after the negative behavior occurs—the sooner the better. As with rewards, immediacy strengthens the link between the behavior and the consequence.

Turn it back on. The reinforcer you would take away should be something you are willing and able enough to reinstate when the positive behavior returns. Imagine a switch within your reach: you will turn it off when behavior you don't want occurs, and other times turn it on so that light shines on the behavior you do want. Turning on the reward for the behavior you do want may require putting aside your feelings about the past, sometimes the very recent past. Try to stay focused on the behavior that is happening now.

For maximum impact on both negative and positive behavior, you'll want to check that you're not still keeping your distance the following night, when he comes home sober, because you are still mad about the night before. You don't want to accidentally punish the behavior you want any more than you want to accidentally reward the behavior you don't want.

Be specific. The reinforcer to be withdrawn should be associated specifically with the behavior you want to discourage. The more specific and targeted the better; in other words, it should *not* be a response you would have to many other behaviors. If not talking to her is your response to everything she does that you don't like, it will lose its power to impact any one of the specific behaviors. When you brainstorm reinforcers, make a short list of more than one to apply to different behaviors.

Leave the reaction up to your loved one. Withdrawing a reward *is not punishment.* We mean that both technically and in practical terms. We'll address punishment later, but the point here is that punishment is doing something *to* a person, whereas time out from positive reinforcement is exactly that: not giving something previously given (and to be given again!) for positive behavior. Here's why it's different: in withdrawing the positive you are not engaging, not getting into it, not—in a perfect world—inflecting the interaction in any way. Withdrawing is simply NOT doing. It avoids the fight and leaves it on your loved one to learn the choice is his.

Withdrawing a reward should not sound (internally or outwardly) like "so there" or "take that." It should be carried out with a neutral expression. Keeping quietly to yourself because your wife came home drunk is a different state of being than the "silent treatment," and it sends a different message. If you withdraw a reward aggressively or emotionally, your loved one may think more about "what an SOB you are for being so withholding" than about simply *missing* the reward.

What's hard about this . . . Unless you're a monk or a nun, you may not have much practice not-doing. Just do the best you can to not-reward as calmly and nonjudgmentally as you can manage. Practice self-care skills that help you manage your distress if you need to. Plan self-care activities to take your mind off the problem.

Communicate. Think ahead to whether and how you will make your intentions known. You may not always choose to be explicit, but positive communication can help clarify the connection between the behavior and your response. You might say, "Oh, you're drinking, so I'm going to be in our room reading. Feel free to get yourself some dinner." Planning this in advance can help you avoid blurting out something less positive in the heat of your disappointment ("I can smell the alcohol from across the room! You're on your own tonight, pal."). Communication can help make the difference between not-doing and punishment.

Positive communication can also help to reduce the emotionality of your loved one's response, if you explain your strategy beforehand. Following the guidelines for positive communication, pick a time when the mood between you is good, be positive, be brief, offer understanding and help, and avoid arguing. You might find a relaxed moment on a Saturday morning when you have some privacy to say, "I love having dinner with you on weeknights when we're both not drinking. I just wanted to let you know that it's actually not much fun for me when you're drinking, so in those cases I'm going to read by myself upstairs, and we can do it another night." Don't forget to include the positive side of the equation, that is, the behavior you do want. Positive communication can make the difference between an explanation and a threat.

Allowing Natural Consequences

With this strategy for dealing with behavior you don't want, you don't do anything, but just step out of the way and allow it to happen. The reinforcement strategies in the last chapter hinged on the positive consequences of substance use for your loved one—what he gets out of it— in order to help channel his motivations toward alternative behaviors. Allowing natural consequences channels, or rather avoids diverting, any negative consequences to maximize their naturally deterring effects. Even more than withdrawing rewards, allowing consequences helps your loved one understand his behavior as his choice. He learns that changing his behavior is his choice, as opposed to something you are pushing on him all the time.

Natural consequences are the direct outcomes of your loved one's substance use that he would experience if no one interfered. They're the costs he naturally incurs by using. They can be emotional costs, such as depression, anger, shame, or feeling out of control; physical costs such as sleep disruptions, agitation, or injuries; and what we call structural costs: loss of relationships, financial problems, legal problems, and so forth. The costs of using may range in severity from mild headaches or embarrassments to deep shame and major deprivations like getting fired or losing custody of a child.

For most people, using or overusing substances results in negative consequences that pretty quickly convince them to limit use to moderation or no use at all. For most people, the costs just don't seem worth it. For others, the benefits of using are greater and/or more numerous, and the negative consequences are fewer and/or less—because their brains are more rewarded by a substance, or life feels more painful to them in one way or another that a substance relieves, or their social group uses more heavily, or any of the other reasons people use. But you would not be reading this book if there were not also significant negative consequences to your loved one's use, and the goal here is to let those consequences speak for themselves. In cost-benefit terms, you aim to not get in the way of or prevent the costs from occurring.

What would happen if your husband was late to work because he was hungover and moving slowly and you didn't rush in to drag him out of bed, pack his bag, or help him find his keys? If your wife passed out at the kitchen table and you didn't carry her to bed? If your son took ecstasy and failed to turn in his assignments the next day and you didn't provide his school with an excuse? Probably trouble with the boss at work, the stark reality of waking up in the kitchen, and having to deal with the principal at school. In other words, if you let it happen, your loved one would feel the impact of his or her behavior and the costs would register in the "costs" column of his motivational accounting, where they belong.

Good News: Costs seed change. Disliking the outcome of a behavior pushes strongly in the direction of extinguishing it. After all, negative consequences are the reasons for your loved one to stop doing what he is doing.

We call this strategy the "quiet confrontation," because allowing natural consequences helps relocate the stress, frustration, and fight to *within* your loved one, rather than *between* the two of you. Instead of arguing with her, let the argument about whether she uses substances reside within her. If you don't deflect them, then she will directly feel the discomfort, alarm, and other misgivings about her own behavior and use that information to make different choices. Allowing her to come face-to-face—the literal meaning of "confront"—with the results of her own actions, without distraction, will help her take her own behavior to heart instead of blaming you.

How to Get Out of the Way

You can use the approach to problem solving that we presented in chapter 8, "Goals (and Problems)," to plan how you will step out of the way of naturally occurring consequences. "Allowing" is not as simple as it sounds.

1. **Define the problem.** What are the potential (and actual) natural consequences of his substance use? Is there anything buffering his experiencing these directly? Is there anything *you* are doing, inadvertently or purposefully, to deflect his costs? We've already mentioned some common ones. Others include:

   - Driving him/picking him up when he's intoxicated
   - Nursing her through a hangover
   - Taking on his household responsibilities, child care, errands
   - Paying bills, giving cash
   - Preventing legal consequences (not reporting theft, abuse, or physical threats)
   - Making excuses for absences, cancellations, or negative behavior ("he had a bad day")
   - Making/canceling appointments and managing his schedule

   Remember, the consequence should be a result of the behavior and perceived by your loved one as negative. Just as a reward is only as reinforcing as its value to the person receiving it, the consequence will impact your loved one insofar as he experiences it as a drawback.
   Nadia was a client whose husband got up so late on weekends after drinking that they could barely get to their kids' soccer games on time. Nadia knew her husband delighted in watching the kids' games and wanted to be there for them. She predicted that if she stopped working

so hard to get him up, he would sleep in and feel the loss of missing the kids' activities. She was right; he couldn't get up on his own and was upset about it. She left the choice and consequences squarely in his lap. He experienced the downside of his drinking, and he couldn't blame her anymore for "so rudely" waking him up and "bossing him around."

2. **Brainstorm.** Try to think of all the subtle or more obvious ways that you could change *your* behavior, as much as you could stand, to get out of the way of the consequences of his behavior. For this step, put *all* your ideas on the page. Don't hold anything back out of fear, as some consequences that seem harsh at first can be helpful. Do you know your wife sometimes has too many drinks when she picks up the kids? If you reported her for driving over the legal limit, which resulted in closer monitoring of her, thus preventing her from drinking and driving with your children in the car, would it be worth it (for your kids and everyone else on the road)? It's at least worth considering, and you won't get very far in brainstorming if you censor your ideas too quickly.

3. **Eliminate unwanted ideas.** After you've written down *all* your ideas, evaluate them:

    Is it safe to allow the consequence? On the nights when Nadia's husband drank too much, she was angry that they had to pay for a cab and manage without their car until he could come back for it the next day. (She didn't drive.) She thought about insisting that he drive anyway, but that would be dangerous, and could get him arrested. The cost of this natural consequence was potentially too high for everyone.

    To be clear, this strategy does not amount to letting your loved one "hit bottom." The natural consequences of people's substance use can be horrific, and we believe that the traditional advice to let people "bottom out" contributes to cycling through relapses, hospitalizations, and rehabs as well as intensifying mental and physical health problems. Not all consequences are reasonable to allow, for your loved one's health and well-being and for your peace of mind. This is especially true for parents. Being strategic means doing what works—in this case, allowing certain meaningful consequences within your limits of safety and sanity.

    You should be able to live with the consequence. Consider the potential costs of letting the consequences happen. What are the risks—financial, emotional, and physical—to you, your family, and your loved one? How severe could the consequences be and how much could you stand? On second thought, you may decide that it's too scary. It's one thing to allow her to be late in the morning; it's another to think she could lose her job when it's your family's only source of income. A consequence of your declining to pick him up could be the inconvenience of finding his way home, or it could be the risk of his driving drunk. Eliminate any consequences that seem too dangerous or too upsetting for you.

4. **Identify and address potential obstacles.** What might get in the way of allowing the consequences? Consider:

   Would problems arise for you (or other family members) as a result of allowing the consequence? By letting him sleep in, Nadia would miss her husband's company at the games, and knew the kids would too. She decided, however, that they could tolerate these drawbacks temporarily, knowing that the potential benefits were worth it. She also anticipated some logistical challenges on days when the girls were in different games—historically she would go to one and her husband to the other. She could arrange for the girls to get rides with other teammates, but one of their kids would not have a cheering parent on the sideline. She would let them talk to their father about that if they missed him.

   How will your loved one handle the consequence? In Nadia's case, she knew her husband would feel upset with himself and worry about how their kids took it. She did not think he would be angry with her. Emotional discomfort is an effective natural consequence, but you may need to prepare for the possibility that your loved one will initially take it out on you. They may be used to your protection or even depend on it. You leaving him exposed will probably stir up confusion, anger, and fear. You can use your distress tolerance skills to manage his initial reactions, and do what you need to do to take care of yourself. If violence is a possibility, review our suggestions in chapter 6, "Have Your Limits," to know your limits and make plans that keep you and yours as safe as possible.

5. **Assign task(s).**

   Decide how and when you will communicate the plan. Nadia used positive communication to tell her husband about her new approach to weekend mornings. She planned to talk to him in a calm moment before they went out the night before, as she thought this would get a better reception than if she sprung it on him either in front of people as he was reaching for a drink or the next morning when he would be feeling lousy. She wrote herself a script and practiced: "I want to talk with you about our weekend plans. It's hard for me to get the girls ready for the games and also make sure you're up and ready too. I know sometimes Saturday mornings are tough for you to get going—and I'm sure you'd rather I didn't stalk you! So for now I plan to leave the getting up part to you and hope that we can all enjoy our Saturdays together."

Nadia also planned what she would say to the kids if their father didn't get up in time: "Your dad seems to be having trouble getting up this morning, so we're going to go ahead and perhaps he can meet us there, otherwise we'll see him afterward. You know how much he enjoys your games, so I'm sure he'll want to hear all about it later. For now, let's get going with our day and make sure we get there on time."

6. **Get out of the way.** Now that you've selected a natural consequence for its potential to impact your loved one's decision to use, it's time to get out of the way and see what happens. Nadia let her husband sleep and she went to watch the girls. After this happened a few times, she heard him decline a drink at a party "because he had to get up early for the kids." When Nadia realized that her plan was working, she even went so far as to schedule appealing morning activities if there were no "naturally occurring" sports events. She felt so pleased by the changes she saw that she was able to do this in the spirit of family fun rather than punishment, a difference that was not lost on her husband. He awoke with so much energy when he hadn't overdone it the night before that he readily joined in whatever activity she had planned.

One kind of opportunity to get out of the way comes with other people's comments about your loved one's behaviors. Family members often field questions ("How is he?" "Should I be worried?") from other friends and family. Usually we recommend that these family members encourage the person asking the question to speak directly to the one they are concerned about. The more feedback that your loved one gets directly from other people, the better—much better than when the message comes from you, which might feel to your loved one like tattling or gossiping, even though you don't mean it that way, and this can put you, as the messenger, in position to get bitten.

This Isn't Punishment Either

As you let your loved one experience natural, real-world consequences, stay aware of the attitude you take while it is happening, as conveyed by your tone of voice, eye contact, and body language as well as your words. As we discussed in the previous section on withdrawing positive reinforcers, the best strategy is to be as matter of fact as possible and not punitive, righteous, or angry. Remember, a punitive attitude interferes with the goodwill and collaboration upon which everything positive depends. If you decide to stop nursing her through her hangovers, don't make the alternative a lecture on how you think she deserves it: just stop nursing her through it. As best you can, get on with your day, and let the natural consequences speak for themselves.

"But I Care Too Much to Let Anything Bad Happen"

Even if allowing consequences seems reasonable to you in theory and maybe even a relief, you may worry about seeming uncaring or mean. But you're not being mean; you're creating an opportunity. And you're doing it because you care. When you let people face the consequences of their actions directly, you let them learn. They can learn the steps it takes to clean up a mess or how to ask for help. They can learn to accept responsibility and apologize to others for canceling plans, showing up late, hurting feelings, and so on. And most important, once they decide their behavior is not working, they can learn new alternative healthy behaviors.

What's hard about this . . . everything. We can't put a box around it this time because the whole thing is hard. We naturally want to protect those we love. No one wants to see a loved one suffer. You may reheat dinner when she's late because you don't know when she'll get a healthy meal. Or pay his rent because you don't want to see him evicted—where else would he go?

You may smooth the rough edges of your loved one's natural consequences to protect other people you care about as well. You may help make excuses because you don't want others to worry. You may call in sick for him because other people depend on the paycheck. And, of course, the consequences affect you too. Making excuses to yourself may help you feel better. Making excuses to others can save you some embarrassment. You may clean up a mess because you don't want to look at it and it seems easier to just do it yourself. This all makes perfect sense. The problem with protecting people from negative consequences, however, is that it can inadvertently support use. Positive change depends on the experience of positive consequences for positive behavior and negative consequences for negative behavior.

These natural inclinations to protect and rescue people you love from the negative consequences of substance use are the "enabling" behaviors that self-help books and treatment providers discourage. It's a normal response to pain in relationships, and a good and reasonable attempt to reduce that pain or avoid conflict. Often it works in the short term. But in reinforcement terms, it rewards the behavior you don't want. You don't mean to, but there it is: in attempting to minimize the distress to yourself, your loved one, your family and friends, you can in effect be making it easier for your loved one to keep doing what he's doing.

Ignoring Negative Behaviors: The Art of Doing Nothing

Another way to influence behavior is simply to ignore it. When a behavior is not reinforced, it is gradually extinguished. Ignoring gives the least amount of reinforcement that you can give: nothing. No reward, no interaction, no response, no attention at all. Ignoring takes not-doing to a whole other level. It should not be confused with cold-shouldering, sulking, or other ways of communicating displeasure through body language that aren't really ignoring; they're dishing it right back. The message of ignoring is "I am not interested in this behavior" whereas giving someone the cold shoulder says, "I'm mad at you."

We don't recommend ignoring substance use very often, as withdrawing rewards and allowing consequences are more effective strategies. However, ignoring is helpful for dealing with your loved one's *reactions* to those strategies. When your loved one tries to engage you with some version of "why are you doing this to me"—for example, being provocative out of anger or indignation, yelling, swearing, pouting, or sulking—ignoring is the best way to discourage those reactions.

If you respond to the sulking, you reinforce sulking (whether fighting about it or comforting it away). If you yell at your loved one for yelling, you reinforce yelling. Humans are such social animals that even negative attention like complaining, pleading, or fighting can be rewarding, especially when a relationship has broken down to the point where there is little to no positive attention at all. In these situations, negative attention may seem better to your loved one than no attention.

We can't sell ignoring without a product label warning. Sometimes ignoring the behavior you don't want results, initially, in an *escalation* of the behavior, a phenomenon called a "behavioral burst." Bursts are often seen right before the behavior extinguishes, or stops altogether, and they are hard for everyone involved. Luckily, they don't tend to last long. In fact, they're often a sign of the end stage of a behavior. As the person realizes that this behavior that previously worked for him doesn't anymore, he makes some last, desperate (often confused and disbelieving) attempts.

Bursts end, but only if you don't respond to them. If you respond at the peak, which is often the most painful point for everyone, it just sets a new peak, the person having learned that if he takes you to that edge, you will give in—and that the behavior still works. It can feel brutal, but we encourage you to stay firm and use every self-care skill you have to ride out a burst. You might have to do it a couple of times, but the behavior will likely burn out.

To deal with a burst, the most effective strategy is ignoring in combination with positive reinforcement. The moment your loved one stops yelling, sulking, or otherwise acting out, give her your attention. If your husband comes home sober, be willing to sit and visit and give him your time and care. When your daughter stops cursing, ask her if she would like some dinner. (This is consistent because ignoring relates to the behavior rather than the person. You don't ignore your daughter; you ignore her cursing.)

Finally, make sure everyone on your team is prepared to cooperate with your ignoring. Nothing disrupts the effectiveness of ignoring more than someone else's stepping in and giving attention—for example, when you have just made the effort to ignore your daughter's outburst, your spouse walks in and asks her, "What's wrong, honey?" and undoes all your hard work. Identify the specific behaviors you plan to ignore and explain this to the other members of your household.

A Case Against Punishment

The last option when someone does something you don't like is to do something they don't like in response. Many of the examples of consequences in this chapter might sound like what people normally call "punishment," but for the sake of clarity and for the purposes of this book, we define *punishment* more narrowly: using an aggressive or punitive tone (yelling, cursing, name-calling, or threatening violence), mocking (imitating how his face looks when he's stoned, taking pictures of her passed out), or being physically aggressive (slapping, hitting, pushing).

We don't recommend punishment as an option among options or even as a last resort. Punishing someone might make you feel more powerful and "right" in the short term, but it doesn't help; and it causes problems over time. Remember, most people change because they want to, not because they are told to. Also, punishment only suppresses a behavior; it doesn't teach a new behavior—"I won't do this right now so she doesn't scream at me," versus "If I get my homework done, I can stay out later tonight." The best way to help someone change is to teach her or expose her to a competing behavior. Punishment contributes nothing positive to the world of alternatives you're trying to help your loved one build.

Punishment seldom helps to extinguish unwanted behaviors, either; it simply silences them for the duration of the punishment. This unfortunately can lead to the behaviors going underground, including hiding, sneaking, and lying, which effectively cuts off your opportunities to respond to the behavior in more helpful ways because you don't know when it's happening.

And probably the worst thing for you as a loved one trying to stay connected and help is that punishment sets up an adversarial relationship. It puts you in the position of bad cop instead of spouse, parent, or friend. Punishment destroys empathy and impedes understanding, which you know now is critical to positive communication and a collaborative approach to change. It breeds black-and-white thinking, because the subtext is always "I'm right, you're wrong." It can also leave your loved one with the feeling that resentment and rebellion are his only options for expressing himself.

In short, punishment undermines people's autonomy, pisses them off, starts a tug-of-war, and detracts from the point of change.

What's hard about this—especially for people with ADHD . . . If you are a parent of a teen or young adult with ADHD and substance problems, you have an extra reason to find alternatives to punishment. The only positive value of any punishment is that it can be anticipated and therefore avoided by behaving well. People who are particularly impulsive or struggle with ADHD symptoms are not good at anticipating the future and seldom think through consequences before they experience them. As a result, for these people, punishment as the only consequence can lead to a profound sense of learned helplessness, defeat, and generally feeling bad about themselves.

Kelly's husband said terrible things to her when he was drunk. He had developed a pattern of coming home drunk about once a week, usually picking a fight with her at some point later in the evening. Kelly would get sucked into the argument. The following day, she would be exhausted and somewhat traumatized by the name-calling and things he said, such as that he never wanted to see her again. Working with her therapist, she realized why she stuck around for these fights: a desire to punish him with anger at the only time it felt "fair" to unleash it. When he was drunk and they were fighting, she took it as permission to unload all her pent-up anger and frustration. Although she was succeeding at punishing him, the consequences for her were bad (that next day was horrible) and she was not attaining her higher goals of his drinking less and their relationship improving.

And she discovered other reasons for their fights. When she stayed up to fight with him, she could keep an eye on him. She worried that he might fall in the house or use sharp tools or appliances, and she saw that in her vigilant hovering, she was an easy target and to some extent even provoked him because he felt judged and trapped. Kelly weighed the new options her CRAFT therapist helped her consider: she could continue the status quo, which was not what she really wanted, or she could risk allowing an accident to occur if she were to remove herself from the situation. She chose to risk it. Kelly learned over time to go to bed early or occupy herself with her new hobby of knitting and watching old movies, which kept her mind off her worrying. She withdrew the reinforcer of her attention on those nights and planned ways to give him more positive attention when he was sober. When he tried to pick a fight anyway, she ignored it.

Not everyone would be comfortable with the risk of injury involved in Kelly's strategy. If you're not sure, it may help to consult the past. Kelly's husband had broken a few dishes over the years, but he'd never actually fallen or hurt himself and she decided she could live with these odds.

Don't forget the forest. If the "trees" of withdrawing positive reinforcement, allowing natural consequences, and ignoring are your specific strategies to promote certain behaviors and discourage others, the overall objective is still to help your loved one feel like the world and your relationship together in it is a good, satisfying place when he isn't using substances. On the other hand, when he is using substances, the world should seem to him a place with fewer rewards. Even the perfect argument, if you could make it, would not likely convince him of this. Try to rely more on your behavior and his experience rather than arguing for change. Let your loved one experience costs and benefits, causes and effects—and let him choose.

Exercise: Withdrawing Positive Reinforcers

Find examples of behaviors on your part that reinforce substance use or other behaviors you don't want. Using these guidelines for withdrawing reinforcers, consider which of your behaviors you could realistically withdraw.

Your loved one values and will miss it when it is withdrawn.

It is easy enough for you to withdraw.

You feel safe withdrawing it.

You can withdraw it soon enough after the behavior you don't want occurs.

You are willing to reintroduce it when he returns to the behavior you want.

Exercise: Allowing Natural Consequences/Ignoring Behavior

1. Your Behavior Analysis from chapter 2 (pages 67–68) includes a column of negative consequences for your loved one of his or her substance use. Looking back over this exercise, notice if there are any consequences that she is not aware of. Is there anything you could do to help her connect her choices and behavior with these consequences? Is there anything you could do to make the "allowing" more tolerable for you?

2. When your loved one is intoxicated, hungover, or otherwise engaged in a behavior you don't want AND you are a) confident he is not at risk or in imminent danger, and b) not physically at risk yourself . . .

Do:

Go about your day

Find something to do to get your mind off the behavior you don't want

Take a walk to cool off or relax

Get out of the house if you are tense or frustrated

Visit or call a friend or family member

Go to the library; read a book

Listen to music, or a podcast (headphones are great for removing yourself)

Pick something from your distress tolerance lists from chapter 5, "Self-
   Care I: Damage Control" (e.g., take a bath, use relaxation techniques,
   pray, or meditate).
Can you think of other dos? _____

_____

_____

Don't:
Try to punish your loved one with the "cold shoulder"
Lecture or give rational explanations of why drinking or using is "bad"
Nag him to stop
Follow her around to make sure she stays out of trouble
"Cover up" for the behavior
Try to talk to him about important decisions, like career or parenting
Talk about the behavior behind her back, where she can overhear
Threaten him
Resort to pleading or crying
Get caught up in yelling and fighting
Act "crazy" to prove a point
Try to engage in conversation
Can you think of other don'ts? _____

_____

_____

CHAPTER 12.

Treatment Options

The key word here is options, *plural*. As we've seen, everyone is different, and this applies to the specifics of people's problems (what they've been using, how much, how long, and their reasons), as well as to the many ways that people ultimately decide to make changes. It is true also for formal treatment. What helped one person—say, twenty-eight days in rehab followed by couples therapy and 12-step meetings—might not be a suitable plan for another. The next person wants to stay at work, start medication to prevent drinking, and see her therapist twice a week—and her preferences matter. Both paths could help; it depends on the person. As you read, keep in mind what you have come to know about your loved one so far—her patterns of using, underlying issues, openness to support, awareness of the need to change, and so on, because you can use this information to understand what treatment options make most sense for her.

This chapter is about understanding the options—because this is typically a strange new world for families entering into it, and also because one of the most effective ways to encourage someone to change is to present multiple, reasonable choices. In the next chapter, you'll learn how to present the options to your loved one, but first we want you to know what they are. As you take in this information, think of yourself as an ally in decisions about treatment, in keeping with another thing we know about motivation: both the short- and long-term trajectory are helped enormously through respectful collaboration.

The three biggest questions to ask about treatment are:

1. What *setting* makes the most sense to start with (inpatient or residential, outpatient, and so on)?
2. What *intensity* of treatment is appropriate; that is, how often will treatment occur?
3. What *approach* seems like the best fit for your loved one (and what is the evidence supporting that approach)?

These questions will guide you to choices that can be tailored to your specific needs, and to options that may not be immediately apparent.

Unfortunately, many people arrive at the crossroad of choosing treatment in a panic, through a crisis or emergency—she just got suspended at work or school; you just found out about the cocaine and the affair; she got a DUI; you discovered needles in his bathroom drawer. Frantic, people often grab for the first option they hear, and often the most restrictive option they hear about (usually rehab), because it *feels* safest. In other words, when it feels like an emergency (and it might be), *setting* is often the only thing people consider. But even if rehab is the best setting for a person, approach and intensity matter at least as much. Entering treatment is a big decision that deserves more than a gut reaction. This chapter will help you and your loved one make a decision based on information and reason.

After narrowing down treatment settings, intensity, and approaches, you'll want to find out about the training and qualifications of the people providing the treatment, their capacity to work with co-occurring disorders like anxiety or depression, their strategies for including the family, and how they would work with your loved one's goals. We will explain the right questions to ask. We will also help you think through the costs associated with different treatment options, as well as a variety of self-help resources.

The Power of a Good Assessment

The first step to good treatment is a good assessment. The qualifications and approach of the person doing the assessment impact the recommendations they will make. For the person who comes to an assessment with a nightly habit of four big scotches: a nurse might suggest rehab, a psychiatrist might suggest detox, an internist might give the person a Valium, a psychologist might refer him to a physician and an intensive outpatient program, and a counselor might suggest AA meetings. Between two assessors recommending rehab, one might prioritize psychiatric sophistication and willingness to use medications, while another might ignore or even reject those considerations. Ask the person doing the assessment about her preferred approach or treatment philosophy, as it will surely influence her recommendations.

Fortunately, there has been a strong push over the last forty years to standardize assessment procedures, resulting in new conceptual frameworks for assessing people's problems. Perhaps foremost among the new assessment standards is the Addiction Severity Index (ASI), developed by A. Thomas McLellan at the University of Pennsylvania. This standardized interview for professionals led the field to assess people in multiple life areas as a way to understand the extent to which their substance use affects them. The ASI assesses substance use (frequency of use, quantities, types of substances, direct effects of these substances), but it also explores family and relationships, job and household functioning, legal issues, health issues, and more. This helps clinicians develop a fuller picture of the person in front of them, compelling them to go beyond "alcoholic" or "addict" in their conclusions. This broader understanding of the person and his life helps point toward *how much* treatment he needs and in *what setting*.

ASAM and the Patient Placement Criteria

One of the leading organizations concerned with assessment and treatment placement issues is the American Society of Addiction Medicine (ASAM). The ASAM system uses what it calls Patient Placement Criteria (PPC), a standardized matrix to collect information in six life dimensions. A thorough assessment will cover all six.

1. Acute intoxication and/or withdrawal potential—Or, what is the current state of this person physiologically speaking: how much of a substance is he or she using (in general and right this moment) and is there the presence of intoxication and/or potential for physical withdrawal? This is critical in determining the need for detoxification procedures to avert medical crises.

2. Biomedical conditions and complications—Does the person have substance-related medical conditions, or conditions that are affected by his or her substance use, such as liver disease, pancreatitis, history of stroke, prescribed medications that may interact dangerously with the abused substance(s); et cetera? These conditions would point in the direction of more restrictive, medically monitored care, at least initially.

3. Emotional/behavioral conditions and complications—This covers a lot of territory, including other psychiatric conditions (e.g., mood and anxiety disorders, psychosis, the presence of a personality disorder), self-harming behaviors (e.g., cutting), a history of trauma, and other compulsive behaviors including eating disorders, gambling, or sexual acting out. To the extent the person is struggling with such issues, more intensive treatment would be appropriate.

4. Treatment acceptance/resistance—This is the motivational dimension: the more resistant someone is to help, the more treatment he or she may need. Though there is some merit to this idea, it is not such a helpful framing of motivation, and unfortunately, much of the treatment system has evolved in a manner that doesn't manage "resistance" well, setting up power struggles that don't help anyone. More optimistically, providers are learning to work with resistance as the evidence-based motivational model becomes better understood.

5. Relapse/continued use potential—This dimension assesses the risk for relapse to use. Considerations include history (for how long and how early in life use began), prior change attempts (whether periods of abstinence or reduction have been maintained before), and the level of environmental challenge (relationship stress, financial stress, et cetera); as well as aspects of psychological readiness for change such as a sense of determination, strength of coping skills, degree of impulsivity, and perceptions of use and nonuse (amount of pleasure expected from use and amount of discomfort expected from abstaining).

6. Recovery environment—Environmental factors like the degree of substance use in one's close relationships and living environment can increase or decrease relapse potential. Someone who lives with an active substance user or lives in a "drug-intensive" environment is at higher risk for relapse than a person with a strong support network of nonusing family and friends and accountability at work.

Setting and Intensity: ASAM's Levels of Care

The ASAM system can also help you organize your thinking about what treatments are available. Specifically, ASAM describes four Levels of Care, where setting and intensity meet. Each level is a measure of structure or restrictiveness in the setting (residential or not, degree of medical monitoring, staffing pattern, including the amount of time an MD is present, ability to come and go), and the intensity of the program (how many hours a day and days a week there are treatment activities).

Remember, ASAM recommends starting with the *least* intensive level of treatment that is safe.

Level I—Nonintensive Outpatient Care

Setting—Clients schedule appointments week to week and commute to treatment. There is no structure other than attendance requirements.

Intensity—Less than ten hours per week, to as few as one visit. Treatment can last anywhere from three months to several years.

Examples of Level I care:

- Onetime consultation or brief intervention—Typically an evaluation with a substance abuse specialist, independent practitioner, or treatment program. (It is important to assess for mental health issues, so consider training/degree.)
- Weekly individual, group, couples, or family therapy (or any combination)—services may be provided by any level of practitioner (as recognized and licensed by your particular state) in the context of a treatment program or by private practitioners.
- Monthly medication check-ins with a psychiatrist—These are part of an outpatient treatment regimen or, less often, *the* treatment regimen. Medications alone, unaccompanied by any psychotherapeutic support, are often less effective, but certainly viable in relatively stable, uncomplicated situations.
- DUI programs (six to eight weeks, once a week)—These are, by definition, mandated programs, most often provided by a state agency, although sometimes by private practitioners. The quality of these programs is variable and depends almost entirely on the person leading the class. Program length varies, depending on the mandate.

Good News: Many detoxifications can be safely, medically managed on an outpatient basis. Historically, "detox" is a place people go in a hospital setting to physically withdraw from substances; alternatively (and commonly), it is a process people go through in agony at home, sometimes at great risk. In medically supervised outpatient cases, however, clients live at home and go daily to their doctor to have their vitals checked and receive medications to manage withdrawal symptoms for that day. Outpatient detoxes are less disruptive (for instance, no need to explain multiday absences from work); the question is whether they're safe and doable for a particular individual. Can the person tolerate the discomfort that often accompanies detoxification (even with the most state-of-the-art medications, most people experience some distress while they are detoxing) without deciding to return to use? A successful outpatient detox also requires that a person remove himself from (or tolerate) triggers to use, as well as be organized enough to take the medications exactly as prescribed.

And a warning: Certain substances (alcohol and benzodiazepines like Xanax and Valium) are dangerous to withdraw from without medical management. In severe cases, doing so can result in death. Withdrawal symptoms typically express themselves as a syndrome ranging from being physically very uncomfortable (itchy skin, sweating, vomiting, insomnia) to emotionally uncomfortable (heightened depression, paranoia, anxiety, and "anhedonia," a very-difficult-to-endure state of no feelings at all). If a person is unlikely to tolerate the physical and/or emotional distress of withdrawal, a short stay at a Level IV facility (described below) is advised.

Level II—Intensive Outpatient Care

Setting—Clients attend a structured program week to week and commute to treatment. Structure includes attendance requirements and often drug testing.

Intensity—Services are provided more than ten hours per week and typically take place in a clinic setting rather than through an individual provider. Treatment length is variable (three to nine months), but typically somewhat more time-limited than Level I.

Examples of Level II care:

• Intensive evening programs (e.g., five evenings a week) designed to accommodate daytime working.

• Intensive Outpatient Programs (IOP)/"partial hospitalization" programs (e.g., five days a week, three to six hours per day)—IOPs can serve as a starting point for clients returning from inpatient stays or they can be the step people take before deciding to go to inpatient treatment. (Many insurance companies require that you have "failed" at IOP before they will pay for inpatient treatment.) Because of the hours and structure, these programs are well suited to those needing more support and/or monitoring, including a psychiatric component to help people to deal with emotional instability, anxiety, and depression, to work through trauma, and to develop healthy relationships. IOPs can also help clients manage their use of medications and provide support in the areas of job or school functioning.

Level III—Residential/Inpatient care

Setting—Clients live at the facility while in treatment. Treatment is highly structured, with set programming for participants, often in groups.

Intensity—Treatment activities are intensive, typically occurring throughout the day, five to seven days a week. Treatment length varies widely at this level of care, from two weeks to two years.

Examples of Level III care:

- "Rehab"—Typically a four- to six-week highly structured inpatient stay that provides medical monitoring of physical problems and medication. Therapy is usually intensive, occurring throughout each day, and can include self-help, professional counseling, and a psychiatric component. Rehab offers safety from substance use, as well as an opportunity to focus on psychiatric and emotional difficulties along with substance problems.

  This level of care and type of facility has stood, in many people's minds, for what treatment is. Begun in the early 1950s as a hospital-based treatment, rehab has grown into a multimillion-dollar industry with "high end" rehabs advertising "cures" and costing anywhere from $10,000 to $80,000 dollars a month. It is an odd fact (true mostly in the United States) that the treatment *approach* in rehabs is almost invariably 12-step, though this is starting to change.

  This puts the onus on you to investigate each and every facility you consider, especially if your loved one needs more sophisticated psychiatric care. For a well-researched and insightful examination of rehab care, see Anne Fletcher's 2013 book *Inside Rehab*.

- Therapeutic communities ("TCs")—Traditionally a twelve- to twenty-four-month program, TCs are highly structured and, traditionally, confrontational in their approach. The TC approach is unique in the field in that treatment is provided largely by other recovering community members. This setting has often been used for more criminally delinquent populations, as well as (oddly) for adolescents.

- Extended care—Residences are often suggested by inpatient rehab facilities as a step-down from their more treatment intensive rehab services. They provide less supervision and clients typically are allowed to interact with the outside world, going to off-site self-help meetings, getting jobs, returning to school, and so on. Many extended care programs provide extensive therapeutic support and specialize in underlying issues like trauma or personality disorders. Supervision in these programs varies and regulations are different from state to state. Our experience is that some are helpful, thoughtfully run programs and residences that give clients a safe place to live while they go about building a life. Others are less safe, and/or poorly managed. Unfortunately, at times some manipulate families with fear. We recommend that you investigate carefully and visit in person before you consider signing up. Most important: while some extended care programs are licensed to provide treatment, sober living is not treatment; at best, sober living residences offer a supervised (via drug and Breathalyzer tests), safe place to stay—often a critical ingredient to sustaining change.

Level IV—Medically Managed Intensive Inpatient Care

Setting—Clients stay at the facility, typically a hospital-based program with intensive, twenty-four-hour medical management. Services focus on stabilizing acute substance or psychiatric crises.

Intensity—Monitoring is intensive and more medically oriented than psychotherapeutic in nature, including managing medications, stabilizing psychiatric symptoms, managing symptoms of substance withdrawal, ensuring bodily safety. A stay of three to five days is typical, depending on the substance (and insurance company).

Examples of Level IV care:

• Inpatient hospital detoxification ("detox")—This level of service is for one purpose only: to safely, medically taper someone off (with medication) substances of abuse on which they have become *physically* dependent. Not all substances of abuse cause physical dependence (some behaviors, like gambling, cause distressing symptoms when a person stops, but are not in any sense physically dangerous to him), and some are more medically dangerous to withdraw from than others (alcohol in this sense is more dangerous than opioids, despite the discomfort of both withdrawals). Characteristic of this setting/level of care is the combination of intensive medication/medical monitoring with very little psychotherapeutic treatment. The treatment team is there to monitor safety; in fact many people are somewhat cognitively impaired and physically uncomfortable during detox, and not so open to talking anyway. (This is also why so many people relapse after detox if they don't get further help: it is only the first, physical step to making change.)

Absent any additional medical or psychiatric complications, detox from alcohol requires the shortest duration of medication-assisted tapering off (two to five days), while also being potentially the most medically dangerous of substances to stop using when dependent due to the physical risks of the withdrawal syndrome. Opioids (e.g., heroin or prescription painkillers like Percocet and Vicodin) can take anywhere from five to fourteen days to comfortably taper off, depending on the dose or amount at which the individual started. An opioid taper can be uncomfortable, but it is far and away less dangerous than alcohol withdrawal. Finally, benzodiazepine dependence usually requires the longest tapering period. Depending on the length of use and degree of tolerance, tapering can go on for months. As a result, the process cannot be completed in a short detoxification stay, though it may start there with a "taper schedule" handed off to the next treatment provider (whether it be longer inpatient stay or outpatient psychiatrist) to monitor and complete.

• Psychiatric hospitalization Also a hospital-based service, including around-the-clock physician and nursing care to medically manage acute psychiatric issues. We mention it here as a service that is sometimes appropriate for people in the throes of acute substance problems—for example, a psychotic reaction to intoxication or withdrawal, acute exacerbation of other psychiatric issues (depression, panic, dissociation) through substance use, or because it's the only unit in your local hospital that does detox. For all the psychiatric reasons listed here, it's a fine, utilitarian place to land (though never a lot of fun).

If your loved one needs to consider an inpatient stay for detoxification or psychiatric emergency, they (and you) should not necessarily expect to be treated with the utmost respect and TLC—it's most unfortunate, but substance users are typically viewed with some degree of suspicion and contempt in the modern inpatient hospital system. Tell your loved one to take a deep breath (or a hundred) and approach it as a medical procedure. It does not last long for most, and there's more choice and comfort on the other side, where it matters most.

Other Ways to Add Structure

As you get feedback from treatment providers about what might be helpful to your loved one, there are other strategies you should know about for
adding structure and safety to an outpatient level of service: medications,
drug testing, and sober companions.

Medication Strategies for Increasing Support

There are several medications available specifically for substance problems that can contribute to structure (we will revisit these in more detail
in the "pharmacotherapies" section).

   Antabuse (disulfiram) is a deterrent medication prescribed specifically for people abusing alcohol who desire to abstain. Unfortunately, its
long and storied history inflames sentiment among consumers and professionals. Leaving those flames aside, what is important here is that Antabuse, especially when taken in a supervised fashion, provides a degree of
safety and structure to the treatment of alcohol problems that effectively
increases the level of care without more treatment.

   Naltrexone is a medication (monthly injectable form called Vivitrol)
that blocks the effects of opioid drugs. Unlike Antabuse for alcohol, Naltrexone does not induce sickness; it blocks the euphoric effect (the fun
part) of taking opioids, thus removing the reason to use them. It is a
medication support for maintaining abstinence, improving treatment
retention, and preventing relapse.

Drug Testing/Blood Alcohol Level (BAL) Monitoring

Drug testing and Breathalyzer tests (for alcohol) increase structure and
safety. Drug testing may be performed by treatment providers, as well as
by family members with home testing kits (with a wide range of accuracy).
While testing can provide important feedback, consider the following if
you think it might be helpful for your loved one:

- The impact on relationships—Specifically, drug testing can cause
  people to feel "policed," putting family members in the position of
  monitoring, which can introduce conflict. On the other hand, you
  can frame it as a way to increase trust, and an ongoing opportunity to
  positively reinforce negative (drug-free) results.
- The accuracy of the test—Many substances are not picked up by tests,

especially more exotic drugs like "bath salts" or "spice," as well as many specific types of opioids and benzodiazepines.

Drug traces last for varying periods of time in urine and breath. Many substances are difficult to pick up. For example, alcohol lasts a very short period of time (usually less than twelve hours), while many other substances are detectable for only one to two days.

- Supervision of the test—There is no accuracy if the sample does not come from the person being tested! Substituting urine samples is fairly common, and the only way to prevent it definitively is by supervising the sample collection process. Nobody likes this, including the supervisor, and it raises the "policing" quotient, but if you need certainty, for example if safety is at stake, then supervision is the only way to legitimately go (and this is not something you should consider doing yourself, only through a lab or facility).

"Sober Companions" and "Recovery Coaches"

There has been a recent uptick in people providing these services as an option for supporting abstinence and ensuring safety for a person not in residential (inpatient) care. "Sober companions" are hired to accompany your loved one throughout her life as a friendly monitor of her positive direction and a wedge against negative behaviors. Sober companions are not police officers or enforcers of any sort; rather, they are often people in recovery themselves who work for themselves or an agency to provide these services. Companions can live with a person in her home for a period of time, providing round-the-clock support. Alternatively, companions may be present for a limited number of hours during a week, for key times of high risk like after work or special events. "Recovery coaches" typically provide less intensive coverage in terms of hours, with the goal of teaching day-to-day skills to help a person remain free from drugs, alcohol, and other self-harming actions or compulsive behaviors (sex, gambling). They can support a client through everyday challenges such as returning to school, work, and family life and help them establish healthier routines. We call them "on-the-ground" support. A qualified coach should have a certification from an International Coach Academy or a Recovery Coach Academy.

Clients have reported to us that these relationships have helped them stay on track, especially in the early days after Level III rehab treatment, when they may be feeling a bit shaky and uncertain about establishing their new routine. Companions and coaches can also serve as healthy role models for a sober life.

The downsides? Sober companion service can be expensive, as high as $1,500 a day or $250 an hour, and is an out-of-pocket expense not covered by health insurance. Clients who have sober companions hired for them might feel intruded upon and policed, which in turn can cause them to lose a sense of their own motivation for change. Last, to date there are no state regulations for this job title and the business is unregulated—we have heard reports of unprofessional conduct, where companions failed to provide the expected support, or conversely, where clients got more intrusive, threatening "support" than they wanted. Careful checking and referencing is a must, but a good sober companion can be very helpful early on.

Treatment Approaches

Separate from setting (where) and intensity (how often) is the *type* of treatment offered, or treatment approach. For example, one IOP may offer a treatment based on 12-step ideas, while another provides training in DBT (Dialectical Behavior Therapy) skills and approaches clients from a motivational perspective. While both may run five days a week, five hours a day, the content will be very different.

Does it matter? For a long period of time in mainstream American addiction treatment, when treatment was assumed to be only one thing, no one gave much thought to comparison. Researchers, however, have done the head-to-head comparisons now for forty years, and found that some approaches consistently outperform others. We describe some of the more strongly supported approaches.

Brief Interventions

This category does not involve therapy as we usually think of it, but more time-limited (one- or two- or four-time) interactions that can have a dramatic impact on the direction of a person's behavior. There's strong evidence that brief contacts such as SBIRT (Screening, Brief Intervention, and Referral to Treatment) do have an impact. These interventions typically take place in health care settings, such as in an emergency room, clinic, or doctor's office. Also in this category: brief assessment and feedback in a college setting (BASICS) and a two- to three-session protocol for adolescents, involving their parents, in school settings have been found to be effective in lowering alcohol and drug use.

The main components of a brief intervention are 1) a personalized assessment (pertaining to that specific person, not generic psycho-education), 2) feedback that is nonjudgmental, 3) clear options for taking action, emphasizing goals that the person feels he can actually achieve, 4) given in an overall empathic style. Brief can mean a ten-minute talk with a primary care doctor to discuss risks associated with drinking or smoking, or four meetings with a school therapist who knows about substance use. When they are nondogmatic, nonjudgmental, and empathic, brief interventions are highly effective.

Don't forget, most people get better without treatment. Brief interventions highlight the importance of understanding substance problems across a broad continuum. Your loved one's problems may be quite severe, or they may be "drinking a little too much." The treatment world has an unfortunate history of turning a blind eye to people with less serious problems, and waiting until (if) they melt down into the depths of dysfunction before helping. This split leaves many people out in the cold, when they could have a discussion or three that would change their entire trajectory. For many people, a brief intervention may be all they need for a shift in perspective that puts them on a new path.

Where to Find It

Brief interventions occur in a number of different settings, but the most likely provider for many people is their physician. (One of the most frequently cited reasons for stopping smoking is "My doctor told me to.") As you look for resources, you should include anyone who is in the position to have a conversation with your loved one about her use—school counselors, general practitioners, and employee assistance program counselors are all good candidates.

Motivational Approaches

Since the late 1970s, our understanding of the role of motivation in change has shifted both in addiction treatment and the larger arena of human psychology. Motivational approaches can help to motivate people in *any* treatment. In fact, brief interventions are in large part based on motivational concepts and strategies. Chapter 2 ("Motivation: Why Do People Change?") explains what motivational approaches are about.

Where to Find It

Most purely, in the clinical treatment approach called Motivational Interviewing (MI). A modified version of this approach, standardized to a few brief sessions, is also sometimes used in treatment programs, and is called MET, or Motivational Enhancement Therapy. Unfortunately, some programs have responded to the increasing interest in MI by saying that they do it, even if their clinical practices have not changed much. MI is not easily mastered, in part because, aside from the specific MI strategies and techniques, there is also a "spirit" to delivering MI that is difficult to teach. Look for a program where the staff has had substantial training in MI, including follow-up supervision. Another alternative is to seek out a private practitioner who has been trained in MI or, better yet, is a part of the Motivational Interviewing Network of Trainers (MINT).

Cognitive Behavioral Therapy (CBT)

CBT has been disseminated in the substance abuse treatment system more than motivational approaches. It has been around since the 1950s and is widely used in treatments for other disorders, including anxiety and depression. This approach encompasses a range of protocols, but, as the name implies, they all share the goal of helping people learn new ways of thinking and new behaviors. Treatment includes training in communication skills (both positive communication and assertiveness skills), relapse prevention skills (including drink-refusal skills, problem-solving skills, and relaxation and stress-reduction strategies), and cognitive strategies for dealing with negative self-talk, rumination, thoughts about substance use, and planning for the future. CBT can include practical matters such as job seeking and money management. It's a pragmatic therapy, with daily and weekly goal setting, homework assignments between appointments to practice new skills in real life, and a focus on solving problems. In CBT, homework is critical to success.

Community Reinforcement Approach (CRA)

This specific CBT-oriented therapy has perhaps the single largest research base of support for its effectiveness for substance problems. (Alas, in our field, the most effective treatments are the least well known, and CRA is a prime example.)

As you might guess from *reinforcement* in the name, CRA is based on the idea that people tend to participate in behaviors that are reinforced and pleasurable, and continue with behaviors to the extent they are reinforced. As you have learned, substances are reinforcing. CRA takes this simple premise and widens the circle of reinforcement, asking providers to help clients examine their life and surroundings for what they find enjoyable and sustaining—reinforcing—including family, friends, work, health, and so on. CRA leverages these systems (the community) to compete as reinforcers with substance use. People need reasons not to use substances, and CRA helps them fill their lives with reasons.

One of the benefits of 12-step involvement (if it fits an individual) is that it offers a positive community to join. People welcome you, encourage your hard work, ask you to run meetings, ask you for advice, and so on—all rewarding activities and experiences that compete with using substances. Conversely, we see people come out of rehab and fall immediately back into using, because they haven't developed a life to compete with substance use. It's hard work building that life, but it is the long-term strategy that will keep changes in place.

CRA uses CBT procedures, in a combination unique to CRA. Research evidence supports CRA across many types of substances, groups of people, and settings. As you might imagine (given that some of the early CRA developers expanded the ideas into CRAFT), CRA includes family as a powerful part of the recovery environment, and asks for your participation in your loved one's treatment.

Where to Find It

It may be hard to find in practice, especially in the private treatment system, but CRA has begun to show up in publicly funded programs (where government funding insists on proven treatments). There is also a substantial effort toward training in the adolescent version of CRA, called A-CRA. If you can't find CRA, look for other CBT approaches.

Behavioral Marital Therapy/Couple-Centered Treatments

BMT is a robustly supported approach that involves working with the couple (if there is one), as opposed to the patient alone, which is good news if it's a spouse or partner you're worried about. (If not, you can still take in the basic idea that *relationships impact substance use*.) BMT includes you as a primary participant who is crucial for change to occur. People hear marital therapy and think no holds barred, everything's on the table ("I finally get a chance to talk about that thing you did when we were in Mexico ten years ago"), but the behavioral bent of this approach makes it more contained and focused on present-day problems.

BMT is a short-term behavioral approach that can supplement other treatment. The couples treatment, which takes place in anywhere from six to twenty sessions, initially focuses on helping the loved one achieve abstinence while also reducing overall tension and conflict between the partners. Abstinence skills include standard CBT strategies such as substance-refusal skills and coping strategies for trigger situations.

Then therapy focuses on increasing pleasurable activities for the couple; improving communication, trust, and hopefulness; developing conflict resolution strategies; and discussing the ways partners will specifically support change. BMT may include supervised medications when appropriate, such as Antabuse (see below). The couple produces a contract in this process, to clarify what each person in the couple is agreeing to do.

BMT is the epitome of a behavioral approach: structured, with homework, including goal setting, tracking, and a focus on present and future events as opposed to reviewing the past.

Where to Find It

BMT is so specific that it's easy to identify a prospective provider who has been trained in it. To broaden your options for couples therapy, you can look for other well-researched couples approaches (e.g., Emotion-Focused Therapy, or EFT).

Pharmacotherapies

Medications can be a powerful component of treatment, especially in conjunction with a behavioral therapy program.

There are several important categories of medications, which correspond somewhat to the stage of treatment in which they are used: detoxification agents to manage withdrawal; long-term maintenance or "replacement" agents; craving reducers; or "blockers" against the effects of a substance (either by blocking their effects or causing sickness if the substance is used). These types of medications all come under the heading of addiction-specific medications.

Separately, your loved one may want to consider psychiatric medication for underlying issues (ADHD, depression, anxiety, paranoia, et cetera). This can be crucial to a person's ability to make long-term changes in his or her use of substances, as indicated by a thorough initial assessment.

Managing medically uncomfortable or dangerous physical withdrawal is the first order of business in certain situations. As well as saving lives, proper management of this stage can dramatically improve retention and success rates.

Here, we will cover only medications *approved* for use in addiction treatment, which as of this writing means only for alcohol, opioid, and nicotine use. To date, there are no medications approved for the variety of other drugs of abuse, including marijuana and cocaine, but researchers are working on it.

Medication is not a magic bullet. It is also not something outside of treatment, to be avoided, feared, or used as a last resort. It *is* a crutch, and that's a good thing: if your loved one had a broken leg, you wouldn't hide her crutches from her so she could learn to walk on her own. You would make sure she was never without her crutches, especially after the doctor has said the bone would reset badly if she tried to walk without them. For some substances, in some situations, it can be downright dangerous not to consider medication.

Medication Options in the Ongoing Treatment of Alcohol Use Disorders

Two medications help people to reduce or abstain from using alcohol. A third medication, acamprosate (Campral), was initially found to have anticraving effects but only in studies where subjects were abstinent. All three of these medications are FDA approved for the treatment of alcohol disorders:

Antabuse (disulfiram)—Antabuse interferes with alcohol metabolism, blocking its proper breakdown in the body. Once started (as a daily dose of at least 250mg), people will experience its effects for two to fourteen days after stopping, that is to "feel really sick" if they drink. Specifically, the person regularly taking a daily dose of Antabuse will quickly (five to fifteen minutes) experience a variety of unpleasant physical reactions upon starting to drink alcohol, which will worsen if he continues to drink: a racing or pounding heart, headache and nausea, and flushing, which increase if drinking continues. These symptoms kick in after just a small amount of alcohol, typically with the first drink, making the experience of drinking totally unpleasant and aversive.

A major problem with Antabuse is lack of compliance: people stop taking it (including "cheeking" it, spitting it out, or switching pills). In studies, Antabuse has been found to be very effective, especially in the early stages of treatment, but only when compliance is assured. The best way to ensure compliance is by administering the medication with supervision. Finding a person and place to supervise ingestion that don't make it feel like a prison scenario can be tricky, but it's important, in order to minimize resistance. Ideally, the person taking Antabuse recognizes its usefulness as a tool and agrees to supervision as a helping hand, but reaching that point may take discussion and a collaborative spirit.

Antabuse can be helpful later in the change process, too, when a person is mostly stable but anticipates some extraordinary, higher-risk circumstance where the urge to drink will be greater than usual. By taking Antabuse, the decision is done when the person takes the pill; case closed, not open to renegotiation later that day. Restarting Antabuse for five days would be a completely reasonable strategy at such times.

Antabuse has a number of substantial benefits, including:

- Reduction in family worry—By ensuring abstinence in a clear, verifiable way, Antabuse can help to lower the emotional temperature in the household, reduce suspicion, and reestablish trust.
- Reduction in "slips"—Especially early in the change process, when there are many new tools to grapple with, emotions to deal with, relationships to navigate, and behaviors to learn, people are particularly vulnerable to a return to using. Antabuse significantly reduces the likelihood of a slip and therefore increases the likelihood of practicing other skills for managing triggers (versus drinking), so that forward momentum develops.
- Reduction in agonizing daily decisions—In our experience, many people who start Antabuse immediately experience tremendous relief from obsessing throughout the day or night over whether they will drink or not. It's as though they flip a worry switch to off in the morning when they take their medication, and are not then troubled throughout the day, having already, definitively reaffirmed their decision to be abstinent.
- Increase in opportunities for positive reinforcement—Antabuse will help achieve sobriety. Achieving goals makes us feel more capable of achieving goals, especially if we've failed at those goals previously.

Naltrexone (Revia)—A fairly recent entry (approved in 1994) to the alcohol treatment medication scene, Naltrexone's targeted effect is to reduce the desire ("craving") to drink, as well as to reduce the amount consumed if drinking begins. Unlike Antabuse, Naltrexone has no adverse impact if one does start to drink, so in that way it does not discourage drinking, other than the hoped-for reduction in desire. Interestingly, this medication can also be used to achieve a goal of moderate drinking, as it has been shown empirically to reduce heavy drinking. This type of moderation goal, however, is typically not discussed in American treatment settings, where moderation goals are not well accepted. Studies have shown that this medication has greater effectiveness for men (specifically) with a paternal history of alcohol problems in their family.

From a motivational standpoint, the differences between these two medications are pronounced, as one presents a black-and-white barrier and decision to be totally abstinent, while the other offers a softer leading edge. People more readily accept the latter, but naltrexone is not necessarily the best path. The ultimate effectiveness of naltrexone is less dramatic, as it has been found to be effective with a relatively small percentage of people, whereas Antabuse almost always has the expected effect.

Medication Options in the Ongoing Treatment of Opioid Use Disorders
There are several medications approved for use with opioid users. These fall into two categories: 1) blocking the effects of opioids, and 2) replacing the abused opioid with a different, longer-acting opioid for maintenance on that medication. *Opioid replacement or maintenance therapy has a long and documented history of effectiveness and safety.* Opioid blocking medications, while basically safe, have been poorly received by the client community. We hope that the effectiveness profile of blockers changes with the advent of new, long-acting (one-month) injectable blockers (Vivitrol), but evidence is still being collected.

Blockers: Naltrexone/Vivitrol: This blocks opioid receptors (yes, the same naltrexone from the alcohol category, but used for opioids for an entirely different effect). Naltrexone is given daily and orally and therefore has compliance problems because people can simply stop taking the medication and get high within a couple of days. Vivitrol, an injectable form of naltrexone that blocks opioid receptors for one month, is showing promising results in improving compliance. This medication does not reduce cravings and as a result is less effective for many people who suffer from not-uncommon painful and protracted craving states.

Opioid Replacement Medications: Buprenorphine (Suboxone) and Methadone: These medications are themselves opioids, so the decision to begin their use is a decision to remain on an opioid, including being physically dependent on that opioid (stopping the medication would produce withdrawal). This may seem counterintuitive ("Aren't we trying to get him off drugs?"). However, evidence shows that people who have become physically dependent on opioids (whether heroin or prescription opioids like OxyContin, Percocet, and so on) have very poor track records of getting off and staying off them. The problem is not so much with getting off of opioids (detoxing)—which can be accomplished by completing a medically managed detox. The problem is *staying* off opioids. Opioid replacement medication is most effective when people stay on it for a more extended period of time (eight to twenty-four months), stabilizing at a dosage and using the time to stabilize their life in ways that support abstinence and positive change before they consider coming off the medication. Typically, coming off or tapering is then best accomplished over an extended period as well, a matter of months, not weeks.

People trying to overcome a physical dependence on opioids often experience prolonged craving states and relapse frequently. They are also at high risk of overdosing when they relapse, as the risk of overdose is higher after stopping for a period than it is with regular use, because tolerance is reduced. Maintenance opioid medication substantially reduces the risks involved with relapse in three ways: 1) by reducing cravings for opioids, 2) by reducing most of the high if there is a relapse, and 3) by buffering the brain against the possibility of inadvertent overdose in the event of a relapse.

The usual course of treatment for opioid dependence actually *increases* the risk of death by overdose: inpatient detox and inpatient rehab rarely include an opioid maintenance medication *or* an opioid blocker, while the evidence could not be more clear that both of these treatment options decrease the risk of death by overdose. The procedure of withdrawal from opioid use in detox or rehab is too short for most people and leaves them at their highest craving level and greatest vulnerability to overdose when they leave the safety of the inpatient setting.

A doctor can't prescribe methadone (another long-acting opioid maintenance medication) on an outpatient basis; you must enroll at a specially designated methadone dispensing clinic. For a multitude of historical reasons, methadone programs have often been underfunded, not well staffed, and not psychiatrically sophisticated, so personalized care is in short supply.

The advent of Suboxone/buprenorphine in this country in the early 2000s was a huge step forward; prescribed by a trained physician from her office (a week or more's worth at a time), Suboxone can be taken like any other medication. It is important that your loved one get a thorough assessment and think through his personal needs in deciding whether to go for maintenance, to detoxify completely from all opioids, or to use blockers. In any case, we urge you to support what works, and not give in to the pull of "getting him off of everything."

What's hard about this . . . "Isn't this just Suboxone abuse"? As outpatient providers, we have heard many people express concern about the abuse potential for opioid replacement medications like Suboxone, including those who have tried to manage it without any real medical support. These clients may have bounced between opioid use and Suboxone use without any real, consistent plan, trying to detox themselves and then relapsing back to use. We think that much of the ambivalence about using these medications effectively comes from the ambivalence clients are exposed to within the more traditional treatment systems. When they hear the message that they are "not really sober" or are "not in real recovery" if they are on these medications, it is natural for them to feel bad about taking them. As a result, clients often take a dose that is too low (and therefore ineffective) or take the medication for too short a time (and then are at risk for relapse). Bottom line: using maintenance medications in the treatment of opioid-dependent people decreases their level of risk.

Even beyond opioid maintenance medications, many settings still promote the concept that "a drug is a drug," and that any use of medications is just replacing one drug with another, including effective medications. This *philosophical* stance regarding medications may hide behind a seemingly more inclusive program description. More times than we care to remember, we have had the experience of inpatient programs promising to maintain clients on opioid maintenance therapy only to taper them off while still inpatients, leaving them in a very dangerous state of craving and maximal vulnerability to overdose immediately upon discharge. Likewise, it can be difficult to find a provider willing to discuss Antabuse or Vivitrol as a standard part of treatment. All we can say is, ask a lot of questions about whether medication might be a helpful part of treatment.

Where to Find It
We recommend starting with a physician who is certified and experienced in treating substance problems. This could be a nonpsychiatrist certified through the American Society of Addiction Medicine (ASAM), or a psychiatrist who has been board-certified in addiction psychiatry. To prescribe Suboxone, MDs must have completed a special eight-hour training.

Medication Options for Smoking Cessation
There are two categories of treatment for cigarette smoking approved by the FDA: over-the-counter nicotine replacement therapies (NRT) and prescription medications not containing nicotine (Chantix and Zyban). The four most highly recommended methods (in order) are: 1) a combination of more than one NRT option (patch and gum/inhaler/lozenge), 2) Chantix, 3) Chantix with single NRT, and 4) Zyban with single NRT. Treatment

length is typically at least ten weeks. People with substance abuse problems have higher rates of cigarette smoking and have historically been advised to address other substance problems first; yet we know that nicotine acts powerfully on the reward centers of the brain and that cigarette smoking is the single largest preventable cause of death worldwide. Evidence shows that if someone wants to quit smoking, they should be encouraged to do so regardless of their stage in addressing substance problems and should consider all the pharmacological support they need to be successful.

NRT: Available in gum, patches, lozenges, nasal spray, and oral inhaler, NRT is specifically designed to relieve withdrawal symptoms by providing some nicotine and slowly reducing the amount over time. It does not enter the lungs and is pure nicotine, so it has none of the carcinogens that cigarette smoke delivers. Because NRT does not give you a spike in nicotine like cigarettes do, you don't get the "high" sensation, which helps to prevent relapse. People were initially advised to discontinue their NRT if a lapse occurred, but more recent studies show that adverse effects are rare and that continuing NRT increases quit rates.

Prescription Medications: Chantix (varenicline) works on the areas of the brain that are affected by nicotine, which eases withdrawal and blocks the impact of nicotine from cigarettes. This can be a very effective medication, but some people experience aversive side effects, the most common being gastrointestinal problems, strange dreams, and depressed mood or irritability. Zyban (bupropion) affects the dopamine pathways of the brain and there is evidence of its relieving nicotine withdrawal symptoms.

Where to Find It

Most NRTs are available at drugstores, and prescription medications can be obtained from general practitioners or psychiatrists.

What Else Do You Need to Know?

Who is providing the treatment? MDs? Psychologists? Counselors? And what are their qualifications specifically for treating substance problems? In the United States, substance treatment evolved in a tradition of recovering people providing clinical care, with the premise that those who have been through it can help best. In fact, this has never been shown to matter in studies that have measured outcome differences based on the recovery status of the counselor. What has been demonstrated to matter is the treatment provider's ability to feel and show genuine empathy for another's situation and struggles.

An empathetic substance abuse counselor without advanced training and degrees may provide good treatment; what he won't likely have, though, is expertise in and experience with the additional mental health and medical issues that must be addressed in order for your loved one to succeed.

What is the provider's level of training in the approaches he or she uses? Some evidence-based approaches involve specialized training and supervision (e.g., CRA, CRAFT, Motivational Interviewing, and Dialectical Behavior Therapy) while others are available for professionals through manuals, and less so through certification trainings. You can inquire into a practitioner or a program's use of supervision after their training. Do the clinicians get follow-up supervision in that method? Do the supervisors get follow-up supervision in a particular method? Plenty of data indicates how difficult it is to train clinicians up to a level of competency in a new treatment approach. It helps to ask how much training they receive and how much ongoing supervision is given to keep them trained to a level of competency.

Is the provider or program capable of assessing and working with co-occurring disorders? If your loved one has other psychiatric or emotional issues, can the treatment provider identify the problem and work with it effectively? Co-occurring disorders are common. While prevalence rates depend on many factors, including the substances being used, gender, age, etcetera, across the board estimates are that 50 percent of people with substance use disorders also have other psychiatric disorders, most commonly depressive disorders, anxiety disorders, and personality disorders. It is not always clear what explains the link; it can be different for different people. Equally unclear is the course these co-occurring issues will take in response to treatment for substance problems. For many years, it was assumed that when a person stopped using substances, other problems would vanish. And sometimes that was true. And sometimes it wasn't. Sometimes they got worse. Following a thorough assessment, you'll need to know if the clinicians are trained to understand, assess, and treat these other issues.

For years, many treatment programs claimed to offer dual treatment, meaning they dealt with both substance and psychiatric problems as part of a comprehensive treatment. More often in practice however, clients would encounter a 12-step oriented program that provided the opportunity to talk to a psychiatrist once, or a psychiatric program that told clients to go to 12-step meetings. We are not being cynical; this is how it was, and it was not enough. Now you can find more integrated services in practice, but you still have to be careful. Tag-on services that are not really robust in their own right are not so helpful, and the more severe your loved one's co-occurring issues, the more this matters. Overlooking major psychiatric challenges can lead to years of no progress, frustration, ruined relationships, and hopelessness.

There is a high prevalence of trauma in the history of substance-abusing clients, including childhood trauma, sexual trauma, violence, accidents, and war trauma. A trauma history can be a complicated and insidious player, exacerbating erratic behaviors, apparent lack of motivation, an uneven route of progress, and self-destructiveness. It can also be difficult to treat. Sometimes there's a definitive diagnosis of post-traumatic stress disorder (PTSD), for which there are effective treatments, but in other cases more diffuse trauma symptoms cause a confusing clinical picture that can change over time. A comprehensive assessment can help discover if previous traumas are contributing to a person's engagement with substances or other compulsive behaviors, although many people do not disclose the extent of trauma until much later in treatment, after a trusting therapeutic relationship has formed.

What is the cost of the treatment? Treatment costs are widely variable, with the highest costs typically associated with treatments at the higher levels of care. Detox is often covered by health insurance as a medical procedure when it happens in a hospital setting. Some private settings, however, do not accept insurance and the fees are per day. Traditional twenty-eight-day inpatient residential programs (rehabs) vary tremendously, from $10,000 to $80,000 a month depending on the facility and staffing. You should know that many adjust their fees on a sliding scale, sometimes dramatically. It never hurts to ask! And be aware that health insurers have become more restrictive for this level of care. Most insurance companies would prefer to pay for intensive outpatient services, while many rehabs do not have the administrative support to manage insurance plan reimbursements.

Outpatient providers, who may or may not accept insurance reimbursement, typically offer sliding scale options. Ask what coverage is accepted by the facility and talk to your insurance company. Try to take a long view as you calculate the costs. We have had the painful experience of trying to help our clients get outpatient treatment after they have spent retirement and college funds (often in a panic) paying for inpatient and residential care. The reality is that some people need support for an extended period and often need additional specialized treatment for co-occurring problems—and remember, many people don't need inpatient care.

Do families/spouses have a role in the treatment? In our chapter "During Treatment," we will help you consider the role(s) you may want to play while your loved one is in treatment, as well as after that, but you should also know how a provider or program wants you to participate. Their recommendation can range from "This is his treatment, not yours; you need to let go" (not so helpful), to educating you about addiction issues (variably helpful), to active engagement in behavioral skill training and support for you (helpful). If the expectation is minimal, we recommend that you negotiate with them for more involvement or find another option. How much involvement your loved one wants from you, as well as how much you want to be involved, are both factors, and both can change over time.

Is abstinence the goal, or the only goal possible? (These questions are relevant only to outpatient care, because inpatient is focused solely on abstaining.)

How will a treatment provider handle your college kid who wants to drink moderately instead of bingeing, or your husband who wants to have a drink on special occasions but is giving up pot? How will they handle your sister who wants desperately to stop using cocaine but lapses occasionally? What does "harm reduction" or "moderation" mean? These are all important questions, and ones that certainly will come up in your loved one's mind as she enters treatment. Since people often begin treatment with ambivalence about their goals and with uncertainties about the future, you will want to watch out for treatment providers who cannot work effectively with a range of goals.

At first glance, people who struggle with substances enough that they seek treatment should consider the goal of total abstinence. But in fact it is more complicated than that for many. National research data indicates that a significant number of people change their substance use patterns in ways that have nothing to do with the traditional view in which complete abstinence is the only valid goal of treatment. In fact, one subgroup that qualified diagnostically as "alcohol dependent" (the most severe category) became unproblematic drinkers without treatment.

Harm Reduction means doing no harm to the person struggling (by refusing to let her engage in treatment), accepting her starting point and goals without insisting on yours, and making it easy to get help. In this way of thinking, the provider mandate of abstinence in order to start treatment is an unnecessary hurdle. For many people, it is a barrier to seeking help, for example for those who don't believe they can succeed at this goal or are not quite ready for it to be the goal even if they think it should be. Some might want this goal for one substance but not another. From a harm-reduction perspective, why scare these people away from getting help? Why not start where they want to start and go from there?

Does this mean the goal should *not* be abstinence? No. Different people have different goals. And people's goals change over time. Abstinence probably makes the most sense initially for many people, for any number of reasons including:

- experiencing thinking, feeling, and functioning without substances for a period of time to understand what that is like, which will often be a rewarding and reinforcing experience.
- feeling a sense of achievement and effectiveness in dealing with a problem that often makes people feel bad about themselves.
- making a decision about longer-term goals from a position of clear-headedness, uninfluenced by use or craving.

If a person has the goal to moderate his use of alcohol, it can be helpful to start with a clean slate and break from old habits (by learning new ones). Even the self-help organization Moderation Management (which gives guidelines and support to people who wish to moderate) suggests an initial period of abstinence before embarking on this path. CRA takes up this idea of a trial approach in the practice called "sobriety sampling," where therapist and client negotiate a window of time for abstinence (a week, a month, whatever they can agree on that seems doable). This works *with* ambivalence: get your feet wet, start to see that you can do this and don't have to "fail" again, see what it is like being abstinent. It's a fine way to start, and often leads to an ongoing recommitment to abstinence goals incrementally, avoiding the overwhelming prospect of changing forever.

In our own clinical experience, most people want to attempt abstinence and they just need encouragement and help to problem-solve their way to the goal. Others state that they want to moderate, yet when allowed to set their own goals and work them through, they often come to realize for themselves that moderation doesn't seem to be a viable path because they can't control their use to the extent that they want to. When they come to this decision voluntarily, it is a powerful choice, because it *is* a choice and *they* are choosing.

Some people really can moderate, though the data would suggest that the heavier, longer, and more consequential the use was initially, the less likely moderation will be successful. We do not consider it to be a laissez-faire setting. It is not a default option for people who do not want to deal with abstinence. We tell people all the time: true moderation is not easy to achieve. And in outpatient treatment, we encourage limits to how long people try moderation before rethinking their goal.

What is the relationship of self-help to treatment? Self-help and professionally provided treatment are really different buckets. If you are paying for and expecting treatment, a program's providers should be trained in evidence-based approaches, not just offering something that your loved one could get for free every day of the week outside. Self-help is helpful for some, and not for others, and there is somewhat limited evidence about a basis on which to judge who will benefit from it and who will not. We encourage our clients to get involved in self-help, based on evidence that it increases odds of reaching abstinence goals and maintaining change; and we help them to overcome their self-help fears of talking in groups, or hearing about "God," and urge them to give it a chance or three to see what they think.

We recommend self-help, most of which is 12-step based, not because it's the only thing that works but because at the very least it offers a new, nonusing social environment and is one of the only forums where adults can freely confide all the terrible and wonderful things they are thinking, feeling, and experiencing, and be accepted rather than judged. Some of our clients are profoundly changed by 12-step involvement.

At the same time, we know that for some, the pressure to join a 12-step group is painfully problematic. Without any intent to bash, and fully recognizing that individuals and groups vary, we list some of the issues that sometimes come up: a) the requirement to identify as an "addict" with a "disease," which can feel burdensome and even cultlike to some, b) the practice of counting abstinence days, which can make it feel intimidating to admit use, and demoralizing to start over, c) depending on the meeting, a certain negativity toward professional treatment (therapy or medications), d) overly intrusive sponsors who are directive and harsh in their involvement, and e) a sense of religiosity that turns some people off. Perhaps the most problematic 12-step tenet has little to do with actual 12-step concepts, and more to do with group psychology: the common perception that people are in denial if they are not interested in this approach. Many people have legitimate concerns or reasons for not wanting to be involved, but end up feeling burdened with the insecurity that they are not really doing it right if they are not attending meetings. We have seen family and friends also carry this burden, as many place great expectations on 12-step attendance and are confused and frightened when their loved one doesn't take to it.

Self-help, like treatment, works best when it suits the individual.

Group or individual therapy—can this be an individualized decision? Some people benefit more from group than individual therapy or vice versa. However, not all programs have the flexibility to individualize this preference in the treatment planning. Some programs are group only, with no individual therapy component, and some practitioners (usually those in private practice) have only individual therapy options. The level of care will influence the group-to-individual therapy ratio, since the usual way to intensify treatment is to add groups. Different people benefit from each or both together.

The Power of a Good Therapist

It's true that many people get better without treatment. It's also true that good therapy, based on a strong therapeutic alliance—the rapport between therapist and client and their ability to work together—helps change lives. The variables that contribute to therapeutic alliance have been studied in almost every type of therapy approach, and one thing is clear: no matter the approach, the alliance accounts for much of what works in therapy, including therapy for substance problems. What is it exactly? Trust, empathy and a positive, nonjudgmental attitude on the part of the therapist (and the relief from shame and humiliation that comes with that attitude); on the client's part, the freedom to make mistakes and still feel accepted, and feeling understood for who he truly is (not needing to hide, including hiding behaviors like substance use).

Secretly or explicitly, many families wish for treatment providers to be hard on their loved ones—to "get tough," bring her "in line," "not fall for his crap," and so on. But good therapy is not punishment, and if it feels that way, it's probably not helping your loved one, evidence-based or not. Encourage your loved one to expect the qualities of a good relationship in therapy: trust, empathy, a positive, nonjudgmental attitude, understanding, and freedom to make mistakes, and encourage her to look for another therapist if she doesn't find an alliance with the first person she tries.

Reading about treatment options may heighten your own sense of readiness for your loved one to get treatment, like a breath of fresh motivational air to *do something*. This may, in turn, increase your frustration if your loved one isn't ready for treatment. Remember, treatment isn't the be-all and end-all, and this book is filled with other things you can do. Start where you are, and meet others where they are. The next chapter will help you talk to your loved one about treatment in a way that he or she will be most likely to hear.

Exercises: Quality and Cost

Questions to Ask Treatment Providers

What is your approach? Is it motivational or behavioral? If so, can you tell me more about that? (Too many providers claim to offer whatever's in demand. Ask for more than a yes or no answer.)

Can you tell me about the training and licensure of you/your staff in this approach?

Do you have a psychiatrist on staff? What is your approach to underlying psychiatric issues?

Do you allow patients to take medications? If yes, what kinds, and are any prohibited?

Do you offer individual as well as group therapy?

Do you involve families in treatment? If so, how exactly?

Do you have a detoxification facility, and if so, who supervises it?

What happens if my loved one relapses?

How do you handle misconduct or rule violations?

How will I be informed of progress and concerns?

Do you do drug testing or other monitoring? Will I be informed of the results?

(For providers of higher levels of care:) What might an aftercare plan look like for my loved one?

Can I speak to others who have used your services?

Do you track outcome, and how do you know if your recommendations work out in the long run?

Questions to Ask Yourself and Your Insurance Provider

How much does treatment cost? Are there additional expenses that I should anticipate?

What will insurance cover? Does the treatment provider give me bills to submit or does the provider submit directly?

What other help might be available to pay for it?

CHAPTER 13.

Suggesting Treatment

You probably don't need convincing that treatment for your loved one would be helpful. Your loved one may be less clear. So, how do you get her to go? Happily, our answer—this chapter—is relatively short, because so much of what you've already done lays the groundwork for her to consider entering treatment. Remember: people are more likely to engage in treatment when they have a choice among treatment options, a rationale they agree with, and an intensity of treatment that matches their needs; when their obstacles are addressed and they participate in the decision.

Maybe you can't imagine your loved one ever being willing to talk about treatment, let alone go. Maybe you've talked about it but he has refused every time. Maybe he's gone to treatment and it didn't seem to work. This chapter will help you optimize the process of suggesting treatment. With your understanding of motivation and the skills you now have at your disposal for taking care of yourself, communicating, and influencing your loved one, you'll have a better chance of success than ever. This chapter will show you how to capitalize on the work you've already done to collaborate with your loved one.

Inviting Strategies That Work

Based on this collaborative foundation, there are proven strategies for eliciting your loved one's interest in getting help. Specifically, we'll elaborate on two major components of CRAFT you have learned: first, seeing things from her perspective—what motivates her, what barriers she perceives to treatment, what options make sense to her—and second, using positive communication—timing the conversation(s), planning what you will say, and, as always, rehearsing before you go live.

If you doubt that there's any approach to suggesting treatment that could work in your case, it should reassure you to remember that the studies evaluating the effectiveness of CRAFT *only* included people who were initially unwilling to enter treatment. In those studies, the treatment-refusing substance users decided to seek help after their family members had completed only five (on average) out of twelve CRAFT sessions. So, if your loved one is expressly unwilling, then he is precisely the person these strategies were designed to help.

Remember Motivation?

To prepare to invite your loved one into treatment, first brush up on the motivational principles in chapter 2. Motivation is enhanced by:

- Having a choice among options
- Having reasons that make sense for a particular choice
- Having a sense of competence about what you are doing
- Getting information without pressure
- Feeling acknowledged, understood, and accepted as you are
- Getting positive feedback for positive change

You'll recognize these factors in the following guidelines for suggesting treatment.

Helpful Guidelines for Suggesting Treatment

See it from your loved one's point of view. Her point of view may be the same as or very different from yours, but either way, the appeal of your invitation to treatment ultimately depends on why it might be important to *her*. What issues matter to her and how can you link these to her desire to change? If continuing a theater project she's involved in at school is important, the treatment options you suggest should reflect that. Perhaps he hasn't liked group therapy in the past, especially ones with "women talking about their feelings," but he would go for individual sessions with a male therapist. When you put your suggestion in terms that are meaningful to your loved one, he will more likely consider it.

Use your positive communication skills. If you haven't already started to put positive communication (see chapter 9) into practice, do! As strange as it may sound, you must (re)learn to talk, and suggesting treatment probably isn't the easiest place to practice with at first. Ideally, you'll have some fluency in positive communication (being positive, brief, specific, keeping a behavioral focus, labeling your feelings, offering understanding, taking partial responsibility, and offering to help) going into this particular discussion or series of discussions about treatment. Positive communication does not aim for everyone to be in agreement or like what they hear, but to increase receptivity and understanding, both of which are crucial when suggesting treatment to your loved one. The point is to lower defensiveness in conversation, so that everyone involved can hear each other, consider, and collaborate.

Consider past attempts. If you've already tried in one way or another to suggest treatment and he declined, take heart. Failed attempts are not reasons to believe it will never work, but clues to what could work better next time. The Communication Analysis exercise in chapter 9 (page 172) will help you examine what could go differently. You also know now that change takes time and practice. You can try to engage your loved one in the idea of treatment and if he declines, learn from the experience and try again.

Address barriers to treatment. Treatment location, cost, approach, schedule, how simpatico other people in the program are (if group treatment), and other such logistics not only contribute to people's initial willingness to say yes to treatment; when these issues are not adequately addressed, they are also common reasons people give for dropping out of treatment. You can't anticipate or ultimately remove every obstacle, but it is certainly worth brainstorming what might get in the way for your loved one and what could at least reduce the barriers. Is the AA meeting you found attended by young twentysomethings like your son or mostly retired sixtysomethings? Are the program's groups available at a convenient time for your mother-in-law to babysit or only at times when child care coverage will be problematic? If your loved one is afraid, what could you do to make it less scary? Validating obstacles to treatment as your loved one sees them will also help you address them as problems to be solved together rather than positions she has to defend.

Unfortunately, many geographical locations lack treatment options, and the only treatment option available may require sacrifices from your loved one and perhaps your whole family. For this reason, think carefully about what you can manage. Think creatively, but be realistic.

Use motivational hooks. You know what pushes your loved one's buttons and what catches his interest. Use this knowledge to plan what you will say and how you will say it. Make it easy for him to say yes. "I'm seeing someone who is helping me think about our marriage in a positive way. Maybe you'd like to come with me for a session?" This presentation probably would get a better reception, knowing as you do that he is worried about your marriage, as opposed to "You need to see someone about your drug problem."

Other hooks could include proposing a consultation (versus "starting treatment"); describing how he can choose what to address in therapy, including non-substance-related problems (perhaps he is motivated to get help for his depression but not his marijuana use), and viewing therapy as a path to obtaining something else that he values (if he gets help quitting marijuana, he could apply for that job he knows has a drug test up front).

Look for hooks in your Behavior Analysis from chapter 2 (pages 67–68) as well. When you considered negative consequences of your loved one's use, which ones did you asterisk because you thought he would agree? In the example we gave, Janie knew that both she and her husband, Oscar, worried about their finances. She also knew that Oscar was a "numbers guy" who would feel more comfortable talking about numbers than feelings. Janie did a little math in order to present treatment options to Oscar in terms of how much less they would cost than the money they currently spent on substances. (She included her own wine consumption as a gesture of taking partial responsibility.) She showed Oscar that weekly outpatient treatment could save them enough in a year to take a trip to Yosemite, where he had long wanted to go, and the option of less intensive, less expensive treatment was a revelation to him. He hadn't considered it because he hadn't known it existed.

Have treatment options (plural) ready. Because motivation fluctuates, it's helpful to do research and make contact with viable treatment facilities beforehand, in preparation to seize a good moment. This is why we preceded this chapter with the one on "Treatment Options."

When the moment comes, having more than one option will lessen pushback and increase the chances of forward movement. This changes the conversation from yes/no (where a single no can shut down the discussion) to a range of possibilities to consider. Of course, a person can still answer "none of the above," but a menu of options is harder to dismiss, invites participation, and promotes collaboration.

Timing matters. As with any positive communication, there will be better and worse opportunities to suggest treatment; if you figure these out now you can be ready for them when they occur (and resist the impulse to have the discussion when you'd better not). Some general pointers for timing the conversation:

- Don't suggest treatment when she is high or hungover. There's a greater chance at those times for irritability, guilt, reactivity, and instability.

- Look for *windows of opportunity*. These include times when your loved one is feeling particularly remorseful in the wake of a sub-stance-related crisis or when someone has said something to him about his use that has given him pause. Windows can happen at positive moments too, like when he expresses interest in your therapy or curiosity about changes he has seen in you—for example, if you started exercising or he noticed you seem calmer. At these times he may be more receptive to the idea of joining you, because he can see the upsides of making changes.
- Consider when and where your loved one tends to be the most approachable in general. If she gets irritable when she's hungry, talk to her after a meal. If she needs time to decompress after work, don't pounce on her when she walks in the door. If she is less guarded when you're in the car or walking the dog, plan your communication for then.
- Consider what else is going on in his life, so you can pick, say, a night of the week that isn't the night before he has a performance review with his boss. The more you can see it from his point of view, the better you'll anticipate timing that could work for or against your purpose.
- Don't displace something else she likes. No matter how strongly you feel that this subject is more important than something she wants to watch on TV, finding a time that doesn't conflict with something else she wants to do will avoid unnecessary antagonism and improve your chances of success.
- Don't forget your own windows. It matters when you are feeling calm, optimistic, warm, and balanced. When are you least likely to be inter-rupted? When are you most relaxed? When will there be time for both of you to speak *and* listen without feeling distracted or rushed? Have you gotten enough sleep?

Choose the right person to have the discussion. It may not be you. Typically, as the one reading this book, you will be the one to suggest getting help. Possibly, though, there is someone else your loved one tends to listen to, someone with whom he is less defensive. Consider family members, friends, and mentors, your family doctor, rabbi, or another trusted adviser. Does your son's uncle have a better relationship with him these days than you or your husband? Does your wife's best friend have her ear right now more than you? Use your imagination and try to leave your ego out of it.

However, consider how your loved one will react to someone else knowing he has a problem. If the person already has his or her own reasons to be concerned, all the better. If not, be careful how much you disclose about your loved one's problems. Sometimes people can be helpful without knowing all the details. If someone else agrees to do it and you feel comfortable asking, suggest that he read this chapter and chapter 9, "Positive Communication."

Be positive. Be careful not to present treatment as punishment. This is difficult when you're frustrated, fed up, and impatient for change, but treatment is not a bad consequence of behaving badly. It's an opportunity for change! Also take care not to convey reasons for treatment as criticism. Again, make sure your loved one agrees with the reasons you see for making changes; at the very least, note that while you think they are good reasons, you understand that they might not seem so to him. Positive communication will help you avoid these pitfalls.

Start small. As previously noted, the requirements for people with substance problems to declare readiness to quit forever and go to rehab and/or attend 12-step meetings have prevented *many* people from seeking help or even considering change. Similarly, anxious and upset family members often want to insist on a "program," though an individual therapist or medical doctor is a legitimate—and for some people more approachable—option. It's tempting to lock on to the hope that a certain type of treatment is "it," but it's more helpful to start where your loved one is willing to start.

You can make the idea of treatment easier to chew on by breaking it into bite-size pieces. A single consultation, no strings attached, for example. A "sobriety sampling" experiment rather than a vow to never use substances again. Help may well be more palatable as something to try for a period of time rather than an admission of overwhelming need. Small is a fine and often more feasible place to start.

Rehearse. Rehearse the words you want to use, the tone you know is most effective, and the validation you know you should remember to make about his fears. When people are nervous, they often speak faster, have an "edge" in their tone of voice, say too much, and forget things. When people are nervous but they have practiced, they radically improve the match between what they *want* to say and what they *do* say. You'll be nervous. Practice. You'd take the time to practice giving a speech or a toast, so why not for a discussion where you ask your loved one to change?

Have an exit plan. No matter how perfectly you deliver your lines, your loved one might still object. Planning how you will react if this happens can save the invitation from turning into an argument. If you have a plan for walking away before heavy conflict ensues, you will be in a better position to perhaps adjust your presentation and try again when another window of opportunity opens. Know your own "buttons" that could be pushed and cause an angry response on your part. The world won't stop turning if you get angry, but it won't help your loved one agree to treatment either. Try to foresee what she might say or do that could set you off and plan how you will walk away, calm yourself down, take a break, or otherwise reorient yourself to the path you want to be on.

You get more than one shot if you need it! You will feel more comfortable having an exit plan knowing you will be able to try again. You can step away when the wrong button gets pushed, or you're just not getting anywhere, and circle back. Take some time to analyze what happened, what didn't work well, what did work well, and how you might modify your discussion (timing, tone, what you forgot to mention, and so on). Be patient, and try again.

Here are some examples of what it might look like when you put it all together:

Example 1

Since those layoffs at your job, you seem to be drinking more on the weekends. I totally understand why you would want to forget about work, but you're forgetting about other things too. (Brief, specific understanding statement.) *It upsets me when we go out for dinner with friends and you don't remember the conversation later.* (Brief, specific feeling statement.) *Do you think there might be other ways to deal with the stress at work? Your sister was saying she likes her new therapist. Maybe her therapist could recommend someone?* (Offer to help.)

Example 2

Have you noticed we haven't been fighting as much lately? I've been doing some things to help me be in a better mood, and it's gotten me thinking about ways to make things better between us. (Brief, specific, partial responsibility.) *Can I show you this website I found that talks about science-based approaches to change?* (Brief, specific offer to help.) *It doesn't sound anything like that guy you talked to last year who told you that you have an incurable disease.* (Understanding in the form of acknowledging what the loved one experienced as unhelpful in the past.)

What's hard about this . . . You can only do what you can do. She might say no or ignore you or otherwise brush you off; you might be mistaken about a motivational hook; you might lose *your* temper. This is just one conversation. You will have another chance.

Sharise was a client of ours who felt so empowered by her first session with a CRAFT therapist that she went straight home and announced to her husband that she was taking care of herself, finally, and insisted he get treatment. She told him he was "arrogant" for not thinking a therapist could help. This turned into a four-day argument. While she had initially felt relieved to "get it off her chest," the fight made him more opposed to treatment than before.

Sharise worked with her therapist on how to reapproach her husband and suggest treatment in a way that he would be more likely to accept. She rehearsed how she could react in case he got defensive again, so as not to make it worse. She would be ready to hear no without getting angry and defensive. She knew he was under a lot of stress, but she thought his drinking was making it worse. She also knew that he assumed all therapists would sit silently and analyze him, which he thought was a waste of time. Given these hooks, she decided that the next time he launched into how stressed-out he was, she would say, *I know you're skeptical about therapy and also very busy* (validating). *But the therapist I spoke with sounded smart and funny* (not silent), *and she said some things about skills to manage stress and how that might help with your drinking* (stress management being his goal). *Would you agree to try just having a conversation with her?*

What about an Intervention?

While the evidence suggests that interventions do not successfully engage as many people in treatment as CRAFT, they can be useful in certain cases when your access and/or leverage are compromised, and your loved one is in real, imminent danger.

Johnson Institute Interventions

"JI" interventions are the typical TV intervention, in which family, friends, and colleagues are coached by a designated interventionist to approach someone they have determined to have a substance problem.

With this method, the meeting is a surprise to the person using substances. Usually each participant shares a prepared statement about why he or she believes the person needs help, citing incidents or problems they've witnessed. This is typically paired with appreciation for who that person could be or has been in the past. An ultimatum about starting treatment (usually immediately) is then issued, and the treatment is usually rehab.

There is no licensing body to determine what occurs in an intervention. Some states have a certification process for interventionists, but some interventionists are dramatic and confrontational, which we know undermines motivation (in both the short and long term). You need to be an informed consumer if you choose this route, and at least speak to references for or families who have worked with the interventionist. Try to find an experienced, kind, and nondramatic interventionist who will listen to the information you have about your loved one. You know your loved one best and you have information the interventionist should care to know. The interventionist should indicate that he understands it as a collaborative process.

ARISE Model Intervention

A more collaborative (and motivationally sensible) kind of intervention, called ARISE, invites the substance user to participate in the process from the start, and if he or she declines, it is with the understanding that the family will meet anyway. There's no secret. The ARISE approach treats the person with respect and invites his perspective. Its collaborative orientation lines up with evidence-based approaches. It also allows for a more traditional intervention as a last resort if nothing else succeeds, though in the research trials of ARISE interventions, a traditional intervention was almost never needed. While there is not enough good research to pronounce ARISE unequivocally an "evidence-based" approach, outcomes have been good with this method. Unfortunately, it is unclear whether the approach will catch on in the treatment community. What we can say is that it does integrate elements of the evidence-based motivational approaches we have described throughout this book.

We hear stories about interventions that were life-saving; we also hear people say they were left feeling traumatized and alienated by interventions. Both accounts are true. We appreciate the need for intervention at times, *and* we want to correct the misperception that it is the only way to get your loved one to change.

Give Yourself Some Credit

We applaud your patience, caring, and desire to help. We know that your heart is in your throat sometimes, and breaking at others. Yet here you are, trying to figure out how to talk to your loved one about entering treatment. We hope that he takes up your suggestion, connects with a professional, and pursues help further. We also hope that you won't despair if he doesn't. Success has many faces. Your conversation may not lead directly to treatment, but it may start your loved one thinking more seriously about treatment than he has before. Even if regular sessions do not follow an initial consultation, he might have taken something important from the meeting that sooner rather than later lands him on a path of change.

And if the conversation itself implodes, you know what to do: analyze what happened and plan how and when you will try again. You may need some time to feel sad, disappointed, or angry. Use your acceptance skills and take care of yourself. Change is often slower than anyone would like. As treatment providers, we're convinced of the potential for treatment to help in many cases, but at the same time we know the research shows that many, many people change eventually, without treatment. In any case, we—you, your loved one's friends and family and we treatment providers—can make a difference in how we invite people to change.

Exercise: Preparing to Suggest Treatment

Use this exercise to plan how you will invite your loved one to seek help.

1. Why might your loved one consider treatment? Write down at least one reason he might seek it.
2. When do you think your loved one would be most receptive to the idea of treatment? This could mean time of day, day of week, or time of month, and could accommodate his mood state—insofar as you can predict, what tends to put him in a good mood?—or physiological state such as being rested, fed, and not hungover.
3. What might make it easier for your loved one to say yes? If he has said no before, analyze that conversation and be as specific as you can about what didn't work and what, if anything, did.
4. Is there anyone in a better position than you to suggest treatment?
5. What treatment options will you suggest? Is someone ready to meet with your loved one more or less immediately after she says yes?
6. What will you say, exactly? Referring back to the elements of positive communication, write a script, including a plan B in the event that your loved one says no.
7. Approach someone you trust and ask him or her to role-play with you.

CHAPTER 14.

During Treatment

He's finally talking to someone about his drinking! It is a big moment and an important development. And yet, it is one paving stone on a long, wide path. Families often have an end goal of getting someone into treatment, but it is not the end of the road. Your work is not yet done. More hopefully: it's not the first piece of change you've witnessed, and it won't be the last. Treatment is part of the process, not the destination.

The strategic efforts you've made and the collaboration that got you here will continue to be part of the process. You can't do his treatment for him, but you don't have to stand on the sidelines feeling helpless. At this juncture, you probably feel some mix of emotions: fear, nervousness, excitement, hopefulness, and skepticism. And you will likely be worried and unsure: Is he really going to the sessions? Is the therapist ever going to ask what *you* think? Should you ask him about his treatment or leave him alone? What should you do if you see signs of use? As treatment continues, you will look back and see you didn't cross a finish line when he got into treatment. This chapter is about what the work for both of you can look like now.

The most important thing we can say about supporting your loved one's treatment can be summed up in five words: *keep doing what you're doing.* All of the skills you have worked on so far continue to apply now. They may apply *more* now, because now is the beginning of some new traction: you have help! And at this point your efforts may start to feel more rewarding for you, because his entry into formal treatment may well be part of a more serious commitment. So, stick with it.

Beyond what you are already doing, this chapter addresses specific issues that come up at this stage: dealing with your loved one's ambivalence, allowing for different paces of change, coping with relapse, keeping perspective on the trajectory of change ("Is treatment helping?"), recognizing positive change, reinforcing honesty, and managing your suspicions. Under the heading of "dealing with the system" we'll cover confidentiality,

247

information sharing, session involvement, defining goals (even if they will change), defining roles, and knowing when treatment is finished.

Understanding these aspects of the process can help you pace yourself and your expectations as you go, and recognize progress as it is happening.

Your involvement will be different if your loved one participates in inpatient treatment as opposed to outpatient. We will discuss both situations, although outpatient treatment is more common and longer term. We often tell clients heading off to rehab that it is the "easy part," because despite the disruption, expense, and fear of going away, rehab is usually a relief from the consuming struggle—using substances, hiding it from others, recovering from the effects, and trying to manage a life around all this. The advantage of outpatient therapy over inpatient is also the challenge or the "hard part": to integrate change into day-to-day life. Naturally, this includes the increased risk of lapses to old behavior, which can be frightening, especially for family members. We hope this chapter makes it less so for you.

Ambivalence Is the Nature of the Beast

We bring back the idea of "Stages of Change" here because it is a helpful reminder that change is not linear. And that applies to your loved one's time in treatment as well. People cycle back and forth in their "readiness" to change; between the different stages of contemplation, preparation, action, and maintenance, and it can be unsettling for friends and family when action and ambivalence mix. Remember, ambivalence is normal. If you can take it as something that happens *with* change rather than against it, it will be less upsetting for you.

Motivationally speaking, there are more and less helpful ways to respond to ambivalence. It's helpful to stay calm enough to use positive communication, to validate her feelings while you preserve consistent expectations for her behavior: "I understand you miss using. It sounds hard. Do you want to talk about it?" It's not so helpful to escalate into anxiety, which implies that you don't believe she can handle it, or to fight with it, since trying to talk her out of her feelings sets her up to defend them.

Nor should you try to make the ambivalence go away by removing whatever feels difficult about change. If she's upset by feedback she got from her therapy group members, for example, it doesn't follow that you should side with her desire to drop out of the group. It's important to distinguish between an expression of ambivalence and a plan of action. Hearing "I hated group today," you might understandably leap to fears that she will abandon treatment altogether, and return to a life of drug use. In her mind, she *could* be contemplating quitting therapy, or she might just feel angry and need to vent. If you remain calm, validate her feelings, and inquire supportively, you will more likely learn what's really going on.

Not only is ambivalence normal; it can be a good thing in that the willingness to express it to you is an act of honesty and a sign of trust. If your loved one's ambivalence is hard for you to hear, consider the alternative; she is struggling and you have no idea or, worse, she feels she has to lie about it. Ambivalence, when it is allowed out in the open, makes times of vulnerability more accessible to help. If she says she feels worse rather than better without using substances, that's an opportunity to problem-solve how she could improve her mood. When you identify a target (her low mood), you can work on it. If it stays hidden, she might return to use later because it was not addressed. Allowing for ambivalence will help you handle the next topic: her goals for treatment.

Defining Substance Goals

Beyond particular treatment goals—total abstinence or moderation; abstinence from some things and not others; stopping forever or for now—above all that, helping your loved one embrace his path is the most important and long-term goal.

You may have strong feelings about his goals, and the treatment program most likely has a position on them too. There is a common (and common-sense) equating of treatment with abstinence. It rings true because usually by the time someone shows up for treatment, or by the time you are motivated to pick up this book, the problem is serious. (We hope that with better information, people will seek help sooner.) Abstinence makes even more sense for inpatient treatment, where the severity of use that qualifies someone for admission is incompatible with non-abstinence goals.

What we are addressing here, however, is your role in helping your loved one own his goals, whatever they are. And here, we make two important distinctions: First, what is the most sensible goal? Second, what does he want to do? These don't always converge, and that's where you can help.

Many people come to treatment believing that they need to achieve abstinence from all substances. This is by far the most prevalent goal, and it is certainly the goal that has been researched the most as an outcome measure for treatment effectiveness studies. The problem, as we discussed in the previous section, is ambivalence. One of the few studies to look directly at nonabstinence goals addressed it beautifully. In the early 1970s, psychologists Mark and Linda Sobell published the results of a study on a treatment for alcohol abusers in which a key difference in the two treatment approaches was the *goal* of treatment. Patients were evaluated as potentially eligible for a moderation goal, and then randomly assigned to either an abstinence goal with "treatment as usual" (for example, group therapy or AA meetings), or a moderation goal and cognitive-behavioral procedures. The outcome? The group assigned to a moderation goal not only had a far superior outcome but also a much higher rate of *total abstinence*!

The Sobells' study helped change the way we understand the nature of goal selection and change. People most powerfully learn for themselves whether complete abstinence is necessary. We know from years of experience that even those clients with an abstinence goal often question whether they must be abstinent "forever." The best way to help people navigate these questions (and impulses) is to have them take ownership of the process and answer for themselves. Let them collect the data and interpret it.

You can help most by allowing this "figuring out," without rushing your loved one to conclusions he may not have reached. It's a tough position, given the anxiety you feel and hopefulness about change finally happening. Try to let him continue his process of sorting and deciding by supporting him in his forward movement (with positive reinforcement for nonusing behavior and natural consequences paving the way).

While abstinence is the understandable goal of inpatient care, your loved one may continue to express ambivalence. At every stage you can help by being as nonjudgmental as possible about his thoughts on the matter, offering your opinions and advice without the expectation that he must agree, understanding his perspective on his goals, and then getting behind him and helping him achieve them (to the extent he wants help).

Allowing for Different Paces of Change

When your loved one reaches a goal, it's tempting to move the goal post a little—or a lot—farther away. This is a fairly common (and problematic) dynamic: families start to see changes and they understandably want more. It's natural to think, *Now that she's not snorting all that heroin, she should be able to ace her classes like she used to and dump all those bad friends.* Many of these expectations are just not realistic early on. Consider what it takes: healing a brain from the impact of substances, developing new ways to manage feelings and triggers, *and* doing well in school *and* making a whole new set of friends. Give it time, pay careful attention to how she's actually doing (not how you wish she was doing), and use the advice of her treatment team. Do they think she's ready to return to school? Would it make sense to start with a partial course load? Does she seem to be managing her current responsibilities? Does she appear to have more time on her hands than seems healthy? The treatment team can help you sort out what is healthy, gradual healing, and what are inappropriate expectations for change.

Often, family members have been holding back their expectations for their loved one for so long while she was using substances that with a small opening toward change, the expectations come flooding back . . . ready or not. You're not expected to have no expectations, and in fact your expectations, when they are reasonable, can help to guide and inspire her. Her therapist, meanwhile, can help her cope with these expectations (or advise you that she's not ready).

It's also possible that your loved one is ready to take a next step but doesn't know how. She may need additional supports like job coaching, résumé writing, tutoring, and so on. Depending on how long people have used substances and how young they were when they started, they may have missed a lot of learning about how to get things done.

Charlie had ADHD and had required plenty of support from his parents to get through high school. His parents had gotten in the habit of checking his homework, getting him out of bed, and following up with teachers. Sometimes Charlie complained about his parents' "hyper-involvement," but mostly he had enjoyed school. Smoking pot with his friends on the weekends had worked well enough to tune his parents out. Charlie was excited to be in college on his own but getting himself up and managing his time proved problematic. Smoking pot helped him forget that he felt bad about sleeping through classes. He didn't worry too much; he just assumed things would get better when he started his second semester and stopped making "freshman mistakes." When his next term was no better, he became depressed and slept even more, and pretty much stopped going to class altogether.

That summer, Charlie agreed to outpatient treatment, which he attended regularly in the evenings after his job busing tables. Back at school the next year, he talked to a counselor once a week and his mood and attendance were much improved, but his parents couldn't stop worrying about "the drugs." They called him several times a day to see how he was doing and whether he needed their assistance. Charlie's counselor helped them see that his treatment was as much about learning how to live by himself—to plan his days, manage his time, do his laundry, and so on— as it was about his use of marijuana. Charlie's parents, meanwhile, had to learn new definitions of helping: believing in Charlie and giving him more room to help himself.

Dealing with Relapse

Relapse can be disastrous for some people, but for most people it is part of the process of learning how to live differently. It doesn't mean your loved one isn't making progress, and it doesn't mean he needs to go to rehab. It *could* mean either of those things, but it usually does not. For most friends and family members who naturally associate any return to old behaviors with the pain, frustration, fear, and anger of "before," the possibility and reality of relapse are scary. We hope that understanding that relapse is normal will make it less scary—enough that you won't perceive every slip as disastrous. This is for your sake, so that relapse is not more stressful than it has to be, and for your loved one's sake, because overreacting is not particularly useful to him.

It's not all in the eye of the beholder, however. Here are some objective measures: A relapse is less worrisome when a) it is contained within a relatively short period of time (e.g., one evening), b) the risk to his safety is low, and c) your loved one makes an effort to learn from it in treatment or some other setting, to understand why it happened and what he can do to make it less likely. It can be helpful to notice the overall trajectory and look for shorter lapses, more time in between, and less damage.

You can impact how your loved one deals with lapsing or relapsing. An important concept in relapse prevention is the abstinence violation effect (AVE), by which a person assigns stable ("This is who I am") and internal ("I'm weak"; "I have no willpower") meaning to a lapse. These assumptions lead to negative feelings like shame and hopelessness and may actually *increase* the chances of a lapse becoming a full-blown relapse. Internally this translates to "I've blown it, I might as well keep drinking." You may have these assumptions as well—"He obviously doesn't care" or "He's just a drunk, so this is to be expected." Conversely, if you (and your loved one) remain hopeful about the progress he has made, and understand the process to be step-by-step learning *that might include lapses,* he will be less likely to despair. If you're calm and nonaccusatory, he will be less likely to minimize and defend his return to old behavior, more likely to reflect on the event and share the process with you (or at least with his treatment program), and more likely to invite your help to resume new behaviors and stay on track. All the work you've done to avoid arguing, communicate positively, and reinforce positive behavior will support your involvement now.

Keep Perspective on the Trajectory of Change

If you drew a straight line from where your loved one started at the beginning of treatment to where she is now, does it generally point upward—even a tiny bit—or downward, or lie flat? Today could be a bad day relative to yesterday, or this week compared to three weeks ago, but if you can see the whole line and which way it's going, that is perspective. We wish we could bottle this one up and just give it to you, it is so important to the tenor of your relationship and to your own self-care. Perspective helps you stay calm in a momentary crisis; perspective helps you balance optimism and realism; and perspective will help you evaluate the significance of any given lapse.

"Where she's at" should include a wider range of behaviors than substance use, though the latter is obviously important. You can use the Relationship Happiness Scale (pages 143–44) or any of the tracking methods you have been using to help you reflect on the direction of change. Everything counts. How often did she drink before treatment started? How was she doing in other areas of her life before treatment? If in stepping back like this you see a lack of progress on the whole (which could be the case even if your loved one is abstinent), it may be time for a different plan. For example, if someone is sober but too anxious to leave the house, a psychiatric consultation could be in order. But if the slope points upward and she had a bad night of using for the first time in a month, maybe it's a bad night that she will learn from. Maybe the plan is fine.

Recognize and Reward Positive Change: Mastery

People in treatment for substance problems often feel that their friends and family don't understand how much work it is to get better. Recovering from a substance problem and learning a new way to live is hard. If your wife was learning to fly, you would admire her and praise her (and probably think it was cool). Changing substance use patterns can be as difficult as flying planes, and often takes longer to master. It deserves more than a bare minimum of credit for "just not screwing up." Your loved one may be able to do it anyway, but your acknowledgment and encouragement helps.

In one of our skills groups for people overcoming substance problems, an independent, athletic woman in her forties who was juggling the demands of her teaching position, dating, training a new puppy, and keeping up with her running schedule described phone conversations with her parents in California. Every time they talked, they had a way of asking, "How *are* you?" that they all knew really meant "Are you still not abusing pills?"—as if her whole life could be boiled down to that. She understood that they were worried and meant well, but she missed talking to her parents about other things and felt stuck in the position of "problem child" that was neither very interesting nor empowering. She would hang up feeling more discouraged than encouraged. As the woman spoke, the other group members nodded in recognition.

It is helpful to acknowledge the whole caboodle of changes your loved one is making. Along with "not drinking," he may also be trying not to be irritable in the mornings, as well as finding something to do after work that doesn't include his drinking friends, and going to two AA meetings a week where he doesn't feel entirely comfortable. Meanwhile, he might have problems with his boss at work, deep pride in his daughter's soccer playing, and would love to take a drive through the fall foliage this year. Let him know you see those things too. The more you can help him realize the richness of life, the more life he will have to compete with substances.

Managing Suspicion: How Much Supervision Is Enough?

Ongoing suspicion is toxic to relationships. The question is how to establish a balanced stance of observation without falling into suspicion, anticipating the worst at every turn. This balance is a matter of tone and context. You might decide (ideally, together with your loved one and/or her treatment team) that it will be helpful to do drug testing at home. You might decide (again, ideally together) that your loved one's taking Antabuse in front of you each morning will be a helpful structure. In either case, your approach could be suspicious, angry, punitive, and fearful, or collaborative, loving, and supportive—maybe even with a dose of humor.

Find the sweet spot of supervision in the context of your present situation, in proportion to your loved one's *current* behavior, and be prepared to adjust it as change continues. Has she been abstinent for six months but you still ask her if she's been drinking when she comes home twenty minutes late? That may reflect *your* emotional reality, but it doesn't match her behavior—your nervousness would be understandable, but it's not actually helpful to her.

Better to approach supervision as an opportunity to generate evidence of positive change. Then, when you do see change, you can take it as confirmation of what you already hope and believe she is capable of doing, and reward her with recognition and increased trust. Conversely, if she is changing in positive ways but you still treat her as flawed and failing, you will miss opportunities to reinforce progress, and inadvertently discourage change. Consider the continuum of risk involved, and where her behavior falls on it in different areas. What has she always (or for quite a while) done well and safely? You can leave those areas of competence and responsibility free from active oversight. It's common for people to lie and obfuscate about substance use and *not* about other things. Don't assume your loved one is lying about everything and needs supervision over every part of her life.

What's hard about this . . . For a family member who has witnessed terrible things, one day, week, or even one year of improvement on the part of your loved one may not be enough to erase the fear or expectation of a return to hell. The truth is that you may recall much more than she does about those dark days (her mind was altered, after all). Tracking can help you resist the pull of bad memories and outdated expectations and stay focused on the present. If her expectations for herself can change, so can yours.

Monitoring for Use

Drug and Breathalyzer tests are tools to assure you about the absence or presence of substances. It's up to you (and your loved one) to shed any draconian associations and conjure the motivational, collaborative spirit that makes these tools compatible with the other strategies in this book. It may help to broach the subject by identifying what might be in it for *him*. What's in it for *you* is clear: if the test is "negative" (no evidence of substances), you get reassurance and peace of mind. If the test is "positive" (evidence of substance use), this can be reassuring for you too, if it helps explain your observations. Many people find it more unsettling not knowing whether, for example, a loved one is hyper from normal excitement or from cocaine than knowing for sure that it is from cocaine. In fact, many people report feeling chronically unsettled and on guard from having suspicions with no way to know for sure. It is not good for them, and not good for their loved ones. Drug and Breathalyzer tests let you know.

What's in it for your loved one? In a collaborative approach to testing, your loved one gets to demonstrate positive behavior (to which you can attach rewards). And certainty is a relief for him too—that you know he has not been using. You can reassure him that in case of negative test results, you understand your job is to step back, manage your own anxiety, and refocus on what is going right.

One of our clients, Tony, had some big reasons not to drink. He had pancreatitis, and he could not see his kids if he had been drinking. In his mind, he knew he didn't want to drink. But his impulse to have alcohol could be so strong he would do it anyway if he thought nobody would find out. Tony was the first to say that Breathalyzers were helpful for him. He knew his therapist and others he had enlisted to monitor him could check at any time and see if he had been drinking. He knew he was going to be tested before he saw his kids. It helped him say no to his impulses, knowing that he would have to answer for them.

Testing can be helpful, but it is not foolproof. Breathalyzers can't be faked (as long as the person blows through the tube), but drug tests can be. Here are some guidelines to help keep testing on the up and up:

- Talk about it—Talk about testing as a way to provide consistent, reliable structure and affirm what is going well. There's nothing to be apologetic about, and it doesn't have to be a judgmental interaction: "I need to feel safe with how you are doing. It's been a struggle, and I understand it can be hard to tell me what's really going on sometimes. How about we take the personal judgment out of it and just do the tests, so I'm not guessing and you also know what to expect?"
- Talk about it, part 2—Use your validating skills to openly discuss his possible feelings of ambivalence, shame, and don't forget pride! Knowing he can talk with you about these feelings, he may have less reason to fake a test. Then it can be a tool for him, to increase trust in his relationship with you.
- Don't do random tests at home—That's what the parole department does, not you. Agree to a regular schedule, and test often enough that use would be detected if it occurred (two to three times a week).
- Understand the test—Know what it can and cannot detect. If your loved one is motivated to get around the test, she will certainly find out what it won't detect, so you should too.
- Our preference? Have a lab or treatment program do it—there's no

glory in testing at home. If it is more convenient or it works better between you, go for it. Otherwise, find a local testing facility or see if his treatment program will supervise testing. A lab typically requires a physician to write an order for the tests, which may add to the expense and logistics, but it may be worth it to keep the testing out of your relationship while you benefit from the results.

Drug or alcohol testing at home appeals most to people in two kinds of circumstances: 1) when they aren't using and want to have "proof," and 2) when they want to earn a privilege, and making you happy with a negative drug test can get them that privilege. If your son has gotten into intermittent trouble with OxyContin, for example, and he would like to use your car to go out somewhere with his friends, you could agree to lend him your car, contingent on a negative drug test before and after he drives. If your husband acting strangely is making you tense, a Breathalyzer could reassure you, and he would share the benefit of your being less suspicious and more relaxed.

Managing Relationships with Treatment Providers

While your loved one needs space to do her own treatment, ideally you will be involved in some way, since the evidence is clear that family involvement promotes change. When you're invited, showing up and participating with a loved one says, implicitly if not explicitly, that she doesn't have to do it alone. It demonstrates your investment in the process—you may have said how important it is to you before (even many times), but actions speak louder than words, and this is an opportunity for action. As your loved one enters treatment, ask her what kind of involvement she would like from you.

There are some limits to your participation, however. They are in place for good reasons, and you can work better with them when you know what they are. We strongly suggest taking time at the outset of treatment to define these therapist-family expectations, even though they can change over time. It's helpful to mark, initially, everyone's expectations for confidentiality, information sharing, your involvement in sessions, your role, treatment goals, monitoring, and when treatment will end.

Confidentiality

If your loved one is eighteen or older, she has the legal right to a confidential relationship with her therapist. This means that in order for her therapist to speak with you, your loved one must sign a release of information. A release can be unlimited, allowing the therapist to discuss all aspects of your loved one's care, or limited in some way. It is your loved one's choice. For example, she might approve your right to receive attendance and drug test results but not allow her therapist to share details of the content of her therapy sessions.

Your own therapist, if you have one, can help you think through different scenarios to identify what limits would work for you. Defining your involvement can be reassuring for you, and it provides "containment" for your loved one, that is, knowing you are in the loop to some defined extent can help her stay on course. In lieu of your own therapist, you could have regular (perhaps monthly or bimonthly) family sessions, to share your perceptions, hear your loved one's perspective, and understand what she is working on, even in a general way.

The frustrating thing about confidentiality limits for family members is that you may feel closed out of a system that has a direct impact on your life. Your loved one could choose to release nothing. And that is her right. Don't assume, however, that the therapist or program is encouraging this choice. Most providers prefer some access to family members, because they know that your involvement helps. In these situations, you can use positive communication to suggest to your loved one that she allow you some access to what is happening in her treatment, if only because you would be calmer with input to keep your speculation in check. If you support her treatment financially, we usually recommend that you ask for some access to information from the treatment program in exchange. If nothing else, getting reports about attendance helps cut down on missed sessions that you didn't even know were missed.

We can tell you that it is frustrating as a provider not to be able to include a family member at times. We may be working hard to get your loved one to be open with you. We may know that she is having a hard time while she refuses to ask for your support. But unless she expresses suicidal intent or risks harming another person or endangering a child, we cannot breach confidentiality, though we often wish we could. Some family members assume that treatment providers are uncooperative or have been swayed by their loved one's "BS," when the more likely problem is that they are bound by confidentiality. Try to keep in mind that our hands are often tied as much as yours. And we know it's painful.

One-Way Information Sharing

The therapeutic relationship depends, in part, on privacy. In our experience, most family members understand this and respect the boundaries of their loved one's relationship with his therapist. But what if you believe

d the sessions? Will you come in by yourself or with
e?

urpose of the session(s):
formation providing and treatment planning?
onal sessions that offer general information about addic-
ues in general (often done in rehabs)?
training (positive communication, self-care, and so on)?
king on issues with your loved one?
ill be the frequency of your attendance? Will it be ongoing
ement, or more sporadic check-ins and progress updates?

e gets a say in these issues: your loved one and his treatment
) will certainly have ideas about how your involvement should
red, and *you* have a voice in this too. We urge you to explore
e's understanding and preferences at the outset, and circle back
on the issue over time as well.

Treatment Ever End?

le struggles with substance use can last a long time, treatment doesn't
d to. Six to twelve months is typical for treatment focused on substance
oblems. Many people, however, do need ongoing support. Therapy for
nderlying emotional, psychiatric, or life management problems can go
n productively for (sometimes) years. Some people need less (remember, some don't need any treatment at all). In any case, timelines should
depend on 1) open communication with the treatment provider(s) about
progress, and 2) your loved one having developed a life outside of treatment that supports the positive changes she put in place. Before she leaves
treatment, you'll want to have seen real changes in her daily life, mood,
interests, support network, and her attitude toward substances. These are
the predictors that treatment can be safely tapered or ended.

When Your Loved One Enters Inpatient Treatment

Inpatient treatment is quite a different world. She may love it, she may
hate it, or she may have mixed feelings, but hopefully your loved one
will experience some of the benefits of this level of care: time for her
brain to be unaltered by substances, a period of rejuvenation in which
to (re)introduce healthy behaviors (non-substance-related activities
and interests, plus self-care such as sleep and regular, nutritious meals),

the therapist doesn't kn
What if you suspec
at risk in some wa\
could suggest that he
it with his therapist, or)
Your loved one, howevei,
with safety; his therapist n.
but nothing prevents you fro

Sharing information withou
wedge between you and your lov
therapist, but it might be worth it. .
ing an early warning about potentia
now that could become big if left unad
can often sense when things are going v
great deal more contact with your loved c
could possibly have—this makes you an ide

On the other hand, sometimes the most .
is learning to step out of your loved one's treat.
love is suffering, going in—even taking over—to
natural first response. Once he engages in his own
ever, family members must adjust to a less active role

Tracey was a nineteen-year-old who took a leave o.
lege after her first year due to cocaine problems and d(
was committed to her treatment and motivated to get
was less keen on living at home again and struggling in fro.
ents. The more they micromanaged her behavior, the worse
to function—lying on the couch playing video games, sleepin
the more she pushed them away. Tracey's therapist asked her pa
remember that Tracey was in treatment and working on her pro
with her providers. She encouraged them to "back up" out of the hy
active role that increasingly felt like a burden to them as well as to Trac
They brainstormed how to let reinforcers and natural consequences speak
for them, offering use of their car when she went three days without playing video games, and asking her to pay for therapy sessions she missed
from sleeping in.

Session Involvement

How much and what kind of direct therapy involvement family members
should have, in sessions with their loved one or alone, will be different for
every situation. There are a number of variables and options to consider.

260

1. Who will atte
your loved o
2. What is the
  a. Initial i
  b. Educati
    tion is
  c. Skills
  d. Wor
3. What
  invol

Everyor
provider(
be struct
everyon
around

Doe:

Wh
ne
pr
u

and more intensive psychotherapy to address potentially relevant issues such as trauma, relationship management, and other emotional and psychiatric problems. Whatever the therapeutic approach, inpatient treatment presents a unique opportunity for introspection and feedback from peers and therapists that is more intensive than most people ever have the opportunity to experience.

Rehab typically involves group therapy, psycho-education, and a consistent daily schedule of eating, exercise, therapy, and sleeping. Contact with the outside world is usually restricted—potentially no e-mail, no cell phone, and limited visitation. Depending on the program, someone may be in touch with you about your perspective on events leading to your loved one's choice to go to rehab, as well as her developmental, mental health, and relationship history. Many rehabs have a family week or weekend, and this may be one of the few times you will see or speak with your loved one during her stay.

While your loved one is away, you will likely feel a whole range of emotions: relief, anger, gratitude, fear, hopefulness, and a sense of freedom. If your loved one's struggles have seemed to dominate your life, it can be disorienting to see what it looks like without her presence. A month may sound like a long time when you are used to seeing someone every day, but after the initial shock of the departure, this time will go fast. Here are our suggestions for you during this period.

Rejuvenate yourself.
Hopefully, you have been practicing self-care for a while. To the extent that you have more free time in your day and/or space in your head, make some special plans to rejuvenate yourself. This might include time away yourself, a return to activities that give you something back (like working out, yoga, listening to music around the house, or taking walks), and spending time with other people, possibly including letting some people in on what you have been going through.

Often (despite our encouragement) it is difficult for family members to seek support and counseling to help deal with their own stress. This may be your chance to take those steps—perhaps talking to friends more, starting professional counseling, or finding a support group that feels right to you.

Monitor your expectations.
It's natural to think "He's in, problem solved, we're done," not simplistically, but because he is safe, the pressure is off, and you are hoping

against hope that he will come out in a different place. Remember, going to rehab is the easy part. The harder work comes with slugging it out in day-to-day life. You can be happy about this quality time away, but it is not a miracle cure, and a successful transition post-rehab requires careful planning.

Participate in the treatment if you are asked.

Many rehabs invite families in for a week or weekend, typically to educate you on the "disease of addiction" and counsel you on your role in the problem using concepts such as "codependency" and "enabling." While there is evidence that "education" alone is not particularly effective, we encourage you to go for the validating contact with other families, the relief of seeing firsthand that you're not alone, and the opportunity to learn from each other. Go because it communicates to your loved one that you support her and are on her side. Many people find these experiences revelatory and transformative, others find the information useful. You should feel free to ask questions in advance of going so that you know what to expect from the schedule of events, what will be expected of you, and what contact you can expect (or not) with your loved one.

You may not have much contact with your loved one, as most rehabs don't take this moment to do family therapy. What you also won't typically get (and this is the biggest lost opportunity) is much guidance on how to help when she returns home. We suggest that you ask for some phone sessions with whoever is involved in the aftercare planning, at least on a limited basis where you can stay in touch about progress, expectations, and plans.

Keep your loved one's communications in perspective.

While an inpatient, your loved one is likely to experience a range of feelings from hopefulness to despair. At the beginning, a jumble of emotions may emerge from the protracted withdrawal process (it takes awhile for the brain to settle down) along with fear of change. There will also be times when he feels painful emotions for the first time without substances to numb them out. And it may be a struggle just for him to be around other people, if he had become isolated or is full of shame. At these times your loved one may want to run a million miles away from rehab and you may get desperate phone calls asking you to help him leave. Such a call may push your "rescue" button. Or it may push your "he's full of crap and doesn't want to get better" button. Regardless of the button, you can use positive communication (and distress tolerance) to work your way through it. You can validate and hear him out to see if he calms down with your support. If he reports something that seems of real concern, you can offer to talk with the program. In any case, take care with these calls, as there is probably a lot more going on for your loved one than meets the ear.

Advocate that her current outpatient team (if there is one) or provider is involved.

Not therapeutically, just in terms of information exchange and planning. It is shocking how little treatment providers communicate with each other. Each new team thinks they have to start from scratch. If you have contributed to financing treatment, you can use that leverage to insist that they learn from each other. Many rehabs become "black boxes" that discourage outside therapist involvement (this is true of inpatient psychiatric units as well). This is a huge loss of information, so inasmuch as therapists can be encouraged to share, the better for your loved one (and the more bang for your buck). This applies to aftercare planning as well.

Push for legitimate aftercare planning.

You can push your loved one's outpatient team to be involved, or you can pursue the rehab's inpatient team to coordinate a plan. Ask them (or your loved one) to be sure a release of information is signed so that when the outpatient therapist or doctor calls the inpatient team, there is already a release in place. This way insight about your loved one and her care can be transferred. You can also ask that a discharge summary and any treatment reports (psychological testing, medical scans, etc.) be sent to the outpatient practitioners (again, with a release of information signed by your loved one while she is in treatment). This prevents unnecessary delays as signatures are faxed back and forth after the fact when your loved one is no longer in rehab.

All too often, aftercare planning is a mere afterthought right before discharge, and consists of recommendations to go to 12-step meetings, get a sponsor, and possibly not much else. This is not a legitimate aftercare plan. Your loved one can always go to self-help meetings; they're free and widely available, and may be what she chooses to do. But it is not professional care, and if she was struggling enough to need rehab, she probably would benefit from some professional care, whether a psychiatrist and medication evaluation, a therapist well trained in substance abuse, trauma, or specific mental health issues, or a more comprehensive program that does everything.

You can do the rehab's homework for them by understanding some of the outpatient options available in your area. Rehabs often have a list of people they are comfortable referring to, which may be for good reasons or may not be so good. You can research evidence-based providers in your community. It's a tall task, but worth trying. Three or four calls or ten or eleven Internet clicks may shed some light on resources.

Start thinking about your aftercare plan, not just theirs.
You *can still* help. Don't back off and hold your breath in hope and fear; your loved one does not need to be treated with kid gloves. Return to your helping strategies and keep doing what you were doing. Yes, he has his own responsibility to move forward, but he also needs the help. Your aftercare plan might be, "Who are you going to see in therapy and *how am I going to be involved*?"

Manage your financial reality.
Rehabs are not typically invested in helping you think through the financial reality of long-term support for your loved one beyond their doors. When you discuss aftercare (sober living, treatment options, extended care), you will typically be the one to voice concerns about your family's finances. Gather your facts and get advice. If, to support treatment, you tap into a nest egg, retirement or college fund, or other pools of money that were originally intended for other purposes, be careful to anticipate long-term as well as short-term needs.

After Rehab

With good planning, usually after an inpatient treatment for substance abuse a step-down treatment is recommended in the form of an "IOP" (intensive outpatient program). The rationale is to have a gradual change of treatment intensities. It may be, however, that your loved one is returning to a high level of structure in the form of, for example, work or school, in which case a lower-intensity program may be appropriate.

Whatever the intensity, however, your loved one is most vulnerable immediately after discharge. (As discussed in chapter 12, "Treatment Options," there are medications that can bridge the safety of inpatient care to the less structured setting of outpatient treatment—Suboxone, naltrexone, or Antabuse.) Rehab participants usually fall into one of two camps, either feeling positive and renewed, committed to abstinence, and invested in all the work they've done in rehab or (less frequently) relapse happens quickly upon discharge. Your loved one has likely been cautioned while in rehab that after discharge she may feel great and underestimate her need for help and support, and so should stick with the plan established for treatment while in rehab. Ambivalence is usually minimal when people leave rehab, because they feel the positive effects of being abstinent and they feel committed to change, having been involved in an intense communal process with most everyone pulling in the same direction. It's powerful stuff.

In 12-step lingo, this period of feeling good and downplaying risks for relapse is called the "pink cloud." The most helpful approach for those around someone during this phase is to affirm the value of her new insights, appreciate her effort, and help her create the new life that matches her positive outlook, by sharing in non-substance-related activities and joining in her optimism and joy regarding what is possible now. As the days and weeks go by, she will probably grow more accustomed to regular life. She'll be frustrated by the same things that frustrate everyone else, and she won't have the numbing/pleasure/relief agent that substances once were. As these challenges come more to bear and her outlook changes, try to be flexible in response.

Parents have described the return of a child from inpatient treatment as something akin to bringing her home as a newborn. Spouses and partners are naturally anxious about the transition too. You have good reason to feel on pins and needles, but it's no place for you to live, and not helpful for your loved one. Involve yourself in your own activities, in whatever positive activities you can arrange with your loved one, and involve yourself with others. Your loved one might struggle initially or she might not—try to adopt the long perspective and keep watching that trajectory.

Exercise: Issues During Treatment

1. Is there a particular scenario you are fearful about and would like to know how you would ideally respond (and how your loved one's therapist might respond)? It helps to think it through in advance. For instance, if you suspect that your loved one has used over the weekend, or you have noticed increasingly withdrawn behaviors . . . should you tell the therapist? Where are your dividing lines between something that's worth reporting to the therapist, something that's better to encourage your loved one to raise with the therapist, and something that should be noted and even monitored with your own tracking system, but not necessarily mentioned?

2. Plan for your ideal response to a lapse by your loved one. How would you ideally respond to a lapse to old behaviors in your loved one? How could you help foster a return to healthy behaviors? (Remember the potential abstinence violation effect for both yourself and him.) How would you use positive communication? What self-care efforts would be especially important at that time for you?

PART FOUR

Live Your Life

Glinda: You've always had the power to go back to Kansas.
Dorothy: I have?
Scarecrow: Then why didn't you tell her before?
Glinda: Because she wouldn't have believed me. She had to learn
    it for herself.
                                        —THE WIZARD OF OZ

CHAPTER 15.

Self-Care II:
Building a Life

You've Always Had the Power, Now You Have the Skills

If you're like our clients, you started this book under the assumption that you'll be happy when . . . your loved one goes into rehab, gets out of rehab, stops using, has been abstinent for some time. . . . By now, however, having seen some improvements resulting from her efforts to change along with your efforts to encourage her, we hope you're more receptive to the idea of thriving sooner rather than later, on your own terms. This chapter will help you synthesize skills from throughout this book in the service of building a better life for you.

The coping chapters aimed to help you develop awareness, acceptance, tolerance, and self-caring as well as some limits to prevent yourself from going over the edge. Now it's time to aim higher, to go beyond acceptance and distress tolerance to doing things that make you happy, things you may have put on hold when worry for your loved one consumed you. We hope now you can build on the resilience you have gained through coping with distress and paying attention to your basic needs. It is time for you to set goals for *your* life, independent of your relationship that is affected by substance problems.

Though it may not feel like it now, you have all the skills you need to thrive. You know how to carry on despite lapses and relapses. You can remember that ups, downs, and setbacks are normal, though not inevitable. In fact, as you develop other sources of happiness besides your loved one's sobriety, you're less likely to be knocked over by her struggles. And when you know how to set doable goals and solve problems, you don't have to fear so much what will happen next.

This chapter is structured like one big goal-setting and problem-solving exercise, framing subpar happiness levels as problems to be solved.

Your Happiness, Revisited

Take a minute to revisit the Happiness Scale in chapter 4 (pages 99–100). While it might not look like much, it's both a thermometer for now and a guide for how to proceed in (re)building your life. Just as the Behavior Analysis was your map for helping your loved one, the Happiness Scale can be your map to helping yourself. These exercises will help you develop awareness of what's missing in your own life that you would like to restore, with specific areas you would like to target.

This should be the fun part of helping (remember: helping yourself helps), except that family members often feel conflicted about having any fun themselves, as if it meant they were ditching their loved ones and responsibilities. Few people would argue that a balanced life is a bad idea, but when it comes to actually planning what you're going to do to feel better, you may feel guilty about pursuing happiness independent of your loved one. We hope that after all you have read, you can see that your health and happiness are neither superficial nor irrelevant; they are necessary. If you are stronger and lighter at heart, more confident, more relaxed, less depressed, and less angry, you will be better equipped to help directly. If you're not convinced that you deserve to be healthy and happy for your own sake, remember:

- Role models of good, healthy self-care might be in short supply elsewhere in your loved one's life. Attention to your own self-care can act as an example.
- People struggling with substance abuse often carry tremendous guilt about negatively impacting the lives of people they love and may use substances to numb this awareness. Your happiness can help alleviate that burden and allow your loved one to get on with the business of making changes for himself.
- If you have been labeled "the problem" by your loved one—for being angry, anxious, controlling, or smothering—taking care of yourself can help you keep these emotions and behaviors in check and prevent your loved one from looking at your problems more than his own.

You don't have to deny the problem at hand in order to take care of yourself and enjoy other parts of your life.

Blessings and Potential

Once you have a score for each area of your Happiness Scale, take a moment to consider that *it's normal to not be perfectly happy with every area of your life*. Next, note the areas about which you feel more happy than unhappy, that is, areas you scored 6 or higher. Take a moment now to appreciate this happiness. Count your blessings, but don't just count them; see if you can really *feel* the happiness in your heart. Too often, people let unhappiness in one area cancel out happiness in another.

Then, try to see low scores not as failings, but potential. Let them prompt you to act. Consider friends, family, counselors, spiritual advisers, and other potential sources of support. Consider therapy, where a comforting ear and helpful suggestions could make a difference. Perhaps you could use a break from "the problem," in the form of a vacation or personal day(s) off work. Some people need a more structural change in their relationship, like a temporary separation or sleeping in another room—painful actions to take, but sometimes warranted. Refer to the suggestions and exercises in chapter 6 to determine where your limits need to be and what you can do to protect them.

Your Goals

Pick an area of the scale that interests you. Perhaps it's something you've been meaning to get to or something you'd forgotten all about. It should be an area that could use improvement, but ideally where your happiness score is not too dauntingly low. The idea is to set yourself up to succeed with doable goals.

You may feel inspired to work on more than one area, but in the name of simplicity and achievability, we suggest you start with one for now. Hold those other thoughts, and come back to them later.

Good News: Limiting your goal to one area doesn't limit the effects. Improvement in one area often spills over to others: emotional life improves with sleep or exercise, sex life improves with communication, spiritual activities lead to friendship, and so on.

Some changes are easier to make than others, often depending on how immediate or delayed the rewards. Thriving eventually generates its own momentum—when something makes you happy, you want to keep it going. But it's not all tiptoeing through the tulips, especially in the early stages of making a change. Exercise is a classic example; it may not feel so good at first if you're out of shape. Even the more immediately rewarding activities, like coffee with a friend, or an afternoon catnap, may not come easily if you're not in the habit of doing them. You might sincerely wish to catch up with an old friend, but for that you would need to make time in your already strained schedule. And how are you supposed to nap if all you can do is worry?

So, when the goal is your own change, keep in mind that pessimism, distraction, and inertia will always be obstacles to some degree. You can treat each goal as a problem to be solved, according to the problem-solving steps you know from chapter 8:

1. Define your goal—just one, and make it doable.
2. Brainstorm possible solutions, the more the better.
3. Eliminate unwanted ideas, anything that on second thought you can't imagine yourself actually doing.
4. Select one potential solution that you *can* imagine yourself doing in the foreseeable future.
5. Anticipate possible obstacles.
6. Address each obstacle. (If you can't solve each obstacle, pick a new solution and go through the steps again.)
7. Give yourself the assignment. Decide exactly when and how you'll execute your solution. Then do it!
8. Evaluate the outcome. If you ran into unanticipated obstacles, address them and commit to trying again.

The Value of a Good Comeback

The only person you know better than your loved one is yourself, and awareness will help you see how you get in your own way of change. Many of our clients come to realize that their own thoughts can be one of the obstacles; thoughts like: "I'm too busy," "This is ridiculous," "I don't deserve this," or, "If I have any free time, I should do something 'productive.'" If any of this sounds familiar, try thinking of a really good comeback—to yourself.

Cognitive-behavioral strategies are not just for substance problems; they are among the most effective for dealing with anxiety and depression and for improving self-care. The cognitive parts of these strategies help people change their own judgmental or helpless thinking by working with thoughts as habits like other behavior patterns, to be replaced with healthier, less negative, and more constructive thoughts.

Notice a few of the thoughts that typically get in the way of doing something for yourself. How do you talk yourself out of it? Common ones we hear from clients include "I'll do it later" and "I probably won't like it." After you identify yours, consider alternative thoughts, or what comeback might feel most convincing to you. You might counter "I should do something 'productive'" with "I'll actually be more productive later if I take time for this now," or "I've allotted plenty of time for productivity—this is my time for rest," or "Productive schmucktive, this is important too!"—whatever would be most compelling to you in the moment when you encounter the obstacle thought.

Reinforcing yourself

As you problem-solve, try for a balance of shorter- and longer-term gratification in your range of solutions. Immediately enjoyable goals can even serve as rewards for the work you do toward a longer-term change. Going out to your favorite restaurant with your partner could be a relationship goal, for example, and it could double as a reward for finishing an assignment for a class you're taking. As with your reinforcement strategies for your loved one, your rewards for yourself should cover a range of time commitments and expense. What can you do at a moment's notice and what will take more planning and time to realize? What are some activities that are free or inexpensive? What would you like to do that costs more but would be worth it to your happiness? If you've been in caretaker mode, you may be rusty when it comes to fun for you. But, hopefully, brainstorming rewards for your loved one gave you some ideas. Now is the time to pay all that hard work forward, to yourself.

Take some time now to remember, or imagine, what it is that you like to do. What are activities you used to enjoy that you haven't done lately? Or it could be time to try something new. Asking yourself the following questions may stir up some possibilities.

When was the last time you . . .
read for pleasure?
spent time outdoors?
laughed?

went for a walk?

rode a bike?

went for a swim?

exercised some other way?

got a haircut?

shared a pleasant meal with family or friends?

ate at your favorite restaurant?

played an instrument?

reminisced with an old friend?

felt grateful?

felt pampered?

played a game?

played a sport?

took a road trip?

went camping?

enjoyed nature in some way?

traveled to another country?

had a vacation?

listened to music?

danced?

snuggled?

treated yourself?

had time to yourself?

cooked?

baked?

finished a project around the house?

smelled fresh-cut grass?

rewatched a favorite movie?

got in a boat?

meditated?

got dressed up?

made something from scratch?

learned something new?

helped something grow?

worked for a cause (other than your loved one!) that you believe in?

The point is not to whip yourself into frenzied distraction with too many activities, but to start to develop meaningful, pleasurable pursuits. You might have noticed that this list did *not* include "sat motionless while watching another rerun on TV." At certain times, this could be a much-needed escape, but take care not to confuse inactivity with relaxation or pleasure. If you're literally running around all day, being still may truly be the rest you need; but if you are running around in your thoughts and feelings, vegging out doesn't necessarily rejuvenate. Also not on the list is "took time to worry." Worrying is not problem solving, so worrying more will not better your chances of coming up with a creative solution. In fact, it may take you further away. If you worry when you try to take time out, find a way to distract or soothe yourself.

Coming Back to a Social Life

Social life—a special category of thriving represented in the Happiness Scale by "friendship," "family," "significant other," and "community,"— is particularly vulnerable to the stresses of substance or compulsive behavior problems, which can isolate the person using substances and those close to him. Typically people experience a shrinking social support network as the problem takes over. They may keep it a secret from other friends and family members for some time. Socializing with your loved one, who is perhaps often not in control, may feel embarrassing. Talking about the problem in social situations may not feel appropriate, but *not* talking about it and pretending everything's fine can be stressful too. For these and other reasons, you may have given up on your social life.

This inclination to withdraw, while understandable, is happening right when you need contact the most. You need people to talk to about your problems, and you need people to spend time with to get away from your problems—to distract you and make you laugh, recharge you, and remind you that nobody's life is perfect. We *cannot overstate* the importance of social support and enjoyment independent of the status of the substance problem you're dealing with. If you are low on happiness in any of the social areas in the scale, consider this a priority.

New activities in any area (or ones revived from the past) may organically lead to new sources of social support. You may find yourself making new friends as you volunteer, or start going to church again, or take a spinning class at your gym. Indeed, such activities could potentially be solutions to the problem of limited social support. But if you target one of the social areas for improvement and feel blocked by shyness or awkwardness, don't panic. Social anxieties are more common than people tend to acknowledge. It might help to set your goal around an existing friend or acquaintance rather than trying to make a brand new friend. You can also use positive communication to plan how you will reach out to someone, and practice in advance.

Don't be afraid to come right out and ask for help. The evidence from many areas of behavioral change (including substance use, exercise, and diet) shows that asking for help from others is associated with success in making and maintaining change. Yet some people feel ashamed or embarrassed to admit wanting attention and support. Others don't know what to ask for, or whom to ask. If you feel awkward, afraid, or reluctant for any reason to ask for help, remember this is a skill you can learn. The exercise at the end of this chapter will help you identify different kinds of help you may need and whom you could ask.

Mindful Awareness

Mindful awareness, or mindfulness, is not only helpful in times of crisis or intense distress; it also helps people thrive. At CMC, mindfulness is woven into everything we do. We teach mindfulness because it helps people achieve all three of our ACT goals (awareness, coping, and tolerating). It increases awareness. It is a coping skill. And it helps people improve their ability to tolerate the trials of change. We teach it to our clients and practice it ourselves. The more you practice mindfulness in everyday life, the better your mind can serve you in times of distress and point you toward happiness, because with mindfulness you can choose what you will attend to in any given moment.

Mindfulness can make the difference between actually enjoying the enjoyable activities you pursue and hardly registering any pleasure because you can't stop thinking about a problem. If you invest the effort in making changes to improve your life, we hope you will notice change when it comes and allow yourself to feel joy when it happens.

As scientific evidence has accumulated for the effectiveness of mindful awareness to improve outcomes for depression, pain, substance use problems and other afflictions, so have the resources and training options to help you develop this skill. We include some favorites on our website.

What If Things Don't Change Enough?

What if, after some period of time and some amount of effort, you feel things have not changed enough? What if you have worked hard to develop your empathy, patience, and understanding—and your loved one's behavior still pushes you over your limits? What if you are taking better care of yourself and still find you're falling apart? What if you have worked in earnest to change the way you communicate, reinforce the behavior you want, and not reinforce the behavior you don't want, to little avail? What if your loved one seems oblivious to every natural consequence you can stand to allow, as he careens toward ones you would never wish for him to experience?

First, we want to acknowledge how hard you've been trying. Then we want to encourage you to go back to chapter 6 and reassess your limits. You may need to consider more radical lines in the sand between you and your loved one, maybe for the time being, maybe for a very long time.

Though we are optimistic and cherish our work every day because people do get better, we also know that substance problems sometimes end marriages, break apart families, and cause monumental losses of financial, emotional, and physical well-being; for the person with the problem and everyone who cares about him or her. This is the heartbreaking reality: some people just don't change enough, or don't change fast enough, or don't change, period. Sometimes, all the evidence-based treatments and loving support systems in the world don't seem to touch them. Sometimes, for whatever painful internal, historical, genetic, lifestyle, or other reasons, a loved, cherished family member cannot or will not let himself be helped. Our hearts break for him, and for you if you happen to love someone like this.

Which brings us back to acceptance, a hard, sad valley to walk through in such cases. But this valley of acceptance is still the place—the only place—for letting go and starting on a new path. It may not be the path you hoped to walk, the one you bought this book for, and not the one we would wish for you, but we do want to support you in taking the path of reality. If you have reached your limits and need a break, short-term or long-term, in your relationship, we encourage you to focus on your own self-care and problem solving and to build a better life for yourself even if you decide that your life cannot include your loved one. If you've done your best, and can't do any more, we hope that you can go on treating yourself kindly and go forward with the care and support in your life that you deserve.

We wanted to write a book you can keep on your shelf in case you need to refer to it again, because on the one hand change takes time, and on the other hand, even if you separate, divorce, stop financial support, stop talking, or otherwise detach from your loved one, most likely your love will continue. In your life or in your heart or both, as long as you love her, she will be a part of your life and we hope this book will be helpful to you for as long as you need help.

This Is Not the End

Substance problems *can* end. Books *must* end. Change, however, goes on, especially when you know how to keep it going—as now you do—and the skills and understanding in this book are for life. Which is a good thing, because nobody, not even the experts, knows how long it will take.

If you started this book with problems that you just wanted to be over and at this point all your problems aren't quite gone, we hope at least to leave you with more reasons to keep going. We hope that if you can't close the book and say that's the end of that, you nonetheless have a better idea of what you *can do* than when you started: knowledge to hold onto, skills to keep practicing, and strategies that will keep helping you and your loved one in any and every stage of change. We hope you found sources of calm to keep tapping into, and optimism to keep on keeping on.

We started the book with ten principles. We hope the rest of the book helped you apply the principles to your unique situation, and your reasons for optimism deepened in the process. Consider how much you may have changed since you first read these principles and what they mean to you now: You *can* help. Helping yourself helps. Your loved one isn't crazy. The world isn't black-and-white. Labels do more harm than good. Different people need different options. Treatment isn't the be-all and end-all. Ambivalence is normal. People can be helped at any time. Life is a series of experiments.

Remember, your optimism helps change happen; sure-footed, grounded optimism. We've shown you the ground. You have our optimism. We hope that your optimism will grow in you from here and more change in your life will follow.

Exercise: Asking for Help

This exercise will help you identify the kinds of help you need and whom you can get it from. Keep in mind that certain people may be helpful in some ways and not others. Be specific!

Ways of Helping	Who Can Help
Distracting you during tough periods	_____
Tolerating you when you are irritable or down	_____
Openly appreciating you	_____
Spending time with you during difficult moments or hard days	_____
Letting you complain	_____
Respecting your needs	_____
Doing activities with you	_____
Giving you perspective	_____
Cheering you up	_____
Other:	_____

Pick one person to ask for help using the positive communication guidelines. If you are still reluctant to ask after you have planned what you will say, why do you think that is? Sometimes it's enough just to be aware of your uneasiness and give yourself permission to go ahead anyway. Or you may be able to take steps to minimize your anxiety, such as calling instead of asking in person. If you identify an obstacle to asking that you don't know how to address, you might consider asking someone else.

Exercise: Mindfulness

You can practice mindfulness anytime. The literature overflows with specific exercises and examples, but the basic instruction is to pay nonjudgmental attention to what you're doing when you're doing it. Your mind will wander, or sprint, to other thoughts; it's what human minds evolved to do. It may cover great (or more often not-so-great) distances before you notice that your mind is gone and you're lost in thought, but as soon as you do notice, gently but firmly—as nonjudgmentally as possible—bring your attention back to what you are doing. You don't have to "meditate" to practice being mindful—just try to do One Thing: to practice mindfulness of eating breakfast, close your laptop, don't try to have a conversation, just eat. To be mindful of walking, take the earphones out of your ears and just walk. If you want to be mindful of music, don't relegate it to the background of something else . . . just listen.

Exercise: You Are Here, Continued

In chapter 4, we asked, "How are you?" and offered some tools for building awareness.

How are you now?

It's important to keep asking. We leave you with this question, and this exercise to help you assess how you're doing in all the areas we've covered in this book.

Motivation/Energy Level

1. How motivated are you feeling about doing the work (learning strategies, increasing your understanding, etc.) needed to help your loved one and change your situation?

   1   -   2   -   3   -   4   -   5
   Not motivated   Very motivated

2. How much emotional/mental energy do you have available?

   1   -   2   -   3   -   4   -   5
   Little energy available   A lot of energy available

3. How much physical energy do you have available?

   1   -   2   -   3   -   4   -   5
   Little energy available   A lot of energy available

Optimism

4. How optimistic do you feel about your loved one making positive changes?

   1   -   2   -   3   -   4   -   5
   Very pessimistic   Very optimistic

5. How optimistic do you feel about your relationship improving with your loved one?

   1   -   2   -   3   -   4   -   5
   Very pessimistic   Very optimistic

6. How optimistic do you feel about your life starting to feel better day-by-day?

1	-	2	-	3	-	4	-	5
Very pessimistic						Very optimistic		

Self-Care

7. How are you sleeping?

1	-	2	-	3	-	4	-	5
Poorly								Well

8. How are you eating?

1	-	2	-	3	-	4	-	5
Poorly								Well

9. How frequently are you engaging in exercise?

1	-	2	-	3	-	4	-	5
Not often						Very often		

10. How involved are you with your interests and/or hobbies?

1	-	2	-	3	-	4	-	5
Not involved						Very involved		

11. How involved with/supported by outside friendships/relationships are you?

1		2	-	3	-	4	-	5
Not involved						Very involved		

12. When you consider your life as a whole (relationships, work, responsibilities, emotional life, etc.), how well balanced do these areas feel?

1	-	2	-	3	-	4	-	5
Very imbalanced						Very well balanced		

13. How much do you feel your actions and behaviors match your values?

1	-	2	-	3	-	4	-	5
Not at all							Completely	

Emotional State

14. What is the level of anger you feel in relation to your loved one?

1	-	2	-	3	-	4	-	5
Very angry							Not angry	

15. What is the level of worry/fearfulness you feel in relation to your loved one?

1   -   2   -   3   -   4   -   5
Very worried   Not worried

16. When you have negative feelings (anger, fear, hostility, resentment), how constructively are you managing these feelings?

1   -   2   -   3   -   4   -   5
Very destructively   Very constructively

17. How emotionally "resilient" (able to roll with difficulties rather than getting "stuck" in negative emotional states) do you feel?

1   -   2   -   3   -   4   -   5
Not resilient   Very resilient

Use of CRAFT Skills

18. Do you have clear goals for improving your own physical/emotional well-being?

1   -   2   -   3   -   4   -   5
Not at all clear   Very clear

19. Do you have clear goals for positive behaviors you want to see more of in your loved one?

1   -   2   -   3   -   4   -   5
No goals/very vague   Clear goals

20. Do you have clear responses/ideas for positively reinforcing your loved one's positive behaviors?

1   -   2   -   3   -   4   -   5
Not at all clear   Very clear

21. Are you aware of some natural consequences that could result from your loved one's behavior?

1   -   2   -   3   -   4   -   5
Not aware   Very aware of several

22. How able do you feel to allow those natural consequences?

1   -   2   -   3   -   4   -   5
Not able at all   Quite able to allow

24. How positive is your communication with your loved one?

1   -   2   -   3   -   4   -   5
Not positive/mostly negative   Quite positive

25. Do you understand (e.g., from the Behavior Analysis) the reasons your loved one uses substances?

    1   -   2   -   3   -   4   -   5
    Not at all   A good deal

26. How much do you feel like you've been practicing the new strategies of CRAFT?

    1   -   2   -   3   -   4   -   5
    Not at all   A lot

Key

First, know that just taking the time to ask yourself these questions will increase your awareness and insight! Then, examine your scores for each section, as well as overall. Lower scores indicate more of a struggle for you, while higher scores indicate you are actively engaged in change, both for your loved one and yourself (possible totals range from 26 to 130).

Motivation/Energy Level: The lower your score in this section, the less energy you feel, indicating less interest in or capacity for learning, planning, practicing, and problem solving. In this case, it is wise to attend to caring for yourself and improving the moment. What could you do to lower your stress and up your energy reserves? Start with the basics: sleep, nutrition, affection, exercise.

Optimism: This is one of the most useful areas to track, since a consistently pessimistic view (lower scores) over time suggests something significant needs to change; whereas overall increasing optimism (higher scores), while it may include blips of pessimism, indicates that you are on a path of improvement.

Self-Care: This section provides a snapshot of how well your needs are being cared for. The specific items can direct you to areas in need of attention as well as areas you can take a moment to appreciate because your needs are being fulfilled.

Emotional State: This section spotlights prominent negative emotions (anger, worry, anxiety) that may feature in your day-to-day life. Low scores suggest you're running low on emotional resilience, and you might want to pay more attention to self-care or positive communication.

Use of CRAFT Skills: This section focuses on your attention to some of the basic skills of CRAFT, including self-care, communication, and positive reinforcement. Higher scores indicate you have either been working hard to integrate the CRAFT skills into your life or they come naturally to you already!

Acknowledgments

We shouldn't be surprised; everything we know about motivation and change applied to writing this book: the time, effort, and uncertainties, the learning, the joy, and especially the support of family, friends, colleagues, and clients. We're grateful for this community of people who, among their many other contributions, reinforced our conviction that it was worth it.

Thank you to our own loving, supportive families for their unflagging encouragement and patience while we devoted so much love and every free second to this book: Elisabeth, Ben, and Julia; Will, Bruce, and Jonny Bill; Peter, Anna, and Zoe; Ted, Jules, Tim, and Arlene. We look forward to making up lost weekends with you!

To Linda Loewenthal at the David Black Agency for her business and editorial savvy, and for being our sincere champion very early (when we needed it most) and often. Nice pitch! And credit to her assistant, Carrie Lee, for helping Linda do all of the above and more.

To our editor, Shannon Welch, for taking a big swing at it. Thanks to her, we had the talents and care of John Glynn, Gwyneth Stansfield, Benjamin Holmes, Roz Lippel, Kara Watson, Nan Graham, and their colleagues at Scribner going for us—including a handsome cover design by Tal Goretsky that was easy for the four of us to agree on. Also, thanks to Shannon, it's a better book. We can hardly believe we once considered self-publishing.

To our colleague Bob Meyers, without whom there would be no such thing as CRAFT to help families in such a respectful, loving way. To Jane Smith, who helped Bob put CRAFT into writing and training, so that we could all learn it. To Bill Miller and Alan Marlatt for turning on a light in the addiction treatment world that is still burning bright, and all the other fearless and dedicated researchers who put the evidence in "evidence-based" every day in their pursuit of "what works." To Tom Hedrick and his excellent crew at The Partnership at Drugfree.org for their invaluable encouragement, input, and, well, partnership. And to every clinician in the field who values science and kindness as much as we do—in particular John Mariani at Columbia (who, as an addiction psychiatrist, researcher, reader of part of our manuscript, and friend, exemplifies these values as much as is humanly possible).

We especially cherish our extraordinary team at CMC, who have been front-seat drivers on the road to helping people get better. That collaboration has taught us how to pass on what we know about helping others in this book. We thank you for the skill and professionalism that you bring to CMC, no matter what else is going on in the world (and there is always something!).

To our clients and their families, who inspire us and teach us with their courage and perseverance.

Finally, we thank everyone who has wanted to help someone. You are the reason we wrote this book and the reason our field needs to keep changing and accepting new ways to help you.

Appendix:
When Is It an Emergency?

While we cannot tell you from the pages of a book whether you have an emergency on your hands, we can help you assess the risks. There is *always* some risk in using substances, and many variables that increase the risk. Bad things can and sometimes do happen. But living in a constant state of emergency because of this potential will compromise your ability to deal with difficulties as they come along. Eventually, the stress of it will crush you. Most situations are not emergencies; some are. Keeping a calm, rational perspective is challenging in the face of fear, but it's the safest, most helpful basis for action in *and* out of a crisis.

The following questions are designed to help you consider factors that are known to increase the danger for any person using substances. This is a starting place. You don't have to and shouldn't try to do this alone, and there's no substitute for a thorough assessment by a qualified professional. Start with what you know right now. (You can find out more about any of these risk factors from the resources that follow and many more online.) A YES answer indicates increased risk.

Risks Associated with the Type of Substance(s) or Method of Use
- YES/NO—Is s/he using a risky combination of substances (e.g., two substances that exacerbate each other's effects, such as alcohol and benzodiazepines or opiates)?
- YES/NO—Is s/he using intravenously (with needle or IV)?
- YES/NO—a) Is s/he using on a daily basis that might indicate physical dependence? (Common substances on which one can become physically dependent include alcohol, benzodiazepines, and opiates.) AND . . .

- **YES/NO**—b) Is the substance on which s/he is physically dependent one that is dangerous to stop without medical assistance (most common: alcohol and benzodiazepines)? AND . . .
- **YES/NO**—c) Has s/he recently detoxed from (withdrawn from or stopped taking) a substance on which s/he was dependent? Specifically, has s/he detoxed from opiates without beginning a blocking or replacement medication like naltrexone, buprenorphine (Suboxone), or methadone (making her/him more vulnerable to overdose in case of relapse)?
- **YES/NO**—Does use involve or lead to dangerous behaviors (e.g., unsafe sex, buying drugs in a dangerous area, driving under the influence, getting in fights, neglecting children)?
- **YES/NO**—Is the current behavior new or a recent escalation (as opposed to behavior that may be frightening, but has been stable/consistent for a long time)?
- **YES/NO**—Does s/he have a history of overdose?

Risks Associated with Psychiatric/Emotional Difficulties

- **YES/NO**—Does s/he currently have a psychiatric condition (e.g., depression, bipolar disorder, anxiety disorder, PTSD) that could be dangerously exacerbated by substance use?
- **YES/NO**—Does s/he have a history of psychiatric hospitalization, whether or not in combination with substance use?
- **YES/NO**—Does s/he have a history of self-injurious behavior or acting on suicidal thoughts?
- **YES/NO**—Does s/he have a history of trauma (physical, sexual, neglect) and subsequent emotional difficulties (PTSD, avoidance and withdrawal, excessive fear, and anxiety symptoms)?
- **YES/NO**—Does his/her family have a history of psychiatric problems and/or suicidal behaviors?

Risks Associated with Social Support and Interpersonal Relations

- **YES/NO**—Is s/he isolated (socially or physically)?
- **YES/NO**—Is s/he part of a risky social group? (This has less to do with whether you like his/her friends than about whether they support his/her ongoing substance use, criminality, or other antisocial behavior, and/or discourage positive change.)
- **YES/NO**—Does s/he have a history of violent behavior toward others (e.g., domestic violence, child abuse, bar fights)?

Further Reading

Get Your Loved One Sober: Alternatives to Nagging, Pleading and Threatening. Robert J. Meyers, PhD, and Brenda L. Wolfe, PhD.

Inside Rehab: The Surprising Truth about Addiction Treatment and How to Get Help that Works and *Sober for Good: New Solutions for Drinking Problems—Advice from Those Who Have Succeeded.* Anne Fletcher.

Full Catastrophe Living: Using the Wisdom of Your Body and Mind to Face Stress, Pain and Illness. Jon Kabat-Zinn, PhD.

A User's Guide to the Brain: Perception, Attention and the Four Theatres of the Brain. John J. Ratey, MD.

For more resources, go to www.motivationandchange.com.

Other Risks

- **YES/NO**—Does s/he have a physical condition that would be exacerbated by the substance use (e.g., smoking marijuana with a lung condition like emphysema, using a stimulant with heart vulnerability, drinking with liver disease or hepatitis)?
- **YES/NO**—Does s/he have a history of accidents (e.g., car accidents or injuries) when using?
- **YES/NO**—Does s/he have access to weapons or methods that could harm self or others (e.g., gun, poison, vehicle)?
- **YES/NO**—Does s/he have the responsibility of caring for others who would be at risk of neglect or abuse if s/he uses substances while they are in his/her care (especially children or elders)?

Beyond these specific risk factors, you can orient yourself more helpfully toward risk in general in the following ways:

1. **Err on the side of safety.** If you are afraid for yourself or for your loved one, get some outside help such as the police, 911, an ambulance, neighbor, therapist, friend, or other family members. If you are scared (and you know the difference between anxious and scared), get past the inconvenience and embarrassment and get help. If you are not a trained professional, you shouldn't expect to know when it is really dangerous and when it's not. If your loved one is scaring you that much, it's not such a bad thing that he comes to understand the consequences—that you will seek help outside the family to keep him and yourself safe.

2. **Ground your response with actual data**—mostly behaviors you observe. Your feelings can be important data too, but try to stay calm enough to collect other "hard" data from the world, as many facts as you can gather. It's important to respond quickly to an actual emergency *and* it's also important to respond with as much information gathered as possible. For instance, if you feel scared, do these feelings come from your own (understandable) frustration and urge for change, or from your observation of any of the risk factors above? Many urgent situations are a judgment call, and most judgment is better based on information and planning.

3. **Consider in advance how you will respond to an emergency.** Plan ahead! You can't plan for every detail of an emergency (it wouldn't be an emergency if you could), but you can anticipate some things and plan accordingly (see the note on opiates below). If you're wor-

ried about your loved one's physical health or emotional well-being, identify the nearest hospitals or treatment options in your area. If he is isolated, get names and numbers of people near him (neighbors, friends, visiting nurses, social services) who might be able to check in. If you're worried about your own health or safety, make your own emergency exit plan (see chapter 6, "Have Your Limits"). While you can't control all the variables, you will feel more grounded and ready to cope if you identify resources in advance.

Emergency resources

9-1-1

Poison control hotline (US): 1-800-222-1222

Suicide hotline (US): 1-800-273-8255

Domestic violence hotline (US): 1-800-799-7233

About drug effects: www.drugabuse.gov/drugs-abuse

A Special Note on Opiates

Opiates are a commonly abused family of substances that include heroin as well as prescription pain relievers such as Percocet, Vicodin, fentanyl, and OxyContin. If your loved one uses an opiate drug—including recreationally without dependence—it is important to have an overdose prevention plan:

- Be aware of particular overdose risks, such as reduced tolerance after a period of inpatient treatment or incarceration.
- Know the signs of an opiate overdose: blue lips and/or fingertips, loss of consciousness, strange snoring or gurgling sounds, slow breathing (fewer than eight breaths per minute) or no breathing.
- Learn rescue breathing. Lack of oxygen is what makes opiate overdoses fatal, so rescue breathing can be the difference between life and death.
- Get a naloxone rescue kit. In the event you discover your loved one unconscious or starting to lose consciousness from overdose, information will not suffice; you will need to actually have the kit at that moment to save them. These kits are available through overdose prevention programs (http://www.overdosepreventionalliance.org/p/od-prevention-program-locator.html) or with a doctor's prescription (http://prescribetoprevent.org/ has information to help your doctor write a prescription).

Resources

For Information

National Institute on Drug Abuse (NIDA) www.drugabuse.gov/drugs-abuse

National Institute on Alcoholism and Alcohol Abuse (NIAAA) www .niaaa.nih.gov

Substance Abuse and Mental Health Services Administration (SAMH www.samhsa.gov

Robert J. Meyers and CRAFT www.robertjmeyersphd.com/cr

HBO Addiction documentary series www.hbo.com/addicti

Alcohol Answers www.alcoholanswers.org

Drinker's Checkup www.drinkerscheckup.com

The Partnership at Drugfree.org (for parents) www.d

For Help and Support

SAMHSA Treatment Locator www.samhsa.

Association for Behavioral and Cognitive apist—go to the Public tab, choose F

American Academy of Addiction Psy atrist) www.aaap.org/patient-ref

Behavioral Tech (Dialectical Be .com/resources/tools_consu

The Partnership at Drugfree

SMART Recovery (suppor family.htm

Al-Anon, Nar-Anon (s

Helping Others Live

Faces and Voices of Rec andvoicesofrecovery.org

Notes

Introduction: Hope in Hell

3 *we've seen the evidence*: William R. Miller, Alyssa A. Forcehimes, and Allen Zweben, *Treating Addiction: A Guide for Professionals* (New York: Guilford Press, 2011), 78; 198.

4 *a* science of change: William R. Miller and Kathleen M. Carroll, eds., *Rethinking Substance Abuse: What the Science Shows, and What We Should Do About It* (New York: Guilford Press, 2006).

4 *exempt from scientific standards*: William R. Miller, Joan Zweben, and Wendy R. Johnson, "Evidence-Based Treatment: Why, What, Where, When and How?" *Journal of Substance Abuse Treatment* 29 (2005): 267–76.

4 *including our own*: Andrew Rosenblum et al., "Moderators of Effects of Motivational Enhancements to Cognitive Behavioral Therapy," *American Journal of Drug and Alcohol Abuse* 31, no. 1 (2005): 35–58. Jeffrey Foote, Carrie Wilkens, and Peter Vavagiakis, "A National Survey of Alcohol Screening and Referral in College Health Centers," *Journal of American College Health* 52, no. 4 (2004): 149–57. Nicole Kosanke et al., "Feasibility of Matching Alcohol Patients to ASAM Levels of Care," *The American Journal on Addictions* 11, no. 2 (2002): 124–34.

5 *certain approaches*: William R. Miller, Paula L. Wilbourne, and Jennifer E. Hettema, "What Works? A Summary of Alcohol Treatment Outcome Research," in Reid K. Hester and William R. Miller, eds., *Handbook of Alcoholism Treatment Approaches: Effective Alternatives*, 3rd ed. (Boston: Allyn & Bacon, 2003), 13–63.

5 *often a better place*: Patricia Harrison and Stephen E. Asche, "Comparison of Substance Abuse Treatment Outcomes for Inpatients and Outpatients," *Journal of Substance Abuse Treatment* 17, no. 3 (1999): 207–20.

5 *American Society of Addiction Medicine recommends*: American Society of Addiction Medicine, *ASAM Patient Placement Criteria for the Treatment of Substance-Related Disorders* (Chevy Chase, MD: American Society of Addiction Medicine, 1996).

5 *the culture dictates*: Mark L. Willenbring, "New Research Is Redefining Alcohol Disorders: Does the Treatment Field Have the Courage to Change?" *Addiction Professional* (September–October 2008).

5 *reaching people early*: Miller, Forcehimes, and Zweben, 377–80.

5 *many people get better*: Harald Klingemann, Mark Sobell, and Linda Sobell, "Continuities and Changes in Self-Change Research," *Addiction* 105, no. 9 (2010): 1510–18.

5 *Cognitive-behavioral and motivational approaches*: Miller, Wilbourne, and Hettema, "What Works?" 13–63.

5 *good treatment often includes*: Kim T. Mueser et al., (2006). "Comorbid Substance Use Disorders and Psychiatric Disorders," in Miller and Carroll, *Rethinking*, 115–33.

6 *Neuroimaging research*: Bryon Adinoff and Elliot A. Stein, eds., *Neuroimaging in Addiction* (Hoboken, NJ: Wiley-Blackwell, 2011).

6 *the power of neuroplasticity*: Norman Doidge, *The Brain That Changes Itself: Stories of Personal Triumph from the Frontiers of Brain Science* (New York: Viking, 2007).

6 *teenagers respond well*: Ken C. Winters and Yifrah Kaminer, "Adolescent Behavior Change: Process and Outcomes," in Y. Kaminer and K. Winters, eds., *Clinical Manual of Substance Abuse Treatment* (Washington, DC: American Psychiatric Publishing, Inc., 2011), 143–62.

6 *informed by CRAFT*: Robert J. Meyers, Michael Villanueva, and Jane Ellen Smith, "The Community Reinforcement Approach: History and New Directions," *Journal of Cognitive Psychotherapy: An International Quarterly* 19, no. 3 (2005): 247–60.

6 *the most effective behavioral treatment*: Robert J. Meyers, William R. Miller, eds., *A Community Reinforcement Approach to Addiction Treatment* (Cambridge, UK: Cambridge University Press, 2001).

6 *family involvement*: Robert J. Meyers et al., "Community Reinforcement and Family Training (CRAFT): Engaging Unmotivated Drug Users in Treatment," *Journal of Substance Abuse* 10, no. 3 (1998): 291–308.

7 *Drs. Meyers and Smith*: Jane Ellen Smith and Robert J. Meyers, *Motivating Substance Users to Enter Treatment: Working with Family Members* (New York: Guilford Press, 2004), 270–71.

7 *Two-thirds of people*: Ibid.

8 *part of helping people change*: William R. Miller, "Enhancing Motivation for Change," in Hester and Miller, *Handbook*, 131–51.

9 *many people change on their own*: Carlo DiClemente, "Natural Change and the Troublesome Use of Substances: A Life-Course Perspective," in Miller and Carroll, *Rethinking*, 81–96.

9 *it's not the only way*: Helen Matzger, Lee Ann Kaskutas, and Constance Weisner, "Reasons for Drinking Less and their Relationship to Sustained Remission from Problem Drinking," *Addiction* 100, no. 11 (2005): 1637–46. Klingemann, Sobell, and Sobell, "Continuities."

9 *only a few treatment providers*: Robert J. Meyers, personal communication, April 2013.

10 *Chronic worrying*: Jos F. Brosschot, William Gerin, and Julian F. Thayer, "The Perseverative Cognition Hypothesis: A Review of Worry, Prolonged-Stress Related Physiological Activation, and Health," *Journal of Psychosomatic Research* 60, no. 2 (2006): 113–24.

11 *involving family and friends*: Barbara S. McCrady, "Family and Other Close Relationships," in Miller and Carroll, *Rethinking*, 166–81.

11 *Family influence*: Douglas B. Marlowe et al., "Multidimensional Assessment of Perceived Treatment-Entry Pressures among Substance Abusers," *Psychology of Addictive Behaviors* 15, no. 2 (2001): 97–108.

12 *most people stop abusing substances*: Deborah A. Dawson et al., "Recovery from DSM-IV Alcohol Dependence: United States, 2001–2002," *Addiction* 100, no. 3 (2005): 281–92. Wendy Slutske, "Why Is Natural Recovery So Common for Addictive Disorders?" *Addiction* 105, no. 9 (2010): 1520–21.

12 *the more you criticize someone*: William R. Miller and Stephen Rollnick, *Motivational Interviewing, Third Edition: Helping People Change* (New York: Guilford Press, 2012).

13   *The current scientific evidence*: Miller, Forcehimes, and Zweben, *Treating Addiction*, 10–28.

13   *people are more likely*: William R. Miller, "Enhancing Motivation for Change," in Hester and Miller, *Handbook*, 138–40.

13   *Many people don't seek help*: John A. Cunningham et al., "Barriers to Treatment: Why Alcohol and Drug Abusers Delay or Never Seek Treatment," *Addictive Behaviors* 18, no. 3 (1993): 347–53. Jan Copeland, "A Qualitative Study of Barriers to Formal Treatment Among Women Who Self-Managed Change in Addictive Behaviors," *Journal of Substance Abuse Treatment* 14, no. 2 (1997): 183–90.

14   *Giving people options*: Richard M. Ryan and Edward L. Deci, "Self-Determination Theory and the Facilitation of Intrinsic Motivation, Social Development, and Well-Being," *American Psychologist* 55 (2000): 68–78.

14   *coercion may kill their motivation*: James Garrett et al., "The ARISE Intervention: Using Family and Network Links to Engage Addicted Persons in Treatment," *Journal of Substance Abuse Treatment* 15 (1998): 333–43. B. Loneck, James Garrett, and S. Banks, "A Comparison of the Johnson Intervention with Four Other Methods of Referral to Outpatient Treatment," *American Journal of Drug and Alcohol Abuse* 22 (1996): 233–46.

14   *this kind of confrontation*: William R. Miller and William L. White, "Confrontation in Addiction Treatment," *Counselor Magazine* (Aug 2007): 12–30.

15   *One national survey*: Dawson et al., "Recovery."

15   *Psychological theories of motivation*: William R. Miller, "Motivational Factors in Addictive Behaviors," in William R. Miller and Kathleen M. Carroll, eds., *Rethinking Substance Abuse: What the Science Shows, and What We Should Do About It* (New York: Guilford Press, 2006), 134–50.

16   *believing lifelong abstinence*: William R. Miller et al., "What Predicts Relapse? Prospective Testing of Antecedent Models," supplement, *Addiction* 91 (1996): S155–S171.

16   *moderation is a reasonable*: William R. Miller et al., "Long-Term Follow-Up of Behavioral Self-Control Training," *Journal of Studies on Alcohol* 53, no. 3 (1992): 249–61.

16   *more people may find their way*: Mark Sobell and Linda Sobell, "Conceptual Issues Regarding Goals in the Treatment of Alcohol Problems," *Drugs & Society* 1, nos. 2–3 (1987): 1–37.

17   *less resistance to kindness*: William R. Miller and Stephen Rollnick, *Motivational Interviewing, Third Edition: Helping People Change* (New York: Guilford Press, 2012).

20   *It's measurable*: David P. French and Stephen Sutton, "Reactivity of Measurement in Health Psychology: How Much of a Problem Is It? What Can Be Done About It?" *British Journal of Health Psychology* 15, no. 3 (2010): 453–68.

22   *optimism helps*: Charles R. Synder and Shane J. Lopez, eds., *The Oxford Handbook of Positive Psychology* (New York: Oxford University Press, 2009), 304–5.

Chapter 1: What Is Addiction?

27   *compulsive need for*: Merriam-Webster's *Collegiate Dictionary*, 11th ed. (2004).

28   *no evidence to support*: William R. Miller, "Alcoholism: Toward a Better Disease Model," *Psychology of Addictive Behaviors* 7, no. 2 (1993): 129–36.

28   *A label like* addict: A study conducted by the World Health Organization found that drug addiction was ranked the most stigmatized of *all* health conditions. Alcohol

addiction was ranked fourth. Robin Room et al., "Cross-Cultural Views on Stigma Valuation Parity and Societal Attitudes towards Disability," in T. Bedirhan Ustun et al., eds., *Disability and Culture: Universalism and Diversity* (Seattle: Hofgrebe & Huber, 2001), 247–91.

28 *providers had more negative views*: John Kelly and Cassandra Westerhoff, "Does It Matter How We Refer to Individuals with Substance-Related Conditions? A Randomized Study of Two Commonly Used Terms," *The International Journal on Drug Policy* 21, no. 3 (2010): 202–7.

28 *they identified the term* addict: Theresa B. Moyers and William R. Miller, "Therapists' Conceptualizations of Alcoholism: Measurement and Implications for Treatment Decisions," *Psychology of Addictive Behaviors* 7, no. 4 (1993): 238–45.

29 DSM-5: American Psychiatric Association, *Diagnostic and Statistical Manual of Mental Disorders, Fifth Edition (DSM-5)* (Washington, DC: American Psychiatric Association, 2013).

30 *relationship between genes and behavior*: George Uhl et al., "Human Substance Abuse Vulnerability and Genetic Influences," *American College of Neuropsychopharmacology* (2000). Jibran Khokhar et al., "Pharmacogenetics of Drug Dependence: Role of Gene Variations in Susceptibility and Treatment," *Annual Review of Pharmacology and Toxicology* 50 (2010): 39–61.

30 *people metabolize substances*: Marc A. Schuckit, "Low Levels of Response to Alcohol As a Predictor of Future Alcoholism," *The American Journal of Psychiatry* 151, no. 2 (1994): 184–89.

30 *differences in the taste receptors*: Susan Brasser, Meghan Norman, and Christian Lemon, "T1r3 Taste Receptor Involvement in Gustatory Neural Responses to Ethanol and Oral Ethanol Preference," *Physiological Genomics* 41, no. 3 (2010): 232–43.

30 *Differences in baseline levels*: Petra Zimmermann et al., "Primary Anxiety Disorders and the Development of Subsequent Alcohol Use Disorders: A 4-year Community Study of Adolescents and Young Adults," *Psychological Medicine* 33, no. 7 (2003): 1211–22. Arpana Agrawal et al., "A Twin Study of Personality and Illicit Drug Use and Abuse/Dependence," *Twin Research* 7 (2004): 72–81.

30 *the heritability of addictions*: Francesca Ducci and David Goldman, "The Genetic Basis of Addictive Disorders," *The Psychiatric Clinics of North America* 35, no. 2 (2012): 495–519. G. Uhl and R. Grow, "The Burden of Complex Genetics in Brain Disorders," *Archives of General Psychiatry* 61 (2004): 223–29.

30 *These rates are in line*: Kenneth S. Kendler, "Levels of Explanation in Psychiatric and Substance Use Disorders: Implications for the Development of an Etiologically Based Nosology," *Molecular Psychiatry* 17 (2012): 11–21. O. Joseph Bienvenu, Dimitry Davydow, and Kenneth Kendler, "Psychiatric 'Disease' versus Behavioral Disorders and Degree of Genetic Influence," *Psychological Medicine* 41 (2011): 33–40.

30 *Environmental and social factors*: Tracy L. Simpson and William R. Miller, "Concomitance Between Childhood Sexual and Physical Abuse and Substance Use Problems: A Review," *Clinical Psychology Review* 22 (2002): 27–77.

30 *Availability of substances*: Mark J. Ryzin, Gregory M. Fosco, and Thomas J. Dishion, "Family and Peer Predictors of Substance Use from Early Adolescence to Early Adulthood: An 11-Year Prospective Analysis," *Addictive Behaviors* 37, no. 12 (2012): 1314–24.

31 *Local cultural factors*: Robert Blum et al., "The Effects of Race/Ethnicity, Income, and Family Structure on Adolescent Risk Behaviors," *American Journal of Public Health* 90 (2000): 1879–84.

31 *positive family involvement*: Kim T. Mueser et al., "Comorbid Substance Use Disorders and Psychiatric Disorders," in Miller and Carroll, *Rethinking* (2006), 115–33. Daniel Flannery, Laura Williams, and Alexander Vazsonyi, "Who Are They With and What Are They Doing? Delinquent Behavior, Substance Use, and Early Adolescent After-School Time," *The American Journal of Orthopsychiatry* 69 (1999): 247–53.

31 *most individuals at risk*: Ducci and Goldman, "The Genetic Basis of Addictive Disorders."

31 *This is your brain on drugs*: Partnership for a Drug-Free America, *This Is Your Brain on Drugs* (1987), http://www.youtube.com/watch?v=ub_a2t0ZfTs.

31 *old dogs not only can*: Norman Doidge, *The Brain That Changes Itself: Stories of Personal Triumph from the Frontiers of Brain Science* (New York: Viking, 2007).

32 *The brain's reward system*: Ann E. Kelly, "Memory and Addiction: Shared Neural Circuitry and Molecular Mechanisms," *Neuron* 44 (2004): 161–79. Ann Kelly and Kent Berridge, "The Neuroscience of Natural Rewards: Relevance to Addictive Drugs," *The Journal of Neuroscience* 22, no. 9 (2002): 3306–11.

32 *the brain's way of rewarding us*: Eric J. Nestler, "Is There a Common Molecular Pathway for Addiction?" *Nature Neuroscience* 8, no. 11 (2005): 1445–49.

32 *mechanism by which 'instinct'*: Correspondence with John Mariani, December 26, 2012.

33 *focus our attention*: Peter W. Kalivas and Nora Volkow, "The Neural Basis of Addiction: A Pathology of Motivation and Choice," *American Journal of Psychiatry* 162, no. 8 (2005): 1403–13.

33 *the brain compensates*: Steven E. Hyman, "Addiction: A Disease of Learning and Memory," *American Journal of Psychiatry* 162, no. 8 (2005): 1414–22.

33 *these craving states*: Joshua D. Berke and Steven. E. Hyman, "Addiction, Dopamine and the Molecular Mechanisms of Memory," *Neuron* 25 (2000): 515–32.

33 *a huge factor in relapse*: George F. Koob and Michel L. LeMoal, "Drug Addiction, Dysregulation of Reward and Allostasis," *Neuropsycholopharmacology* 24, no. 2 (2001): 97–129.

33 *key structures in the brain*: Nora Volkow and Joanna Fowler, "Addiction, A Disease of Compulsion and Drive: Involvement of the Orbitofrontal Cortex," *Cerebral Cortex* 10, no. 3 (2000): 318–25. Nora Volkow and Ting-Kai Li, "Drug Addiction: The Neurobiology of Behavior Gone Awry," *Nature Reviews Neuroscience* 5 (2004): 963–70.

34 *this part of the brain*: Ibid.

34 *Teenagers have a distinct disadvantage*: Elizabeth Sowell et al., "Mapping Cortical Change Across the Human Life Span," *Nature Neuroscience* 6, no. 3 (2003): 309–15.

34 *part of the brain gets excited*: George Koob, "Neuroadaptive Mechanisms of Addiction: Studies on the Extended Amygdala," *European Neuropsychopharmacology* 13 (2003): 442–52.

34 *learning new habits*: Patricia R. Porto et al., "Does Cognitive Behavioral Therapy Change the Brain? A Systematic Review of Neuroimaging in Anxiety Disorders," *The Journal of Neuropsychiatry and Clinical Neurosciences* 21, no. 2 (2009): 114–25.

35 *have physiological effects*: Daniel J. Siegel, *Pocket Guide to Interpersonal Neurobiology: An Integrative Handbook of the Mind* (New York: W. W. Norton & Company, 2012).

38 *A person can qualify*: DSM-5

39 *It's helpful to educate yourself*: For example, go to www.drugabuse.gov/drugs-abuse for more information.

40 *the least intrusive level*: American Society of Addiction Medicine, *ASAM Patient Placement Criteria*.

40 *most people with substance problems*: Dawson et al., "Recovery."
41 *"Sobriety sampling"*: Robert Meyers and William Miller, eds., *A Community Reinforcement Approach.*

Chapter 2: Motivation: Why Do People Change?

45 *the science of motivation and change*: William R. Miller and Stephen Rollnick, *Motivational Interviewing, Third Edition: Helping People Change* (New York: Guilford Press, 2012).
45 *treatment providers, family members*: Richard M. Ryan and Edward L. Deci, "Self-Determination Theory and the Facilitation of Intrinsic Motivation, Social Development, and Well-Being," *American Psychologist* 55 (2000): 68–78.
45 *push back, hold on tighter*: William L. White and William R. Miller, "The Use of Confrontation in Addiction Treatment: History, Science, and Time for Change," *Counselor* 8, no. 4 (2007): 12–30.
46 *the outward signs of motivation*: Kent C. Berridge, "Motivation Concepts in Behavioral Neuroscience," *Physiology & Behavior* 81 (2004): 179–209.
47 *if the brain's reward system*: Roy A. Wise, "Dopamine, Learning and Motivation," *Nature Reviews Neuroscience* 5 (2004): 1–12.
48 *SDT identifies two types*: Ryan and Deci, "Self-Determination."
48 *it is essential that people develop*: Edward L. Deci, Richard M. Ryan, and Frederic Guay, "Self-Determination Theory and Actualization of Human Potential," in Dennis McInerney et al., eds., *Theory Driving Research: New Wave Perspectives on Self Processes and Human Development* (Charlotte, NC: Information Age Press, 2013), 109–33.
49 *A classic example*: Robert L. Dupont et al., "Setting the Standard for Recovery: Physicians' Health Programs," *Journal of Substance Abuse Treatment* 36, no. 2 (2009): 159–71.
52 *the costs outweighed the benefits*: John A. Cunningham et al., "Resolution from Alcohol Problems with and without Treatment: Reasons for Change," *Journal of Substance Abuse* 7 (1995): 365–72. H. Matzger, L. Kashutas, and C. Weisner, "Reasons for Drinking Less and Their Relationship to Sustained Alcohol Remission from Problem Drinking," *Addiction* 100 (2005): 1637–46.
52 *cost-benefit analysis*: Timothy R. Apodaca and Richard Longabaugh, "Mechanisms of Change in Motivational Interviewing: A Review and Preliminary Evaluation of the Evidence," *Addiction* 104, no. 5 (2009): 705–15.
55 *The more this can be accepted*: William R. Miller, "Motivational Factors in Addictive Behaviors," in W. R. Miller and Kathleen M. Carroll, eds., *Rethinking Substance Abuse: What the Science Shows, and What We Should Do About It* (New York: Guilford Press, 2006), 134–50.
59 *Confrontation undermines motivation*: White and Miller, "Use of Confrontation in Addiction Treatment," 12–30.
60 *Respectful, collaborative approaches*: William R. Miller, Robert J. Meyers, and J. Scott Tonigan, "Engaging the Unmotivated in Treatment for Alcohol Problems: A Comparison of Three Strategies for Intervention through Family Members," *Journal of Consulting and Clinical Psychology* 67 (1999): 688–97.
60 *aftereffects of some confrontational interventions*: James Garrett et al., "The ARISE Intervention: Using Family and Network Links to Engage Addicted Persons in Treatment," *Journal of Substance Abuse Treatment* 15 (1998): 333–43.

67 *chart below*: Adapted from Jane Ellen Smith and Robert J. Meyers, *Motivating Substance Users to Enter Treatment: Working with Family Members* (New York: Guilford Press, 2004), 74–75.

Chapter 3: Change: How Do People Change?

69 *the process is different*: A. Fletcher, *Sober for Good: New Solutions for Drinking Problems—Advice from Those Who Have Succeeded* (Boston: Houghton Mifflin, 2001).

70 *"Stages of Change" model*: James O. Prochaska and Carlo C. DiClemente, "Stages and Processes of Self-Change of Smoking: Toward an Integrative Model of Change," *Journal of Consulting and Clinical Psychology* 51, no. 3 (1983): 390–95.

73 *goal-directed and motivated*: Susan Mineka and Richard Zinbarg, "A Contemporary Learning Theory Perspective on the Etiology of Anxiety Disorders: It's Not What You Thought It Was," *American Psychologist* 61, no. 1 (2006): 10–26.

74 *behavioral approaches consistently*: William R. Miller, Paula L. Wilbourne, and Jennifer E. Hettema, "What Works? A Summary of Alcohol Treatment Outcome Research," in Reid K. Hester & W. R. Miller, eds., *Handbook of Alcoholism Treatment Approaches: Effective Alternatives*, 3rd ed. (Boston: Allyn & Bacon, 2003), 16–63.

75 *we have to learn alternatives*: A. David Redish et al., "Reconciling Reinforcement Learning Models with Behavioral Extinction and Renewal: Implications for Addiction, Relapse, and Problem Gambling," *Psychological Review* 114, no. 3 (2007): 784–805.

76 *"abstinence violation effect"*: G. Alan Marlatt and Dennis M. Donovan, eds., *Relapse Prevention: Maintenance Strategies in the Treatment of Addictive Behaviors* (New York: Guilford Press, 2005).

76 greater likelihood of relapse: William R. Miller et al., "What Predicts Relapse? Prospective Testing of Antecedent Models," supplement, *Addiction* 91 (1996): S155–71.

77 *"primitive" or "lizard" brain*: You can think of the "primitive brain" as the part of the brain that we share with lizards and other very old species, the fight-or-flight part wholly oriented to seeking pleasure and avoiding pain.

77 *people can appreciate intellectually*: Antoine Bechara, "Decision Making, Impulse Control and Loss of Willpower to Resist Drugs: A Neurocognitive Perspective," *Nature Neuroscience* 8, no. 11 (2005): 1458–63.

78 *ten thousand hours*: Malcolm Gladwell, *Outliers: The Story of Success* (New York: Little, Brown, and Co., 2008).

79 *brain functioning hasn't readjusted*: Redish et al., "Reconciling Reinforcement Learning Models with Behavioral Extinction and Renewal."

80 *importance of building a happy life*: Randall E. Rogers et al., "Abstinence-Contingent Reinforcement and Engagement in Non-Drug-Related Activities Among Illicit Drug Abusers," *Psychology of Addictive Behaviors* 22, no. 4 (2008): 544–50.

81 *a fiftysomething eye surgeon*: Doidge, *The Brain That Changes Itself*.

Chapter 4: Start Where You Are

89 *22.2 million Americans*: US Department of Health and Human Services, Substance Abuse and Mental Health Services Administration, *Results from the 2012 National*

Survey on Drug Use and Health: Summary of National Findings (Rockville, MD: SAMHSA, 2013).

90 *caring for a person*: Smith and Meyers, *Motivating*, 3.

91 *reaffirming that awareness*: Shauna L. Shapiro and Linda E. Carlson, *The Art and Science of Mindfulness* (Washington, DC: American Psychological Association, 2009).

99 *The Happiness Scale*: Adapted from Smith and Meyers, *Motivating*, 223.

Chapter 5: Self-Care I: Damage Control

103 *modeling among grown-ups*: Nicholas Christakis and James Fowler, "The Spread of Obesity in a Large Social Network over 32 Years," *The New England Journal of Medicine* 357, no. 4 (2007): 370–79. Nicholas Christakis and James Fowler, "The Collective Dynamics of Smoking in a Large Social Network," *The New England Journal of Medicine* 358, no. 21 (2008): 2249–58.

104 *most basic—and critical*: Marsha M. Linehan, *Skills Training Manual for Treating Borderline Personality Disorder* (New York: Guilford Press, 1993), 91.

106 *Dialectical Behavior Therapy*: Ibid., 96–103.

114 *In this flying shoe*: Susan Cheever, *My Name Is Bill* (New York: Washington Square Press, 2004), 142.

Chapter 6: Have Your Limits

123 *"catastrophizing"*: Albert Ellis, *Reason and Emotion in Psychotherapy* (New York: Lyle Stuart, 1962).

127 *when domestic violence occurs*: Keith Klostermann et al., "Partner Violence and Substance Abuse: Treatment Interventions," *Aggression and Violent Behavior* 15, no. 3 (2010): 162–66.

Chapter 7: Start Where They Are

133 *direct CRAFT helping strategies*: Robert J. Meyers and Brenda L. Wolfe, *Get Your Loved One Sober: Alternatives to Nagging, Pleading, and Threatening* (Center City, MN: Hazelden, 2004).

136 *a single act of confrontation*: William R. Miller, R. Gayle Benefield, and J. Scott Tonigan, "Enhancing Motivation for Change in Problem Drinking: A Controlled Comparison of Two Therapist Styles," *Journal of Consulting and Clinical Psychology* 61 (1993): 455–61.

140 *your best is enough*: Jane Ellen Smith and Robert J. Meyers, *Motivating Substance Users to Enter Treatment: Working with Family Members* (New York: Guilford Press, 2004): 258–71.

141 *This exercise:* "Daily Reminder to Be Nice" exercise from Jane Ellen Smith and Robert J. Meyers, *Motivating Substance Users to Enter Treatment: Working with Family Members* (New York: Guilford Press, 2004).

Chapter 8: Goals (and Problems)

143   *"Happiness Scales"*: "Relationship Happiness Scale" exercise adapted from Jane Ellen Smith and Robert J. Meyers, *Motivating Substance Users to Enter Treatment: Working with Family Members* (New York: Guilford Press, 2004), 39.

156   *Exercise: Goal Setting*: "Goal Setting" exercise adapted from ibid., 203.

156   *Exercise: Problem Solving*: "Problem Solving" exercise adapted from ibid., 190.

Chapter 9: Positive Communication

164   *process it before words*: Andrew Newberg and Mark Robert Waldman, *Words Can Change Your Brain: 12 Conversation Strategies to Build Trust, Resolve Conflict, and Increase Intimacy* (New York: Penguin Group, 2012).

167   *thoughtful advice carefully delivered*: Thomas Bien, William R. Miller, and Scott Tonigan, "Brief Interventions for Alcohol Problems: A Review," *Addiction* 88 (1993): 315–36.

169   *to live with someone using substances*: Robert J. Meyers and Brenda L. Wolfe, *Get Your Loved One Sober: Alternatives to Nagging, Pleading, and Threatening* (Center City, MN: Hazelden, 2004).

Chapter 10: Reinforcement: The Driver of Change

174   *"reinforcers"*: Scott Edwards and George Koob, "Neurobiology of Dysregulated Motivational Systems in Drug Addiction," *Future Neurology* 5, no. 3 (2010): 393–401.

174   *animal training techniques*: Amy Sutherland, *The New York Times*, June 25, 2006. Sutherland later expanded on the idea in her equally delightful book, W*hat Shamu Taught Me About Life, Love, and Marriage: Lessons for People From Animals and Their Trainers* (New York: Random House, 2008).

174   *reinforcement is a staple*: Cognitive Behavioral Therapy, Dialectical Behavioral Therapy, Behavioral Marital Therapy, the Community Reinforcement Approach and CRAFT ("R" for Reinforcement); all, as the names suggest, behavioral approaches.

175   *the core strategy*: Jane E. Smith, Robert J. Meyers, and J. L. Austin, "Working with Family Members to Engage Treatment-Refusing Drinkers: The CRAFT Program," *Alcoholism Treatment Quarterly* 26 (2008): 169–93.

176   *learning and change*: Kathleen Carroll and Bruce Rounsaville, "Behavior Therapies: The Glass Would Be Half Full If Only We Had a Glass," in W. R. Miller and Kathleen M. Carroll, eds., *Rethinking Substance Abuse: What the Science Shows, and What We Should Do About It* (New York: Guilford Press, 2006), 223–39.

188   *Exercise: Reinforcers*: "Reinforcers" exercise adapted from Jane Ellen Smith and Robert J. Meyers, *Motivating Substance Users to Enter Treatment: Working with Family Members* (New York: Guilford Press, 2004), 137.

189   *(Nonusing) Behavior Analysis*: "Healthy Behavior Analysis" exercise adapted from ibid., 162.

Chapter 11: Consequences

191   *work with both to effect change*: Jane Ellen Smith and Robert J. Meyers, *Motivating Substance Users to Enter Treatment: Working with Family Members* (New York: Guilford Press, 2004).

201   *"behavioral burst"*: For example, Christopher A. Kearney and Anne M. Albano, *When Children Refuse School: A Cognitive-Behavioral Therapy Approach Parent Workbook* (New York: Oxford University Press, 2007).

205   *not physically at risk yourself*: Dos and Don'ts mainly from Steven M. Scruggs, Robert J. Meyers, and Rebecca Kayo, *Community Reinforcement and Family Training Support and Prevention (CRAFT-SP)*, http://www.mirecc.va.gov/visn16/docs/CRAFT-SP_Final.pdf, 47.

Chapter 12: Treatment Options

209   *Addiction Severity Index (ASI)*: A. Thomas McLellan et al., "The Fifth Edition of The Addiction Severity Index," *Journal of Substance Abuse Treatment* 9, no. 3 (1992): 199–213.

209   *Patient Placement Criteria (PPC)*: David R. Gastfriend, ed., *Addiction Treatment Matching: Research Foundations of the American Society of Addiction Medicine (ASAM) Criteria* (Birmingham, NY: Hawthorne Press Medical, 2003).

211   *on an outpatient basis*: Raymond F. Anton and Hugh Myrick, "Treatment of Alcohol Withdrawal," *Alcohol Health & Research World* 22, no. 1 (1998): 38–43.

213   *this is starting to change*: In surveys of almost four hundred private and public drug and alcohol programs, 60 to 75 percent are 12-step based. Paul M. Roman and J. A. Johnson, *National Treatment Center Study Summary Report: Private Treatment Centers* and *National Treatment Center Study Summary Report: Public Treatment Centers* (Athens, GA: Institute for Behavioral Research, University of Georgia, 2004).

213   Inside Rehab: Anne Fletcher, *Inside Rehab: The Surprising Truth about Addiction Treatment—and How to Get Help that Works* (New York: Penguin, 2013).

216   *possibility of opiate overdose*: David Gastfriend, "Intramuscular Extended-Release Naltrexone: Current Evidence," *Annals of the New York Academy of Sciences* 1216 (2011): 144–66.

216   *performed by treatment providers*: Karen Moeller, Kelly Lee, and Julie Kissack, "Urine Drug Screening: Practical Guide for Clinicians," *Mayo Clinic Proceedings* 83, no. 1 (2008): 66–76.

218   *strongly supported approaches*: William R. Miller, Alyssa A. Forcehimes, and Allen Zweben, *Treating Addiction: A Guide for Professionals* (New York: Guilford Press, 2011).

218   *do have an impact*: Thomas F. Babor et al., "Screening, Brief Intervention, and Referral to Treatment (SBIRT): Toward a Public Health Approach to the Management of Substance Abuse," *Substance Abuse* 28 (2007): 7–30.

218   *(BASICS)*: Linda A. Dimeff, John S. Baer, Daniel R. Kivlahan, and G. Alan Marlatt, *Brief Alcohol Screening and Intervention for College Students: A Harm Reduction Approach* (New York: Guilford Press, 1999).

218   *in school settings*: Ken C. Winters et al., "Brief Intervention for Drug-Abusing Adolescents in a School Setting: Outcomes and Mediating Factors," *Journal of Substance Abuse Treatment* 42, no. 3 (2012): 279–88.

220 *(MINT)*: MINT: www.motivationalinterviewing.org/.

220 *more than motivational approaches*: Luke Mitcheson et al., "Introduction to CBT for Substance Use Problems," in *Applied Cognitive and Behavioural Approaches to the Treatment of Addiction: A Practical Treatment Guide* (Chichester, UK: John Wiley & Sons, 2010).

220 *Community Reinforcement Approach (CRA)*: Robert J. Meyers, Hendrik G. Roozen, and Jane Ellen Smith, "The Community Reinforcement Approach: An Update of the Evidence," *Alcohol Research and Health* 33 (2011): 380–88.

221 *Couple-Centered Treatments*: Tim O'Farrell and William Fals-Stewart, "Behavioral Couples Therapy for Alcoholism and Drug Abuse," *Journal of Substance Abuse Treatment* 18, no. 1 (2000): 51–54.

222 *Emotion-Focused Therapy, or EFT*: Susan M. Johnson et al., "Emotionally Focused Couples Therapy: Status and Challenges," *Clinical Psychology: Science and Practice* 6 (1999): 67–79.

222 *Medications can be a powerful component*: William R. Miller, Alyssa A. Forcehimes, and Allen Zweben, *Treating Addiction: A Guide for Professionals* (New York: Guilford Press, 2011): 241–56.

223 *only when compliance is assured*: Charlotte H. Jorgensen, Bolette Pedersen, and Hanne Tonnesen, "The Efficacy of Disulfiram for the Treatment of Alcohol Use Disorder," *Alcoholism: Clinical and Experimental Research* 35, no. 10 (2011): 1749–58.

224 *substantial benefits*: Avinash Alan De Sousa, Jaya A. De Sousa, and Hema Kapoor, "An Open Randomized Trial Comparing Disulfiram and Topiramate in the Treatment of Alcohol Dependence," *Journal of Substance Abuse Treatment* 34 (2008) 460–63.

224 *if drinking begins*: James Garbutt, "The State of Pharmacotherapy for the Treatment of Alcohol Dependence," *Journal of Substance Abuse Treatment* 36, no. 1 (2009): S15–S23.

226 *months, not weeks*: Roger Weiss et al., "Adjunctive Counseling During Brief and Extended Bupronophine-Naloxone Treatment for Prescription Opioid Dependence," *Archives of General Psychiatry* 68, no. 12 (2011): 1238–46.

227 *overuse or abuse*: Ibid.

227 *Zyban with single NRT*: John R. Hughes, "An Updated Algorithm for Choosing among Smoking Cessation Treatments," *Journal of Substance Abuse Treatment* 45, no. 2 (2013): 215–21.

228 *single largest cause*: Centers for Disease Control and Prevention, "Fast Facts," http://www.cdc.gov/tobacco/data_statistics/fact_sheets/fast_facts/.

228 *to be successful*: Hughes, "An Updated Algorithm."

228 *nicotine withdrawal symptoms*: Jibran Khokhar et al., "Pharmacogenetics of Drug Dependence: Role of Gene Variations in Susceptibility and Treatment," *Annual Review of Pharmacology and Toxicology* 50 (2010): 39–61.

228 *recovery status of the counselor*: William L. White, *Peer-based Addiction Recovery Support: History, Theory, Practice, and Scientific Evaluation* (Great Lakes Addiction Technology Transfer Center and Philadelphia Department of Behavioral Health and Mental Retardation Services, 2009), 191–95.

228 *show genuine empathy*: Arthur C. Bohart et al., "Empathy," in John C. Norcross, ed., *Psychotherapy Relationships That Work: Therapist Contributions and Responsiveness to Patients* (New York: Oxford University Press, 2002), 89–107.

229 *new treatment approach*: Steve Martino, "Strategies for Training Counselors in Evidence-Based Treatments," *Addiction Science and Clinical Practice* 5, no. 2 (December 2010): 30–39.

229 *Co-occurring disorders are common*: Patrick M. Flynn and Barry S. Brown, "Co-Occurring Disorders in Substance Abuse Treatment: Issues and Prospects," *Journal of Substance Abuse Treatment* 34, no. 1 (2008): 36–47.

230 *war trauma*: Sonya B. Norman et al., "Do Trauma History and PTSD Symptoms Influence Addiction Relapse Context?" *Drug and Alcohol Dependence* 90, no. 1 (2007): 89–96.

230 *post-traumatic stress disorder (PTSD)*: Kathleen T. Brady, Sudie E. Back, and Scott F. Coffey, "Substance Abuse and Posttraumatic Stress Disorder," *Current Directions in Psychological Science* 13, no. 5 (2004): 206–9.

231 *unproblematic drinkers without treatment*: Deborah A. Dawson et al., "Recovery from DSM-IV Alcohol Dependence: United States, 2001–2002," *Addiction* 100, no. 3 (2005): 281–92.

232 *this path will be successful*: Alan Marlatt and Katie Witkiewitz, "Harm Reduction Approaches to Alcohol Use: Health Promotion, Prevention, and Treatment," *Addictive Behaviors* 27, no. 6 (2002): 867–86.

233 *who will not*: R. Moos and C. Timko, "Outcome Research on Twelve-Step and Other Self-Help Programs," in Marc Galanter and Herbert D. Kleber, eds., *Textbook of Substance Abuse Treatment*, 4th ed. (Washington, DC: American Psychiatric Press, 2008), 511–21.

233 *it increases odds*: Reid K. Hester and William R. Miller, eds., *Handbook of Alcoholism Treatment Approaches: Effective Alternatives*, 3rd ed. (Boston: Allyn & Bacon, 2003): 182.

234 *therapy for substance problems*: Kathleen M. Carroll, Charla Nich, and Bruce J. Rounsaville, "Contribution of the Therapeutic Alliance to Outcome in Active Versus Control Psychotherapies," *Journal of Consulting and Clinical Psychology* 65 (1997): 510–14.

234 *first person she tries*: Barry Duncan et al., "The Therapeutic Relationship," in *The Heart and Soul of Change*, 2nd ed. (Washington, DC: American Psychological Association, 2010), 113–41.

Chapter 13: Suggesting Treatment

243 *Johnson Institute Interventions*: Vernon Johnson, *I'll Quit Tomorrow: A Practical Guide to Alcoholism* (New York: Harper & Row, 1980).

244 *ARISE*: James Garrett et al., "The ARISE Intervention: Using Family and Network Links to Engage Addicted Persons in Treatment," *Journal of Substance Abuse Treatment* 15 (1998): 333–43.

244 *outcomes have been good*: Judith Landau et al., "Outcomes with the ARISE Approach to Engaging Reluctant Drug- and Alcohol-Dependent Individuals in Treatment," *American Journal of Drug and Alcohol Abuse* 30, no. 4 (2004): 711–48.

Chapter 14: During Treatment

252 *abstinence violation effect (AVE)*: Susan Curry, Alan Marlatt, and Judith R. Gordon, "Abstinence Violation Effect: Validation of an Attributional Construct in Smoking Cessation," *Journal of Consulting and Clinical Psychology* 55 (1987): 145–49.

253 *stay on track*: William R. Miller, "What Is a Relapse? Fifty Ways to Leave the Wagon," *Addiction*, supplement, 91, no. 12 (1996): 15–28.

257 *supervise testing*: In "supervised" toxicology testing, the urine sample is taken under direct supervision.
262 *"education" alone is not particularly effective*: William R. Miller, Paula L. Wilbourne, and Jennifer E. Hettema, "What Works? A Summary of Alcohol Treatment Outcome Research," in Hester and Miller, *Handbook of Alcoholism Treatment Approaches*: 34–35.

Chapter 15: Self-Care II: Building a Life

273 *improving self-care*: Andrew C. Butler et. al., "The Empirical Status of Cognitive-Behavioral Therapy: A Review of Meta-Analysis," *Clinical Psychology Review* 26 (2006): 17–31.
273 *stir up some possibilities*: Adapted from Douglas J. MacPhillamy and Peter M. Lewinsohn, "The Pleasant Events Schedule: Studies on Reliability, Validity, and Scale Intercorrelation," *Journal of Consulting and Clinical Psychology* 50 (1982): 363–80.
276 *making and maintaining change*: Sheldon Cohen and Thomas A. Wills, "Stress, Social Support, and the Buffering Hypothesis," *Psychological Bulletin* 98 (1985): 310–57.
276 *and other afflictions*: Shauna Shapiro and Linda E. Carlson, *The Art and Science of Mindfulness* (Washington, DC: American Psychological Association, 2009).

Index

Note: A "t" in page references indicates a table.

About the Authors

Jeffrey Foote, PhD, is cofounder and executive director of CMC and psychologist for the New York Mets. He has been a leader in the science and humanity of change for twenty-five years.

Carrie Wilkens, PhD, is cofounder and clinical director of CMC and a dedicated practitioner of the most effective treatments for substance use problems and compulsive behaviors. Her expertise is regularly sought by the CBS *This Morning*; Fox News; *Newsweek*; *O, The Oprah Magazine*; and *Psychology Today*.

Nicole Kosanke, PhD, is director of family services at CMC, where she specializes in working with family members of people abusing substances. In 2008 Dr. Kosanke was featured in an *O, The Oprah Magazine* article about her client's experience in treatment at CMC, which was later published in *O's Big Book of Happiness: The Best of O*.

Stephanie Higgs is an editor and writer dedicated to bridging the gap between helpful ideas and people who need the help.